MANAGEMENT OF AN
INTER-FIRM NETWORK

Japanese Management and International Studies
(ISSN: 2010-4448)

Editor-in-Chief: Yasuhiro Monden *(Tsukuba University, Japan)*

Published

Vol. 1   Value-Based Management of the Rising Sun
edited by Yasuhiro Monden, Kanji Miyamoto, Kazuki Hamada, Gunyung Lee & Takayuki Asada

Vol. 2   Japanese Management Accounting Today
edited by Yasuhiro Monden, Masanobu Kosuga, Yoshiyuki Nagasaka, Shufuku Hiraoka & Noriko Hoshi

Vol. 3   Japanese Project Management:
KPM — Innovation, Development and Improvement
edited by Shigenobu Ohara & Takayuki Asada

Vol. 4   International Management Accounting in Japan:
Current Status of Electronics Companies
edited by Kanji Miyamoto

Vol. 5   Business Process Management of Japanese and Korean Companies
edited by Gunyung Lee, Masanobu Kosuga, Yoshiyuki Nagasaka & Byungkyu Sohn

Vol. 6   M&A for Value Creation in Japan
edited by Yasuyoshi Kurokawa

Vol. 7   Business Group Management in Japan
edited by Kazuki Hamada

Vol. 8   Management of an Inter-Firm Network
edited by Yasuhiro Monden

Japanese Management and International Studies – Vol. 8

MANAGEMENT OF AN INTER-FIRM NETWORK

editor

Yasuhiro Monden
Tsukuba University, Japan

World Scientific

NEW JERSEY · LONDON · SINGAPORE · BEIJING · SHANGHAI · HONG KONG · TAIPEI · CHENNAI

Published by

World Scientific Publishing Co. Pte. Ltd.

5 Toh Tuck Link, Singapore 596224

USA office: 27 Warren Street, Suite 401-402, Hackensack, NJ 07601

UK office: 57 Shelton Street, Covent Garden, London WC2H 9HE

Library of Congress Cataloging-in-Publication Data
Management of an inter-firm network / edited by Yasuhiro Monden.
    p. cm. -- (Japanese management and international studies, ISSN 2010-4448 ; vol. 8)
    ISBN-13: 978-9814324618
    ISBN-10: 9814324612
    1. Business networks--Japan. 2. Business networks--Management--Japan.
I. Monden, Yasuhiro, 1940–
    HD69.S8M3264 2012
    658'.046--dc23

                                                            2011026046

British Library Cataloguing-in-Publication Data
A catalogue record for this book is available from the British Library.

Typeset by Stallion Press
Email: enquiries@stallionpress.com

Printed in Singapore.

Japan Society of Organization and Accounting (JSOA)

Mission of JSOA and Editorial Information

For the purpose of making a contribution to the business and academic communities, the Japan Society of Organization and Accounting (JSOA), a reformed and expanded organization from the Monden Institute of Management, is committed to publishing the book series, entitled *Japanese Management and International Studies*, with a refereed system.

Focusing on Japan and Japan-related issues, the series is designed to inform the world about research outcomes of the new "Japanese-style management system" developed in Japan. It includes the Japanese version of management systems developed abroad. In addition, it publishes research by foreign scholars and concerning foreign systems that constitute significant points of comparison with the Japanese system.

Research topics included in this series are management of organizations in a broad sense (including the business group) and the accounting that supports the organization. More specifically, topics include business strategy, organizational restructuring, corporate finance, M&A, environmental management, business models, operations management, managerial accounting, financial accounting for organizational restructuring, manager performance evaluation, remuneration systems, and management of revenues and costs. The research approach is interdisciplinary, which includes case studies, theoretical studies, normative studies and empirical studies, but emphasizes real world business.

Each volume contains the series title and a book title which reflects the volume's special theme.

Our JSOA's board of directors has established an editorial board of international standing. In each volume, guest editors who are experts on the volume's special theme serve as the volume editors.

Editorial Board

Contents

Preface

Adam Smith (1776) first advocated that supply and demand in the market would be balanced through the market principle (or market price or supply-demand equilibrium price) of the "invisible hand". This is based on the "division of labor" in the market. However, the market cannot necessarily work well especially in the age of depression.

Thus this volume attempts to propose the system that induces cooperation among the inter-firm network, which is a kind of organization against the concept of "division of labor" in the market. We are going to explore how to design such a network and balance the supply and demand, and finally create mutual satisfaction of all participating firms within the network. This mechanism is mainly based on the "incentive price" system, which will take the place of "market price". As such, proposing the antithesis to Adam Smith's initiated market principle is the main theme of this volume. This new viewpoint and mechanism will develop the new world and can help recover the depressed economy when introduced together with the market competition among the various networks in the industries.

From the above standpoint, the book is into subdivided into three parts, in accordance with the framework of the management theory propounded by Robert Anthony.

PART 1: Strategy for Forming an Inter-Firm Network

Since a network organization is a "network of various companies", the presence of a core company that plays the role of headquarters is essential. The strategic roles played by the core company of a network organization are two-fold: Recognition of the functions (roles) to be shared among the companies participating in the network and the selection of the member companies. This involves the *strategic decision No. 1*. The *strategic decision No. 2* that the core company should undertake is to determine the *forms of business combination* of inter-firm relations.

PART 2: Management Control of an Inter-Firm Network

One more role of the core company is to encourage candidate member companies to do a good job in the network. In order to make the performance of the network as a whole attractive, the core company should have some *incentive systems* that motivate the member companies to perform well. Thus the "plan-do-check-action" cycle is conducted by the core company, in which the performance evaluation system for the member companies is crucially important. This role is the *"management control"* functions of the core company. For this purpose various managerial accounting information of the consolidated business group (network) are needed.

As stated earlier, Adam Smith (1776) first advocated that supply and demand in the market would be balanced through the market principle (or market price) of the "invisible hand". However, the market cannot necessarily work well especially in the age of depression. This volume proposes the management control system that induces cooperation among the inter-firm network, especially the joint-profit allocation system as an incentive system of management control.

In this respect, we will also discuss the management of the horizontally allied networks of small and medium companies, as well as the vertically allied networks.

PART 3: Task Control of Production, Sales and Physical Distribution in an Inter-Firm Network

A network usually consists of member companies from the upstream to the downstream levels of a supply chain, and the core company determines the quantitative allocation of goods in supply and demand among the member companies. In response to the fluctuations in demand in the market, the adjustment of supply of the resources relevant to the supply chain should be made quickly throughout the chain under the *direct quantitative control* of the core company. This role is called *"task control* or *operational control"*.

The goals of such operational control include the whole business process efficiency for reducing the lead times in product development, manufacturing and sales processes. The Japanese automobile industry is unique in smoothing the parts usage each hour. The special technique is introduced. It also aims at the logistics efficiency, which includes not only the forward-flowing logistics but also the reverse (green) flowing logistics.

Further utilization of the master data management for integration of an inter-firm as a whole will be explored.

Acknowledgements

I am very grateful to Ms. Juliet Lee Ley Chin, the senior commissioning editor of the Social Sciences in the World Scientific Publishing Company for her invaluable advice to make this volume a reality. The contributing authors of this volume are also amply rewarded when their now ideas or knowledge contribute to the literature on business management and managerial accounting, thereby being of some use to people around the world.

Yasuhiro Monden

March 7, 2011

List of Contributors

Mohammad Aghdassi
Associate Professor, School of Engineering
Tarbiat Modares University, Iran
P.O. Box 1455-4834, Iran
Tel: +021-801-1001 ext.3396
Fax: +021-800-5040
aghdasim@modares.ac.ir

Henry Aigbedo
Associate Professor of Operations Management
School of Business Administration, Oakland University, USA
Rochester, MI 48309-4401, USA
Ph.D. in Management Science and Engineering from
    Tsukuba University, Japan
Tel: 248-370-4959; Fax: 248-370-4275
haigbedo@oakland.edu

Satoshi Arimoto
Assistant Professor, Faculty of Economics, Niigata University
M.A. in Commerce from Waseda University
8050 Ikarashi 2-no-cho, Nishi-ku, Niigata, 950-2181, Japan
Tel/Fax: 025-262-6560
s.arimoto@econ.niigata-u.ac.jp

Kazuki Hamada
Professor, Institute of Business and Accounting,
Kwansei Gakuin University
1-1-155, Uegahara, Nishinomiya, Hyogo, Japan, 662-8501
Ph. D. in Management Science and Engineering from
    Tsukuba University
k-hamada@kwansei.ac.jp

Tadashi Hasegawa
Professor, School of Management, Kyoto Gakuen University
1 Sogabecho-nanjo-ohtani, Kameoka-City
Kyoto-Prefecture, 621-8555, Japan
MBA from Osaka Prefecture University
Tel: 0771-29-2330
hasegawa@kyotogakuen.ac.jp

Shino Hiiragi
Project Research Associate
Manufacturing Management Research Center,
Graduate School of Economics, The University of Tokyo
7-3-1 Hongo, Bunkyo-ku, Tokyo, 113-0033, Japan
Doctor of Business Administration and Computer Science from
    Aichi Institute of Technology
s_hiiragi@nifty.com

Noriyuki Imai
Vice President, Toyota Financial Services Corporation
6-1 Ushijima-cho, Nishi-ku, Nagoya, 451-6015, Japan
Ph.D. from Meijo University
silverstone@mta.biglobe.ne.jp

Tomonori Inooka
Associate Professor
Faculty of Business, Kokushikan University
4-28-1, Setagaya, Setagaya-ku, Tokyo, 154-8515, Japan
M.Eng. from Tokyo University of Science
inooka@kokushikan.ac.jp

Fumiko Kurokawa
Professor, Dokkyo University,
1-1, Gakuen-cho, Soka-shi, Saitama, 340-0042, Japan
Ph.D. in Management from Meiji University
fkurokaw@dokkyo.ac.jp

Yoshiteru Minagawa
Professor, Faculty of Commerce, Nagoya Gakuin University
1-25 Atsuta Nishimachi, Atsuta, Nagoya, 456-8612, Japan
Doctor of Economics from Nagoya University
minagawa@ngu.ac.jp

Yasuhiro Monden
Professor Emeritus of Tsukuba University
Visiting Professor of NUCB, Global MBA
yasuhirom@mail2.accsnet.ne.jp

Farzad Movahedi Sobhani
Academic staff of the Science &
    Research Branch of Islamic Azad University, Iran
P.O. Box 1455-4834, Iran
Tel: +021-801-1001 ext.3396
Fax: +021-800-5040

Yoshiyuki Nagasaka
Professor, School of Management, Konan University
8-9-1 Okamoto, Higasinada, Kobe, 658-8501, Japan
Doctor of Engineering from Osaka University
Tel: +81-78-435-2454; Fax: +81-78-435-2543
nagasaka@konan-u.ac.jp

Junya Sakaguchi
Associate Professor, School of Accountancy, Kansai University
3-3-35 Yamate-cho, Suita, Osaka, 564-8680, Japan
Tel: 06-6368-1121
Doctor of Business Administration from Kobe University

Naoya Yamaguchi
Associate Professor, Graduate School of Modern Society and Culture
Faculty of Economics, Niigata University
8050 Ikarashi 2-no-cho, Nishi-ku, Niigata, 950-2181, Japan
Tel/Fax: +81-25-262-6504
naoya@econ.niigata-u.ac.jp

Part 1

Strategy for Forming an Inter-Firm Network

1

From Adam Smith's Division of Labor to Network Organization

From the Market Price Mechanism to the Incentive Price Mechanism

Yasuhiro Monden

University of Tsukuba

1   Purpose of this Chapter

The father of economics, Adam Smith (1776), was the first to advocate that supply and demand in the market would be balanced through the market principle (or market price) of the "invisible hand". However, the market does not necessarily work well, especially in an age of depression. Thus, in the early twentieth century, large, vertically integrated companies, such as GM, Standard Oil, etc., emerged in Western countries. Chandler (1977) verified and characterized these companies as having a "visible hand", because these big companies directly controlled the supply and demand in their own integrated organizations. These companies also had the drawbacks of monopoly and large fixed-cost burden. Therefore, the author will try to propose a system that induces cooperation among firms, which constitutes an inter-firm network. In particular, in this chapter, the author will propose that the joint profit allocation system, called *incentive price*, be used as an incentive system of management control.

Thus, the structure of this chapter will be as follows:

(1) from Adam Smith's functional division of labor to cell production;
(2) analogy between the cell-production system and the multi-divisional organization;
(3) from the multi-divisional organization to the network organization;

(4) design of an incentive system for the companies participating in a network.

2 Adam Smith's Functional Division of Labor

Adam Smith said at the very beginning of his famous book (5th ed.), *The Wealth of Nations*,[1] that "The greatest improvement in the productive powers of labor seem to have been the effects of the division of labor". In other words, he emphasized that productivity would be improved most by the division of labor.

When Smith used the term "division of labor", he was advocating the effect of the division of labor on the whole society. Thus, it is clear that he was aiming at division of occupations; division of industries, such as agriculture and manufacturing; and division of labor within a certain industry, for example, division of spinners and weavers. As he is known as the "father of economics", it is apparent that he tried to describe the route to becoming a wealthy nation through nationwide productivity increases based on the division of labor.

Smith's idea was that the wealth of nations would be increased through the free transactions of goods in a society as a whole. This was the original point of the market principle or free market mechanism in the modern world. Further, the means of linkage between the free market transactions of goods through division of labor and the improvement of productivity or wealth of the whole society was the so-called "invisible hand".

In order to show the reasons for such effects caused by the society-wide division of labor or the effectiveness of market transactions, Smith applied a microscopic economic analysis that was supposed to verify that the division of labor in an individual manufacturing firm would markedly improve the factory's productivity.

Thus, in this chapter, the author wishes to critically examine the validity of Smith's logic by following his explanations of the firm's division of labor from the viewpoint of modern production management. This chapter extends a different opinion to his verification, thereby showing a modern

---

[1]In this chapter, the author used and quoted *The Wealth of Nations: Books* I–III by Adam Smith, with an introduction by Andrew Skinner; Harmondsworth, Middlesex: Penguin Books, 1970. This book is called Skinner's *Wealth of Nations* (1970).

approach of achieving supply and demand, an approach that will be used together with the market mechanism.

Based on this analysis, the author will depart from Smith's idea of the functional division of labor and instead recommend the cellular manufacturing system or just-in-time (JIT) production system that integrates various functional operations into each group of product variety.

The cell-type manufacturing system can better increase productivity, adapt much more flexibly to changes to the final demands, and improve respect for humanity in the firm.

In addition, it is doubtful whether market transactions based on the division of labor could actually balance the supply and demand in the market. Cases of dysfunctional markets are well known. Moreover, even though supply and demand may be achieved in a market, it is uncertain how long the balancing movement might take to reach full equilibrium. If it takes too long for an individual firm to clear its over-production, the company might go bankrupt. For a certain industry, or the macroscopic economy as a whole, unless the total supply meets the total demand, or unless the total effective demand meets the total supply in each period, the depression of the industry in question or of the macro-economy will continue.

To overcome this problem and establish a system to balance supply and demand, the author wishes to propose the concept of a "visible hand" in the network organization. (This differs from Chandler's "visible hand" within a single, vertically integrated organization.) The structure of such a network organization is based on an inter-functional firms allied organization, which is the basic premise this chapter uses to criticize Smith's division of labor.

Further as the antithesis of the supply-demand equilibrium price as a market control mechanism, the author proposes an incentive price as a network control mechanism.

2.1   *Division of labor in a pin manufacturing plant*

It is said that in the age of Smith, the trade of the pin-maker was an independent occupation or profession (or craft), but it was also divided into many departments (processes), each of which was in turn regarded as an independent occupation. The task of making a pin was composed of about 18 operations [Smith (1789) in Skinner's *Wealth of Nations* (1970), p. 110] such as:

(1) one man draws out the wire,
(2) another straightens it,

(3) a third cuts it,

(4) a fourth points it,

(5) a fifth grinds it at the top for receiving the head;

(6) to make the head requires three distinct operations;

(7) to put it on is a peculiar business,

(8) to whiten the pin (to make it white in colour) is another;

(9) it is even a trade by itself to put them into the paper (to package the pins).

In some plants, all of the above operations were handled by separate individual workers, and in other plants, a few operations among them were dealt with by the same worker.

In order for Smith to show the productivity increase in pin manufacturing with numerical figures, he described a small manufacturing plant case that he had seen:

- Only 10 workers were employed in that plant. (Thus, some of the 10 men were engaged in a few separate jobs as multi-skilled workers.)
- Workers made 12 pounds of pins a day when they worked hard.
- One pound of pins implies more than 4,000 units of medium-sized pins.
- Thus, these 10 workers could have made approximately 48,000 units (= 4,000 × 12 pounds) of pins a day at most.
- Smith says that "[e]ach person ... might be considered as making four thousand eight hundred pins in a day".

This "production quantity per person per day" is a measure of productivity. A similar productivity measure, production quantity per person per daily regular hours, is still used, even in modern production management theory.

Here Smith contended that "if they had all wrought separately and independently, and without any of them having been educated to this peculiar business, they could certainly not each of them have made twenty, perhaps not one pin in a day" [Smith (1789) in Skinner (1970), p. 110].

Now, at this point, a brief comment on the vertical division of labor among multiple companies in a network organization that the author recommends in this chapter: Certainly, no individual company could be most efficient in all of the operations under the constraints in some plant of various resources. Then, it would be most effective for each company only to concentrate on a single operation of core competence and take part in some division of operations. The argument about network organization up to this point may seem to coincide with Smith's logic of division of labor. However, such multiple companies that are engaged in certain divided jobs will have an *operational alliance* or *capital alliance* to form a network organization, which works virtually as a single organization with inter-firm relationships. Such a vertical inter-firm relationship does not exist in Smith's division of labor, and the merit of its integrity is similar to the efficiency of the cellular manufacturing system that we will see later in this chapter.

2.2   *Three merits of the division of labor*

According to Smith, "the great increase of the quantity of work in consequence of the division of labor" is due to the following three reasons [Smith (1789) in Skinner (1970), p. 112]:

(1) "[F]irst, to the increase of dexterity in every particular workman".
(2) "[S]econdly, to the saving of the time which is commonly lost in passing from one species of work to another". This means that when a workman moves from one kind of job to another, he usually loses setup time, which can be saved if each man is engaged in a single functional job based on division of labor among workmen.
(3) "[L]astly, to the invention of a great number of machines which facilitate and abridge labor, and enable one man to do the work of many".

"The great increase of the quantity of work" implies average production quantity per day per person, as explained before.

The above-explained division of labor in a pin manufacturing plant is the so-called division of functional jobs, and the three merits that Smith proclaims above are also based on the division of functional jobs. The problems with the division of functional jobs and the above three merits that Smith proclaimed will be examined in the forthcoming sections in comparison with the cellular manufacturing system.

3   Cellular Manufacturing System as the Antithesis of Smith's Functional Division of Labor

As we have seen in the previous sections, Smith claimed that a production system based on the functional division of labor by specified workmen could improve productivity. However, such a statement is not necessarily correct from the viewpoint of modern advanced theories of production management that promotes a cellular manufacturing system using multi-skilled workers. This cellular manufacturing system is what Smith criticized as a method of production with very low productivity.

For the purpose of this chapter, which tries to show the synergies created through inter-firm cooperation, the most important thing is to be able to adapt to demand changes in the market, thereby minimizing the risk of over-production. This can be attained by shortening the production lead time. The production system of multi-process holding by multi-skilled workers, explained below, enables such a goal.

3.1 Functional division of labor by specialized workers with "lot" production and conveyance

Now, let us imagine a plant that resembles Smith's pin manufacturing plant, which has various machines for various machining operations. Each process has the same kind of multiple machines with specialized workers. This layout of machines is called the job-shop layout. As shown in Fig. 1, the types of machines are lathing, milling, boring, welding, and polishing machines, which are laid out in groups according to type, to which workers are assigned.

Such a machine layout is seen in the horizontal direction in Fig. 1. This is called holding multiple machine units in Japan.

However, if a man has only one machine unit (a lathe, for example), he just sets a piece of work (material) on the machine and pushes the start button, then merely watches the machine until the machine's automatic operation ends. Thus, the worker has wasted waiting time in each of his cycle times. But, if the worker has six lathes, as Fig. 1 shows in the horizontal direction, then he will move to the second lathe after he pushes the start button of the first lathe while that lathe is cutting. In this way, he can increase his productivity.

Machining operations with more than one of the same kind of machine, such as lathes, are usually inclined to make as many units as possible in one lot or batch, and thus are likely to create production with a large lot size (i.e., both the number of units of materials to be introduced and the output units to be produced are large). As a result, the stocks of products or works-in-process from the process will be large, and the total production lead time will be much longer, as the carrying time of the wasteful inventory in question will be added.

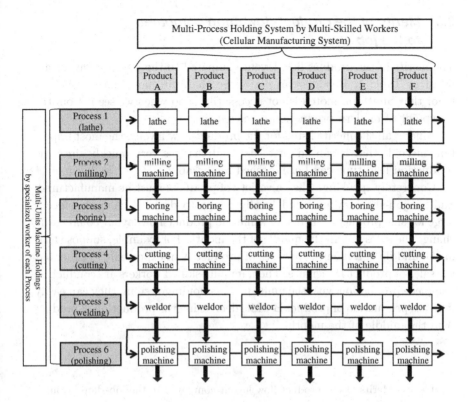

Fig. 1. Job-shop manufacturing and product-flow manufacturing.

3.2 *Product-flow layout with multi-skilled workers for one-piece production*

In order to overcome the drawback of longer production lead time that accompanies the job-shop layout of machines, a multi-skilled worker was introduced who could handle a variety of machines one-by-one according to the timing with which a product would flow along the different machines laid out. Such a machine layout is called the *product-flow layout* or *flow-shop layout* in modern production management textbooks. This layout is also called *multi-process holding* in Japan.

This method of layout is typically done as seen in Fig. 1 in a vertical direction, from top to bottom. A variety of machines — lathing, milling, boring, cutting, welding, and polishing machines — are laid down in this order, and a single worker handles all of these machines at the same time.

3.3 *Merits of the product-flow shop compared to the job shop*

The merits of the product-flow layout compared to the job-shop layout are listed in Table 1. Readers can easily see that the functional division of labor that Smith promoted is not necessarily good when we see it from the viewpoint of modern production management.

Among all the merits listed for the product-flow layout, the most important merit is that it can adapt to demand changes very quickly since the production lead time can be shortened remarkably.

Concretely speaking, when a variety of products must be manufactured, Smith's job-shop layout could hardly adapt to demand changes, since a large lot size production is made, while the product-flow layout could easily change the sales mix in the middle of the month. For example, suppose that in the middle of a month, the sales of product A unexpectedly decline, but the sales of product B increase. Then, if multi-skilled workers are conducting one-piece production with the multi-process holding system, they can easily increase production of product B while decreasing the production of product A in the middle of the month.

Table 1. Merits of the product-flow layout compared to the job-shop layout.

	Product-flow Layout	Job-shop Layout
Lot size	Small (usually, one-piece)	Large
Lead time	Short	Long
Adaptability to demand changes	Speedy	Not speedy
Work-in-process inventory	Few	Many
Detectability of defects	Easy to find	Not easy to find
Skill of worker	Multi-skilled	Single-skilled
Machine	Small and less expensive	Big and expensive
Conveyance	Almost nothing	Much
Detectability of wastes	Easy to find wastes of conveyance, waiting, etc.	Hard to find wastes of conveyance, waiting, etc.
Productivity	Total optimization (productivity increase of the whole plant)	Sub-optimization (productivity increase of each machine)

Smith once claimed that the production system of the functional division of labor by specified workmen could improve productivity. However, such a statement is not necessarily correct. What we have described is a cellular manufacturing system using multi-skilled workers. This cellular manufacturing system is what Smith criticized as a method of production with very low productivity.

For the purpose of this chapter, which tries to show ways of balancing supply and demand through inter-firm cooperation, the most important thing is to be able to adapt to demand changes in the market, thereby minimizing the risk of over-production. This can be attained by shortening the production lead time. The production system of multi-process holding by the multi-skilled workers, explained below, enables us to achieve such a goal.

The multi-process holding system or cellular manufacturing system looks like a network organization. This analogy will be examined in detail in the following section.

4   Analogy between the Cell-Production System and the Multi-Divisional Organization

4.1   *Structural relationship between functional and multi-divisional organizations*

Decentralization means, as the word itself indicates, that many of the decision-making powers that are usually held by the CEO are transferred to subordinate divisions.

Accordingly, a decentralized structure may consist of decentralized units, such as the sales department, the manufacturing department, the product development department and the purchasing department, created as a result of the functional division of a corporate organization. This is the so-called functional organization. (This is the organization schematized in Fig. 2, but viewed laterally.)

On the other hand, there are other types of decentralized organizations classified by product, business type, customer, region, etc., in accordance with the market peculiarity. These decentralized units are generally called divisions, and this type of organization is called multi-divisional. A typical multi-divisional organization consists of decentralized units classified by the product type of the company, and such a system is called a product

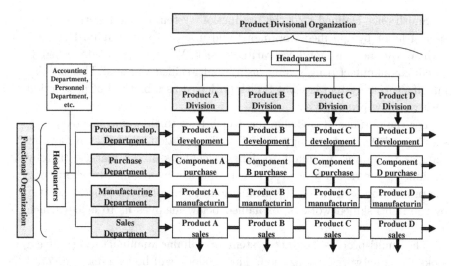

Fig. 2. The relationship between the functional organization and the multi-divisional organization.

divisional system. (This is the organization schematized in Fig. 2, but viewed longitudinally.)

Since the responsibility for a part of the entire company is transferred to each division, each division that is a self-paying organizational unit is also called a profit center.

Please compare Fig. 2 with Fig. 1 ("cellular manufacturing system"). You will notice that the functional organization schematized in Fig. 2 is similar to the functional process layout of the division of labor among the functionally specialized craftsmen referred to by Smith and schematized in Fig. 1; also, the multi-divisional organization illustrated in Fig. 2 is similar to the multi-process layout with multi-skilled workers illustrated in Fig. 1.

Since each division of a multi-divisional organization comprises the management functional departments for production, sales, etc., that are necessary for carrying out everyday tasks, each is a self-sustainable organizational unit to a considerable extent. Panasonic, which had a television division, a washer division, etc., was operated on the basis of a typical product divisional system in the narrow sense. Even now, highly diversified companies in Japan, such as digital merchandise manufacturers, adopt the product divisional system without exception.

Figure 2 illustrates the two organizational forms as a matrix. In the figure, the functional organization is illustrated transversely, and the product divisional organization, which is a typical divisional organization, is illustrated longitudinally. (However, this figure does not illustrate a matrix organization, in which both organizational structures are present concurrently.)

However, in cases where the number of divisions exceeds the span of control by head office, some divisions may be integrated into a higher-level organizational unit called a division headquarter, an internal subsidiary company, or an internal company.

In Japan, in many cases, the actual division system consists of a mixture of the functional division system as a profit center and the product divisional system.

4.2   Merits of the multi-divisional organization compared to the functional organization

From the perspective of supply and demand equilibrium, which is the theme of this chapter, the characteristics of the two organizational forms are as described in Table 2.

First, the weak points of the functional organization are that

(1) coordination among the functional sections is difficult to achieve, and the communication cost therefore is consequently high, because

(2) there is no choice other than to secure the coordination between sales (demand) and production (supply) by way of production and sales meetings in the presence of the president and the directors in charge of production and sales, which means that the communication line becomes long; that is, it becomes difficult to respond swiftly to the change in demand (supply and demand equilibrium). This problem is the same as that posed by pin production based on the division of labor by process (the division of labor by functional process) discussed by Smith; that is, the production of saleable products in a saleable quantity at a saleable point in time (JIT production) is difficult. This problem is especially amplified in multi-product production.

(3) also, in conjunction with this problem, since the cost center (the section that presides over supply) and the revenue center (the section that presides over demand) are separated, it is difficult to secure proper coordination (communication) between the two centers and plan and control

Table 2.   Merits of the multi-divisional organization compared to the functional organization.

Demerits of the Functional Organization	Merits of the Multi-Divisional Organization
(1) The cost of coordination (communication cost) among the various functional sections is high. This demerit is the same as that posed by the pin production based on the division of labor by process discussed by Adam Smith.	(1) The cost of coordination (communication) among the various functional sections is low. This merit is the same as that of the cellular production system.
(2) Since there is no other choice than to secure the coordination between sales (demand) and production (supply) by way of production & sales meetings in the presence of the CEO, the communication line becomes long; that is, it becomes difficult to respond swiftly to the change in demand.	(2) Since the communication line between sales (demand) and production (supply) is short, the supply response to the change in demand is easy to achieve, and swift decision-making according to the market environment, that is, market-oriented management, is possible.
(3) Since the cost center (the section that presides over supply) and the revenue center (the section that presides over demand) are separated, it is difficult to secure a proper coordination (communication) between the two centers and plan and control profit. Above all, profit management by product is quite difficult to achieve, and the only viable profit management would be a company-wide one.	(3) Since each division is a profit center, balancing (profit management) sales revenue (demand) and cost (supply) is easy.
(4) The managers of each functional section are specialists, and it is difficult for the functional organization to foster generalist managers.	(4) Since the employees can directly observe the management activities of the entire division, their morale is higher. Also, it is easy to foster generalist managers. These merits are the same as those of the cellular production system.

profit. Above all, profit management by product is quite difficult, and the only viable profit management method would be a company-wide one.

The multi-divisional organization solves all of the above problems as follows:

(1) the cost of coordination (communication cost) among the functional sections is low. This merit also characterizes the cellular production system, because the supply response to the change in demand, that is, the supply and demand equilibrium, is easily achieved, and swift decision-making according to the market environment is possible; that is, market-oriented management is possible, since production and sales are linked together in the same division and the communication line between sales (demand) and production (supply) is short.

(2) also, since the division is a profit center, it is easy to balance (control the profit) the sales revenue (demand) and the cost (supply) for each product.

(3) furthermore, since the employees can directly experience the management activities of the entire division, their morale is higher. Also, it is easy to foster generalist managers. These features amount to the upgrading of human qualities, which is one of the great advantages of the cellular production system.

As shown above, the functional organization has the same defects as the functional division of labor in the pin factory discussed by Smith, whereas the multi-divisional organization has the same merits as the cellular production system seen in recent years.

5 From the Division-Based Company to the Network Organization

5.1 *What is the network organization?*

In the author's opinion, a good organization is a vertically aligned organization. Such an organization is called a network organization or virtual organization.

The network organization is a structure in which an organization is allied with other companies who have some competitive functional merit in the markets, keeping for themselves functions of their own in which they have core competence, such as research and development, manufacturing, distribution and sales, etc. This is different from using outsourcing from independent companies on the market base; it is a series of long-term alliances (including the so-called *keiretsu*) among vertical functional firms. Thus, this network can be called a supply chain or inter-firm relations.

When making such alliances, the top management of any company should ask themselves, "What is the raison d'être or existence value for the company?" In other words, they have to recognize what their company can contribute to society and what competence they have to sell to customers compared to other companies in the business world.

The network or alliance in this context implies long-term relationships with transactions that include technological alliances, joint development, mutual licensing, joint manufacturing, production consignment (production on commission), sales consignment (sales on commission), capital alliances, and joint ventures, and, moreover, establishment of affiliated companies and mergers. The important point is that the recommendation here is not to establish any single, vertically integrated company, but to construct some inter-firm network.

Let's define the network organization again. It is a network that multiple firms will construct, but it behaves as if it is a single company with mutual cooperation among the constructing companies. The network usually consists of a core company and many other companies that will obey the instructions of the core company. The core company will partake in only the functions in which it is outstanding, and outsource all other functional areas to the others, each according to its own competence.

5.2 Structure of the network organization

The network organization as a whole looks like a vertically combined organization when seen from various functions. It will be depicted in Fig. 3, but readers are encouraged to compare Fig. 3 with Fig. 2, which depicts a typical product-oriented divisional organization.

Observing Fig. 3 for each kind of business vertically, the feature of aligning the strongest firm in each function seems to be equivalent to Smith's division of various firms in various markets, but this is a false notion. This is because Smith promoted the division of firms *in the market*, while the author promotes the division of functional firms *in an organization*, which is a network organization though it is not a single-firm organization.

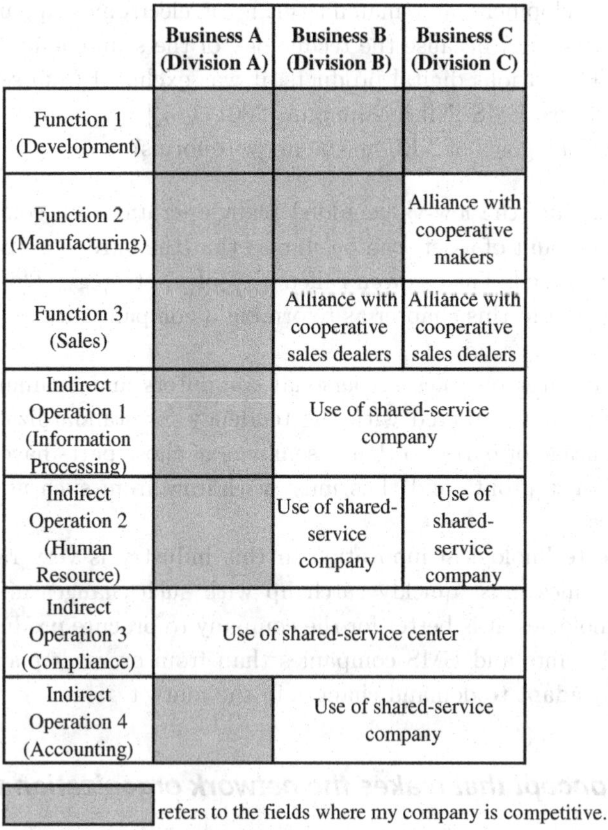

	Business A (Division A)	Business B (Division B)	Business C (Division C)
Function 1 (Development)			
Function 2 (Manufacturing)			Alliance with cooperative makers
Function 3 (Sales)		Alliance with cooperative sales dealers	Alliance with cooperative sales dealers
Indirect Operation 1 (Information Processing)		Use of shared-service company	
Indirect Operation 2 (Human Resource)		Use of shared-service company	Use of shared-service company
Indirect Operation 3 (Compliance)	Use of shared-service center		
Indirect Operation 4 (Accounting)		Use of shared-service company	

▮ refers to the fields where my company is competitive.

Fig. 3. Conceptual figure showing inter-firm organization.

5.3 *A case of an inter-firm network: NEC*

In 2001, NEC sold eight affiliated manufacturing companies in the overseas market of communication instruments to change itself into an asset-efficient company. They also sold overseas personal computer plants. Even NEC's 13 domestic affiliated manufacturing companies for personal computers, printers, cellular phones, and communication instruments, etc. (excluding semi-conductors) were changed into independent electronic manufacturing services (EMS). NEC decided to outsource these areas to EMS, which were going to be independent from the NEC headquarters, since they would be going public in the future. NEC Nagano, for example, which assembles personal computer displays, has established sales and service departments to conduct development and manufacturing of electronics apparatus on commission. However, because the technology of the semi-conductor plant is core to NEC's various digital products, it was excluded from sell-out or being changed into EMS [Nikkei-shinbun (2001/1/5)].

What were the goals of NEC in the above reforms?

(1) By outsourcing the low-value-added plant operations on commission, the total amount of assets can be slim so that the burden of fixed costs can be decreased. This is often called a "fables" strategy. This is what is emphasized in this chapter as reforming a company into an invisible network organization.

(2) The profit rates on sales of personal computers and communication instruments have lowered with the tendency for standardization and common usage of parts, so that assemblers of those parts have become unable to get profits and thus must withdraw from such assembling businesses.

(3) Since the technological innovation in this industry is very rapid and the companies must quickly catch up with such changes in markets and technologies, it is better for the company to procure products from domestic plants and EMS companies than from overseas plants so as to quickly adapt to demand changes in the market.

5.4   *The concept that makes the network organization unique*

The author proposes the following core concept of the network organization: The proper feature of a network organization is that this organization can create new value through the joint activities of participating companies. Further, the decision to participate in this organization by the participants, who are independent companies, will be made based on whether the incentives given by the core company to each participant could be satisfied by each participant.

Such incentives are the allocated amount of anticipated additional value created by the joint cooperative works after participation. Such additional value, created value, or premium value is equivalent to the so-called synergy effect, which may be based on the so-called complementarities.

Such a nature exists neither in the pure market nor in the pure organization. That is, neither in the pure market nor in the pure organization does the concept of incremental value through cooperative activities of multiple independent companies exist. Only the value created by the independent activities of a single company (that is, stand-alone value created by a single company) exists. Therefore, readers can easily understand that the above characteristics of network organization are not derived from any nature of the pure market or the pure organization.

If we consider the relationship between the synergy effect concept and Coase's (1937) transaction cost concept, the transaction cost saved when the transaction is conducted within the internal organization is merely a small portion of the synergy effect. That is, the former is a partial set of the latter. The major synergy effects of inter-firm cooperation include the following:

(a) restructure effect on redundant functions in a combined company;
(b) cost reduction effect through the economy of scale;
(c) increased sales through joint utilization of each other's sales channels;
(d) combination of technologies;
(e) increased sales revenues and profits caused by the new products developed through combination of technologies, etc.

6   Design of an Incentive System for the Companies Participating in a Network

In a network organization, a participating company should not try to make a bargain with another company that is only to its advantage. Such a one-sided bargain will not last long. In transactions between companies, a so-called win-win relationship is necessary. This is the management control role of the core company, and it is achieved by means of the profit-sharing system as an incentive.

Profit-sharing is attained through the internal transfer price, international transfer price, asset transfer price, parts price, acquisition price, or lump-sum subsidy, etc., all of which can be referred to as the incentive price. Upon seeing the shared profit offered by the core company based on this incentive system, prospective member companies decide on their own whether or not they will participate in the network. The prospective companies cannot be coerced into any decision. The only thing the integrator can do is to persuade them to participate using the incentive of shared profit.

When some other competitive company is interested in purchasing this prospective company as a target, then the amount of synergy effect may increase, and thus their proposed purchase price (including the allocated synergy) may increase in the market. However, the theoretical allocation formula for the synergy (See equations (1) and (2) in the following section 7) will not change and it will be consistently applied.

Such flexibility of the incentive price (i.e., purchase price) is not the same as supply-demand equilibrium price, because the former price is determined based on the magnitude of synergy effect and the contribution grade to it whereas the latter price is determined by the numbers of the acquiring firms and acquired firms. Thus both prices will be different in their amounts.

However, with only the economic incentive of shared profit, it may be difficult to form a network organization which is desirable to the integrator.

There are many levels of control in the "control" concept, which can be applied other than the shared profit incentive: (1) Perfect legal ownership of voting rights in the shareholders' meeting. (2) Less than 100% ownership (or more than 50% ownership can control the shareholders' meeting). (3) Sending the parent personnel to the target board of directors to control their decisions. (4) Having the long-term transaction contract (or operational consignment contract) with the target company, such as being a major customer of the products of the target supplier.

If the core company had some of the above control rights they have a power to induce the member candidate firm to be their tighter member. However, if the level of control right is much lower, the control power becomes weaker and as a result even a member candidate firm in the existing network organization may depart or not continue to participate in the network in question.

That is, prospective member companies of the network organization might not participate in the network organization if the incentive is merely a share of the profit. There is a problem in that the profit obtained by maintaining independence and not participating in a complete coalition may be greater than the above-mentioned shared profit. That is, a profit-sharing scheme that is satisfactory for all is difficult to design. Sometimes a partial coalition may be more profitable than a complete coalition.

However, in cases in which a company that is the target of acquisition is a subsidiary of a consolidated business group, it is more likely that the invitation to become a wholly owned subsidiary or be merged will be approved. The approach taken in 2002 by Kunio Nakamura, president of Matsushita Electric (currently called Panasonic), was to acquire full ownership of its five subsidiaries. The advantage of acquiring full ownership of a company is that the president of the parent company can attend the stockholders' general meeting for the wholly owned subsidiary as a stockholder with 100% voting interest, and can fully accomplish the purpose of the parent company in the eventual restructuring of the group's organization (rationalization of the business of the group by splitting some of the businesses of its wholly owned subsidiaries, etc.) using the centralized power of the integrator of the network organization.

Since an affiliated company of the consolidated business group cannot form a partial coalition of sub-groups of affiliated companies departing from the control of the parent company, the profit-sharing through the transaction price will be stable and easily accepted.

Now, the design of the profit-sharing system is essential to the construction of a network organization, but it is also an issue of *financial management accounting*.

The mechanism of profit-sharing among the companies participating in a network is the theme of management accounting, and the setting of the internal transfer prices of goods and services among the vertically allied companies and the setting of the profit-sharing system in the lump-sum total are also problems to be solved.

The issue of setting the internal transfer prices refers to the way the business consignment prices are to be set at the joint of a value chain. The service consignee (or service recipient) would like to consign it at as low a price as possible, whereas the service consignor (or service provider) would like to provide it at as high a price as possible. Now, a profit-sharing scheme satisfactory to both parties is secured by sharing the profit according to the *degree of contribution* of each member company to the joint profit of the network.

7 Examples of Incentive Price

7.1 *The acquisition price of M&A*

The amount of the comprehensive investment contained in their tangible and intangible assets, that is, the standalone market value of each firm before the press release announcement of the merger, can be used as the degree of contribution to the synergy effect or the synergy allocation criterion, and thus the synergy effect can be allotted in advance before knowing the share price on the merger date. This is how merger-involved companies can determine the provisional merger ratio and the acquisition price on the date of the initial press release. The relationships between the standalone shareholder values (A and B) of the acquirer firm and the target firm, the synergy effect C, and the purchase price X are depicted in Fig. 4.

Let us look at the formula for this logic.

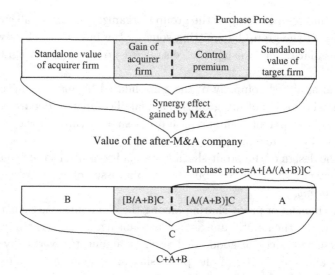

Fig. 4.   The relationships between the standalone shareholder values, the synergy effect, and the purchase price.

Let the shareholder value of non-surviving firm on merger date $= X$, shareholder value of surviving firm on merger date $= Y$, standalone market value of non-surviving firm before the press release for merger $= A$, standalone market value of surviving firm before press release for merger $= B$, present value of synergy effect $= C$, where the present value of the synergy effect (C) is the sum of the present values of RI_t, that is, the expected value of residual profit (or extra profit of often-merger company) at period t.

Then the formula for allocating the synergy effect is as follows:

$$X = [A/(A + B)]C + A \tag{1}$$

    = synergy effect allotment to shareholders of non-surviving firm

      + standalone market value of non-surviving firm before

        press release for merger

$$Y = [B/(A + B)]C + B \tag{2}$$

    = synergy effect allotment to shareholders of surviving firm

      + standalone market value of surviving firm before

        press release for merger

Summing up Eqs. (1) and (2),

Theoretical shareholder value (or theoretical market value)
of the newly formed firm after merger $= X + Y = C + (A + B)$

For details, see Monden (2010).

The above formula will satisfy the condition of the *individual rationality of the cooperative games*. Because the *partial coalition* among multiple firms within the companies of the consolidated business group will not happen due to the control power by capital ownership and so forth of the central parent company, the allocation of profits that merely satisfies the individual rationality will be stable, and all participating companies will be satisfied to participate in the current business group.[2] The above allocation formula is based on the cumulative opportunity cost method that ensures the Φ stability concept of the cooperative game theory applicable to the situation in which all types of partial coalition are not necessarily available. (For Φ stability, see Suzuki, 1959.) For the essence of the cumulative opportunity cost method for profit allocation, please see the appendix (pp. 24–29) to this chapter.

8 Concluding Summary: From the Market Price Mechanism to the Incentive Price Mechanism

Adam Smith (1776) was the first to advocate that supply and demand in the market would be balanced through the market principle (or market

---

[2] As an allocation scheme of the cooperative game, the Shapley value is often applied in academic articles (Shubik, 1962; Hamlen *et al.*, 1977, 1980; etc.), and Moriarity's allocation scheme (Moriarity, 1975a, 1975b) was criticized as neglecting the possibility of partial coalitions. However, since any partial coalition among multiple firms within the consolidated business group will not happen because of the central control through its capital ownership, the author applied Moriarity's allocation formula step-by-step in sequence when any additional merger or acquisition happened. The author has coined the term "cumulative opportunity cost method" to describe this allocation scheme, which will be explained briefly in the appendix of this chapter. Also see "The Role of Intangible Assets in Allocating the Inter-Firm Profit of a Global Consolidated Business", contained in this volume.

price) of the "invisible hand". However, the market does not necessarily work well, especially in an age of depression.

Thus, in the early twentieth century, large, vertically integrated companies such as GM, Standard Oil, etc., emerged in Western countries. Chandler (1977) verified and characterized these companies as having a "visible hand", because these big companies directly controlled the supply and demand in their own integrated organizations. These companies also had the drawbacks of monopoly and large fixed-cost burden.

Therefore the author proposed a system that induces cooperation among firms of the inter-firm network. In particular, the author proposed that the joint profit allocation system, called incentive price, be used as an incentive system of management control.

As an example of an incentive price, the author derived the acquisition price of M&A based on the concepts of cooperative game theory.

In the case where some companies in a network purchase goods or services in market transactions (i.e., in the automobile industry an iron and steel maker trades with an overseas coal-mining company in the coal market), such market transactions are outside the control of the core company (integrator). Similarly, the most downstream of the member companies of the network trade is with the consumer market of the end products. These are the boundaries of the network organization.[3]

Appendix: Cumulative Opportunity Cost Method of Profit Allocation

First, let us see the famous Moriarity formula applied to profit allocation among various departments. Let ϕ_i = profit allocated to the department i, R_i = maximum profit of department i when it works independently, R_N = maximum profit of the grand coalition S_N when all departments have cooperated together.

Under such a grand coalition, the following profit allocation will be made among participating departments:

$$\phi_i = R_i + \frac{R_i}{\sum_{i \in S_N} R_i} \left(R_N - \sum_{i \in S_N} R_i \right). \tag{1}$$

---

[3]For details see Monden (2009), Section 5.5, *Market transactions*.

The last item on the right-hand side $(R_N - \sum_{i \in S_N} R_i)$ stands for the incremental profit earned when all departments work together; in other words this is the synergy effect of the joint activities of all departments. Therefore, Moriarity's allocation method shows how to allocate the incremental profit caused by the joint activities of all departments.

Here, if we assume that

$$\left(R_N - \sum_{i \in S_N} R_i \right) > 0,$$

then the following relationship will always hold:

$$\phi_i > R_i.$$

Because of this relationship, Moriarity's method can ensure the individual rationality of the cooperative game. When some partial coalition can hold, however, Moriarity's allocation method will not ensure the coalition rationality so that the department in the partial coalition in question may reject the allocated profit assigned by the central headquarters of the grand coalition. This is because the profit allocated within the partial coalition in question may be greater than the profit allocated by the center of the grand coalition.

However, in the real world, not all types of partial coalitions may be formed. For example, under the M&A case that is dealt in this chapter, the merging business group is a large group of companies that prepares consolidated financial statements. In such a consolidated business group, the subsidiary companies are controlled by the parent company through capital ownership. The parent company may own more than 50% of the voting shares in a related company, or the parent company may send directors to the related company or may be the biggest customer of the related company in question. In such cases, the parent company is essentially controlling the related company, which will be included in the consolidation of the financial statements.

In short, the subsidiary companies and related companies within the consolidated business group cannot freely make a partial coalition to depart from the central control of a parent company. Here, the author will apply Moriarity's allocation method to such a consolidated business group's M&A with a targeted company when the parent company makes mergers one-by-one, sequentially. Such an M&A is always done in a bilateral relationship and the allocation of the synergy effect is always done between two companies, such that the allocation can be stable due to the assurance of the individual rationality only.

Generally speaking, in M&A, the merger company will combine with a single target company at a time, even though several companies may be considered as candidates for target companies. Even if two companies were merged at almost the same time, it would be usual for one of the companies to be merged before the other.

Thus, there will usually only be one target company at a time. As time elapses, the merger company will continuously add and merge single target companies sequentially. Under such a premise, there must always be profit allocation between two companies. In other words, the synergy allocation between two companies will determine the acquisition price for the merged company.

Now let us formulate the model for sequential profit allocation in the sequential merging process as time elapses.

First, suppose that company X wishes to merge with company Y. The independent profits of each company are denoted as R_X and R_Y. Also, the combined profit or consolidated profit of the combined company $(X + Y)$ will be denoted as R_{X+Y}. Thus, the synergy effect of this merger (or acquisition) will be

$$(R_{X+Y} - R_X - R_Y).$$

If this synergy effect is divided between the two before-merger companies according to the ratio of the independent profits of each company, R_X and R_Y, then the allocated profit for each set of stockholders of the before-merger companies will be ϕ_X and ϕ_Y, as shown in the following equations:

$$\phi_X = \frac{R_X}{R_X + R_Y}(R_{X+Y} - R_X - R_Y) + R_X \tag{3}$$

$$\phi_Y = \frac{R_Y}{R_X + R_Y}(R_{X+Y} - R_X - R_Y) + R_Y \tag{4}$$

Thus $\phi_X > R_X$, $\phi_Y > R_Y$.

Next, after some time elapses, suppose that the after-merger company $(X + Y)$ described above now wishes to merge with company Z. The independent profits of each company are now denoted as R_{X+Y} and R_Z. Also, the combined profit or consolidated profit of the combined company $(X + Y + Z)$ will be denoted as R_{X+Y+Z}. Thus, the synergy effect of this merger (or acquisition) will be

$$(R_{X+Y+Z} - R_{X+Y} - R_Z).$$

If this synergy effect is divided between the two before-merger companies according to the ratio of the independent profits of each company, R_{X+Y} and R_Z, then the allocated profit for each set of stockholders of the before-merger companies will be ϕ_{X+Y} and ϕ_Z, as shown in the following equations:

$$\phi_{X+Y} = \frac{R_{X+Y}}{R_{X+Y} + R_Z}(R_{X+Y+Z} - R_{X+Y} - R_Z) + R_{X+Y} \qquad (5)$$

$$\phi_Z = \frac{R_Z}{R_{X+Y} + R_Z}(R_{X+Y+Z} - R_{X+Y} - R_Z) + R_Z \qquad (6)$$

Thus $\phi_{X+Y} > R_{X+Y}, \phi_Z > R_Z$.

Further, after more time elapses, suppose that the after-merger company $(X+Y+Z)$ now wishes to merge with a new company W. The independent profits of each company are now denoted as R_{X+Y+Z} and R_W. Also, the combined profit or consolidated profit of the combined company $(X + Y + Z + W)$ will be denoted as $R_{X+Y+Z+W}$. Thus, the synergy effect of this merger (or acquisition) will be

$$(R_{X+Y+Z+W} - R_{X+Y+Z} - R_W).$$

If this synergy effect is divided between the two before-merger companies according to the ratio of the independent profits of each company, R_{X+Y+Z} and R_W, then the allocated profit for each set of stockholders of the before-merger companies will be ϕ_{X+Y+Z} and ϕ_W, as shown in the following equations:

$$\phi_{X+Y+Z} = \frac{R_{X+Y+Z}}{R_{X+Y+Z} + R_W}(R_{X+Y+Z+W}$$
$$- R_{X+Y+Z} - R_W) + R_{X+Y+Z} \qquad (7)$$

$$\phi_W = \frac{R_W}{R_{X+Y+Z} + R_W}(R_{X+Y+Z+W}$$
$$- R_{X+Y+Z} - R_W) + R_W. \qquad (8)$$

Thus $\phi_{X+Y+Z} > R_{X+Y+Z}, \phi_W > R_W$.

In each stage of sequential M&As, both the existing coalition company and the additional purchased company have all better gains than the ones in the before-merger situation.

In the second and third mergers (or acquisitions) above, the profits allocated to two companies can be further reallocated to the original existing member companies of the merger company. For example, the profit ϕ_{X+Y+Z} allocated to the original merger company $(X+Y+Z)$ in the third M&A can be reallocated to the company $(X+Y)$ and the company Z based on the ratio of their independent profits of ϕ_{X+Y} and ϕ_Z as ϕ'_{X+Y} and ϕ'_Z. In addition, the profit ϕ'_{X+Y} can also be reallocated to companies X and Y, respectively, based on the ratio of their independent profits of R_X and R_Y. The reallocated profit, to companies X and Y will be ϕ''_X and ϕ''_Y, respectively.

Thus it follows that:

$$\phi_{X+Y+Z} + \phi_W = R_{X+Y+Z+W}$$
$$(\phi''_X + \phi''_Y) + \phi'_Z \geq R_{X+Y+Z}$$
$$\phi''_X + \phi''_Y \geq R_{X+Y}$$

Here the after-merger companies $(X+Y+Z)$ and $(X+Y)$ are the "admissible partial coalitions" in the sequential M&A (business combination) process. The above conditions are called Φ stability conditions.

The above "Φ stability" conditions can hold in any number of grand coalition and its admissible partial coalitions in the sequential M&A process. This proposition can be proved when applying the logic of the mathematical inductive method.

In the actual determination of the acquisition price for the target company in the real-world M&A, the synergy effect expressed in the third merger above, which is

$$(R_{X+Y+Z+W} - R_{X+Y+Z} - R_W),$$

can be measured by directly estimating the synergy effect C, which will be the sum of the present values of the future increase of sales revenues caused by the merger and the future decrease of labor costs due to restructuring the after-merger company.

The independent profits R_{X+Y+Z} and R_W of each company participating in the merger will be expressed by their standalone stockholders' values B_{X+Y+Z} and A_W, respectively. As a result, Eqs. (8) and (7) will be expressed in the following way: (Denote that $A = A_W$ and $B = B_{X+Y+Z}$.)

The stockholders' value or the acquisition price X on the merger date, which will be given to the shareholders of the merged company W, is

$$X = \left(\frac{A}{A+B} \right) C + A. \tag{9}$$

The stockholders' value Y on the merger date, which will be given to the shareholders of the merged company (X + Y + Z) is

$$Y = \left(\frac{B}{A + B} \right) C + B. \tag{10}$$

As a result, the theoretical stockholders' value of the after-merger company (X + Y + Z + W) will be

$$X + Y = C + (A + B). \tag{11}$$

References

Chandler, A.D. Jr. (1977). *The Visible Hand: The Managerial Revolution in American Business*, Cambridge: The Belknap Press of Harvard University Press.

Coase, R. (1937). The nature of the firm, *Economica*, 4, 386–405.

Galbraith, J.R. (2002). *Designing Organization: An Executive Guide to Strategy, Structure, and Process*, New York: John Wiley & Sons.

Hamlen, S.S., Hamlem, W.A. Jr. and Tschirhart, J.T. (1977). The use of core theory in evaluating joint cost allocation schemes, *The Accounting Review*, 52, 616–627.

Hamlen, S.S., Hamlem, W.A. Jr. and Tschirhart, J.T. (1980). The use of the generalized shapley allocation in joint cost allocation, *The Accounting Review*, 55, 269–287.

Imai, K., Itami, H. and Koike, K. (1982). *Economics of Internal Organization*, Tokyo: Toyokeizai Shinposha (in Japanese).

Monden, Y. (1989a). Profit allocation by cumulative opportunity cost method, *Journal of Japan Industrial Management Association*, 40(4), 211–217 (in Japanese).

Monden, Y. (1989b). *Foundation of Transfer Price and Profit Allocation*, Tokyo: Dobunkan Shuppan Co. Ltd. (in Japanese).

Monden, Y. (1991). *Development of Transfer Price and Profit Allocation*, Tokyo: Dobunkan Shuppan Co. Ltd. (in Japanese).

Monden, Y. (2011). *Toyota Production System*, 4th edition, New York, NY: Taylor & Francis, forthcoming.

Monden, Y. (2006). *Toyota Production System*, Tokyo: Diamond Publishing Co. (in Japanese).

Monden, Y. (2009). M&A and its incentive system for the inter-firm organization, in Kurokawa, Y. (ed.), *M&A for Value Creation in Japan*, Singapore: World Scientific Pub. Co.

Monden, Y. (2010). Acquisition price as an incentive price of M&A, in Hamada, K. (ed.), *Business Group Management in Japan*, Singapore: World Scientific Pub. Co.

Mouritsen, J. and Thrane, S. (2006). Accounting, network complementarities and the development of inter-organizational relations, *Accounting, Organizations and Society*, 31, 241–275.

Moriarty, S. (1975a). Another approach to allocating joint costs, *The Accounting Review*, 50(4), 791–795.

Moriarty, S. (1975b). Another approach to allocating joint cost: A reply, *The Accounting Review*, 51(3), 686–687.

Nihon-Keizai-Shimbunsha (ed.), (2002). *Panasonic: Bet for Revival*, Tokyo: Nihon-Shimbun-Sha (in Japanese).

Ohtoshi, T. (2004). Reformation of economy by each functional unit, *Nihon-Keizai-Shimbun*, May 17 (in Japanese).

Shubik, M. (1962). Incentives, decentralized control, the assignment of joint costs and internal pricing, *Management Science*, 8, 325–343.

Shukan-Diamond (2003). Panasonic: Revolution 1000 days, 91(10), 28–47 (in Japanese).

Skinner, A. (1970). *The Wealth of Nations: Books* I–III by Adam Smith, with an introduction by Andrew Skinner; Harmondsworth, Middlesex: Penguin Books.

Solomons, D. (1965). *Divisional Performance: Measurement and Control*, Homewood, IL: Richard D. Irwin.

Smith, A. (1776). *An Inquiry into the Nature and Causes of the Wealth of Nations*, London: W. Strahan and T. Cadell.

Stevenson, W.J. (1990). *Production/Operations Management*, Third Edition, Homewood, IL: Irwin.

Suzuki, M. (1959). *Theory of Game*, Keiso Shobo.

Swamidass, P.M. (ed.), (2000). *Encyclopedia of Production and Manufacturing Management*, Boston: Kluwer.

2

South Korean "Zaibatsu": An Analysis of Its Historical and Financial Characteristics

Tadashi Hasegawa
Kyoto Gakuen University

1 Introduction

The economy of South Korea is chiefly sustained by various financial cliques. It was in the 1970s when those financial cliques were established, though they were chiefly started in colonial times. The basic management structure is the circulation investment and mutual debt guarantee. Any financial clique advances diversification by these, and it either falls into all-out competition or takes the competing limitation act. The problem had already been pointed out in the 1980s. However, the various financial cliques greatly suffered during the Asian monetary crisis, and some collapsed sooner or later in 1997. After that, various financial cliques were facing the global standard for management in exchange for financing from the IMF.

In this chapter we would like to clarify historically why, in South Korea, various financial cliques with this authoritarian tendency came to bear the economic substructure, and what the origin of this mechanism is. In that case, the name Syngman Rhee surfaces. He was the president during the establishment of South Korea though he is not valued so much there now.

In part two, we describe how, in the Korean Peninsula where South Korea exists, it has been invaded by large countries in the vicinity since BC, and how South Korea started in confusion after World War II. At this time, Syngman Rhee appeared. In part three, the features of financial cliques in South Korea are described. In part four, the Samsung Group, which has attained the highest achievement among the South Korean financial cliques, is taken up and both the features and the problems are described.

2   South Korea after World War II

The territory of Korea has been changing bewilderingly since historic times. It has often been invaded by the neighboring large countries and contracted and expanded, though there was also internal division. Remarkably, the nation of Korea has already disappeared three times: during the Han Dynasty of China, Yuan rule and colonization by Japan. During the Han Dynasty from 108 BC for about 400 years, during Yuan rule for about 100 years and during colonization by Japan for 36 years, the national authority of Korea was snatched (National History Textbook, 2003).

In addition, the territory was attacked by the ancient Tang Dynasty; went into ruin by the invasion of Japanese pirates (Wokou) not only at the entire coastline of the Korean Peninsula but also inland; was attacked by the Pohai people, Khitan people and Jurchen people before Yuan rule; the country was further trampled down by Hideyoshi Toyotomi and the Qing in the age of the Chosun Dynasty. In the modern ages the territory was invaded not only by Japan but also the Qing and Russian Empires. After World War II it was ruled by US army politics. The Korean Peninsula was divided into parts, and remains divided into the South and the North (the Soviet Union and also China have intervened in North Korea). There are few other countries so tragic.

Although Korea was liberated when Japan was defeated on August 15, 1945, the relief continued briefly. Because South Korea after independence totally excluded the influence of Japan that was the former colonial power, South Korea did not have any effective power to control her domestic politics. There was only the military occupation of the US and the Soviet Union.

There were already two or more political powers, and when leadership was turned over they were warring with each other. First, there was The Provisional Government of the Republic of Korea that assumed it had succeeded to authority after the 3.1 Movement (anti-Japan independence movement in 1919), insisted on their own validity, and acted in Shanghai and Chongqing in China during the colonial period. Second, there was The Democratic Party of South Korea (the East Asian Daily Report Group was at the center of it, and temporarily supported it) that stayed in the Korean Peninsula during the colonial period since it was strong. And thus there were left and right wings in both parties, which furthermore were conflicting each other. In addition, there was the American military government (Kimura, 2003, p. 75).

The validity of the Democratic Party of South Korea remained in doubt though it was strong especially in the southern Korean Peninsula. This party allied with Syngman Rhee who escaped to foreign countries during the colonial period and fought for independence; in that sense he had validity. Syngman Rhee's charisma grew when he formed the Liberal Party in 1951, establishing a distance from the Democratic Party of South Korea, and introduced the direct presidential election system in 1952. However, an economic rebuilding in the postwar days could not be achieved and the rot by despotism extended too.

Historical importance is not so attached to Syngman Rhee in South Korea now. He has only the position of the mediating president from the colonial age to the age of the "Miracle on the Han River". However, he marked the starting point of the political system and the economic framework of this country after the 8.15 Liberation half a.century ago. You could say that a close connection between political power and the financial cliques, "Zaibatsu", started here.

Because Park Chung-hee, who assumed political power (1963–79) after Syngman Rhee, did not have charisma like the latter, he could not do anything except through human rights violations and suppressing democracy movements, and so aroused the people's repulsion in politics. However, he differed from Syngman Rhee, since Park depended entirely on help from the United States; in terms of economic growth he advanced industrialization in South Korea, which was one of the poorest farming nations in the world, expanded exports rapidly, and got economic development. It was important that there was financial support (300 million dollars) free of charge, financial support (200 million dollars) with a fee, and capital cooperation (100 million dollars) from Japan from the beginning of Park Chung-hee's political power, and that there were Vietnamese special procurements since about 1970, too, because South Korea's exports were only worth several tens of millions of dollars in the 1960s. Moreover, the political power gave preferential treatment to the big enterprises and the financial cliques (Chaebol) in terms of finance and the tax system, allocated the foreign currency and the "letter of credit" to the importers, applied the substantially negative interest rates, exempted them from tax, and reduced tariffs. This economic growth, called the "Miracle on the Han River" continued until the 1980s.

It was Chun Doo-hwan (1980–88) who received political power after Park Chung-hee's assassination in 1979. He was in power after all through the military coup. However, since this, because of excessive and redundant investments in the heavy and chemical industry sector, disregarding domestic and foreign demand, the economic concentration on the financial cliques, inflation and evils such as the wealth gap expansion has occurred. The global competitiveness of manufacturing has decreased due to the delay of technological development and the undeveloped capital-intensive industry, especially since the latter half of the 1980s.

The South Korean economy expanded the fabrication sector, but had stronger characteristics of simple processing and assembly of end-products than that of the advanced countries is weaker and in areas like pure research and applied research, etc. Moreover the number of affiliate companies of 30 large financial cliques, which was 250 in 1984, increased rapidly to 660 in 1995. Naturally, because every large financial clique in South Korea has a full set structure to hold almost all types of business, there is all-out competition in the market. The Asian financial crisis in 1997 pursued and attacked these companies. Thirty large financial clique enterprises such as Hanbo Steel, Kia Auto, Jinro, Ssangyong, Hanhwa and New Core were driven into management failure one after another. Therefore bad loans held by financial institutions were 28 trillion won and the external debt swelled to about 100 billion dollars. The Won fell rapidly. Kim Dae-jung, who was the symbol of South Korean democratization, had to request relief from the IMF and Japan-US-Euro. So, what on earth are these financial cliques that have led the South Korean economy to failure?

3   Korean Financial Cliques, Chaebol

Financial cliques in South Korea are a kind of corporate group (large-scale corporate group). Companies in a chaebol are linked officially or informally in management, human resources and financial affairs and this is characterized as medium-degree uniting. That is, they are neither united by a strategic partnership nor a legal single enterprise (therefore, a chaebol is not one enterprise with federal decentralization). The business is diversified across various industries (therefore differing from the cartel, Zunft and the industry association).

However, the entire corporate group as the entity composed of member enterprises or affiliated enterprises is the financial clique. It is different from the corporate group in Japan. In Japan, the corporate group is characterized by the interdependent relationship and the mutual stock-holding relationship between groups, but in South Korea the founder and the clan have dominion and the property right in the financial clique (Table 1). According

Table 1. Ownership situation in South Korean chaebol.

Financial Clique	Number of Enterprises	Number of Financial Clique Business Sections	Holding Ratio (%)		Internal Person Holding Ratio (A+B) (%)	Property Stocks/Equity Ratio (%)	Ratio of Stocks Listed (%)	
			Owner Clan (A)	Enterprise + Self-ownership (B)			Capital-base	Corporate-base
Hyundai	46	38	15.39	46.02	61.40	20.99	44.31	34.78
Samsung	55	30	2.97	46.04	49.01	32.70	55.22	25.45
LG	48	29	5.97	33.91	39.88	24.20	60.21	22.92
Daewoo	25	27	6.35	35.35	41.69	22.91	86.19	36.00
SK Avr.	32	24	16.10	32.54	48.64	23.27	56.86	15.63
1~5 Plc	41.2	29.6	8.20	39.65	47.85	25.14	62.34	26.69
1~30 Plc	22.3	18.8	10.32	33.82	44.14	22.34	62.08	25.56

to the continuance of the enterprise, ownership and management are separate in the corporate group in Japan but in the financial clique succession
is by heredity or divided when two or more successors exist. The financial
clique is not allowed to own financial institutions in South Korea but in
Japan it gets a lot of loans from that.

Financial cliques in South Korea were given a lot of advantageous business chances by the government by the protection of the domestic market and
preferential financing from the national management bank at the period of the
high economic growth in the 1960s and 1970s. The financial cliques became to
have to use the resources forcibly in order to reserve the growth chance well,
and therefore introduce more and more business capital and resources from
the outside. In this case the important thing is that they do not have healthy
management ability but have a personal connection with the bureaucrat of the
government and get preferential treatment financing from the national management bank (Lee, 2000, p. 100, South Korean Fair Trade Commission).

In general, however, when the capital amount grows, the stockholder's
dominion becomes weak. So how did the financial cliques in South Korea
maintain domination? It was through circulation investment and mutual
debt security (cross-debt guarantee). As a result, the founder owner-
manager was able to rule the entire corporate group by the little stock
that the clan owned. The financial aligues did not make a new operation
division, but the financial aligues always set up a new company when a new
business was started up, and the capital was procured from other member
companies and banks. This debt was secured mutually between affiliated
companies. It was unusual for the financial aligues to procure the capital
from the stock market.

For instance, company A in a financial clique has a capital of 100 billion
won; it invests 20 billion won in company B and 10 billion won in company
C. Next, company B invests opposite circularly 15 billion won and company
C 10 billion won in company A. Then, company A will have a capital of
125 billion won on the accounting book. Company B can invest in company
D and company D invests the capital in company C (see Figs. 1 and 2).
Thus, the capital swells each other in appearance. This assumes so that two
or more companies in the corporation exist. It is not possible to do with
one company. And it is also necessary that the account information or at
least a part of it is closed-door.

Thus, the clan of the owner-manager made it such that overwhelming
dominion can be exercised with few financial assets. The financial cliques
in South Korea have also promoted an authoritarian tendency. Almost all

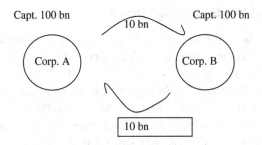

Fig. 1.   Circulation investment (simple case).

Capital 125 bn

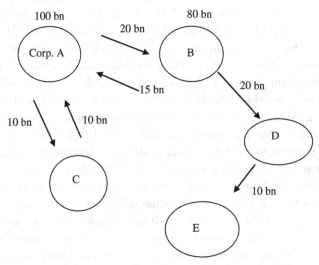

Fig. 2.   Circulation investment (complex case).

these financial cliques diversified their business, restricted competition and created an oligopoly situation. So they spoiled the resource from a view point of the entire country. And the South Korean economy went forward on failure.

Enterprises or corporate groups with good achievement seem now to come up to a global standard for management in South Korea though several years have passed since an Asian monetary crisis. Next, I will describe the Samsung Group, which is the most typical corporate group in South Korea.

4   The Case of the Samsung Group

In South Korea the Samsung Group has been often compared with Sony, which is the global company in Japan. The corporate center of the Samsung Group is Samsung Electronics Co., Ltd. The latter has developed into a global company with about 65.68 trillion won in aggregate market value, overtaking Sony's 63.56 trillion won on April 2, 2002, according to the announcement of the New York Stock Exchange. That was just after the information technology recession that started in 2000.

During the information technology recession the spot price of 128MB general-purpose DRAM (writing/reading memory for which storage was necessary at any time) was 18 dollars a piece in the middle of 2000, but fell sharply to less than one dollar a piece in November 2001. At this time, the achievement of electronics-related enterprise in Japan such as Hitachi Ltd., Panasonic Electric Industrial Co. Ltd., Toshiba, NEC, Fujitsu, and Mitsubishi Electric Corporation in fiscal year 2001 deteriorated rapidly too and almost all were in deficit. However, Samsung Electronics did well; in 1999 it had a surplus of 3.17 trillion won (317 billion yen), in 2000 a surplus of 6 trillion won (chiefly from the semiconductor section), and in 2001 (the year of the slump in the global information technology market) a surplus of 2.9 trillion won (the operating profit of DRAM was 0.7 trillion won, telecommunication (cellular phones, etc.) 1.4 trillion won, digital media 0.3 trillion won and consumer electronics 0.2 trillion won).

Samsung is a large-scale corporate group, or chaebol. It has very diverse companies though there are 63 companies in all, according to Samsung's website. There is the electronics industry division such as Samsung Electronics Co. Ltd., the financial services division except banks, the chemical industries division, the machinary and heavy industries divisions, among others.

The initiator of this huge financial clique is Lee Byung-chull (1910–87), father of the present chairman Lee Kun-hee (b. 1942) and it is assumed that its establishment was in 1938.

Lee Byung-chull had a lineage of Confucianism (Taikei school), but was a good money-maker. He was the youngest child among two sons and two daughters. Current chairman Lee Kun-hee is the elder brother of the youngest daughter among three sons and five daughters. It is not Confucian as the eldest child did not succeed. It can be called one of the features of the Samsung Group.

Lee Byung-chull was born in Gyeongsangnam in 1910. Therefore, he undertook a Japanese education early. He studied also at Waseda University in Japan. He started businesses in rice cleaning, shipping and real estate (land investment) with 300 koku (land value for tribute purposes expressing the quality and amount of harvested rice) from his father in his hometown in 1936 and became a large landowner with an annual income of 10,000 koku and 660 million m^2 of land but was failed by the sudden fall in the price of land etc., because of the outbreak of the Japan-China war in 1937. At this time, it is said that he obtained the following lessons in the active conduct of business:

(1) to watch both the domestic and international situation,
(2) to know one's ability and limit one's rash desires,
(3) not to speculate, and
(4) to cultivate the power of intuition and at the same time make second and third preparations (Yanagihara, 2003, pp. 12–13).

After he had examined China and various places in 1938, he started to trade in vegetables and fruits, groceries, and miscellaneous goods in Daegu, Gyeongsanbuk, and established the "Three-Star" (Samsung) Company with a capital of 30,000 yen. This was the starting point of the Samsung Group. He also entered the flour mill trade, the noodle-making business and the brewing industry. His third son, Lee Kun-hee, was born in 1942. Lee Kun-hee also studied in a junior high school and university (Faculty of Commerce at Waseda University) in Japan. Afterwards, he studied for one year at a business school in the United States. The management sense might have been supported by these experiences. Because the eldest brother and the second elder brother left the father's business after that, Lee Kun-hee succeeded the business. When he was a child, it is said that he liked taking toys apart very much. This "technology-oriented management" continues until today.

When the Korean War broke out in 1950, Samsung was selected as the foreign currency-lending enterprise by the Bank of Korea. Though the Korean War continued until 1953 and there was inflation too, Samsung accomplished further rapid growth. It was an age where the more a business expanded, the more it made a profit. By the way, Lee Byung-chull had been an acquaintance of Syngman Rhee's since his father's generation. However, when Park Chung-hee began to step on the accelerator from industrialization to heavy and chemical industrialization with higher added value in 1972, Lee Byung-chull had already seen the prospects of the electronics industry and cooperated with Sanyo, NEC, Corning Glass and HP in the United States (Samsung had produced 12-inch black-and-white televisions for Sanyo as an OEM since 1969). Lee Byung-chull died in 1987. At this time, the Samsung Group was a large financial clique with a capital of 631 billion won, sales of 17.4 trillion won, an ordinary profit of 266.8 billion won, exports of 125 million dollars and 160,596 employees. The third son Lee Kun-hee assumed leadership in the second generation in accordance with Lee Byung-Chull's will though it is the Confucian way that only the eldest son succeeds.

In 1988 Lee Kun-hee declared "the second establishment" and reorganized the businesses, with advancement into new fields like the aerospace industry and genetic engineering, etc., and amalgamation of the electronics, semiconductor and communications divisions into one. Moreover, he strengthened the structural adjustment headquarters (corporate development division in Japan) and gave it the function of not mere document management but the dissemination of information, situation assessment and planning. This structural adjustment headquarters forms a triangle with Chairman Lee Kun-hee and the managers of Samsung Electronics Co. Ltd., and will play an important role. For instance, Chairman Lee Kun-hee presents the direction of the management and the strategies such as the advancement into the semiconductor business and the integration of Samsung Electronics Co. Ltd., and Samsung Semiconductor & Communication, etc. The structural adjustment headquarters draws up the overall strategy for the future in cooperation with Samsung Economic Research Institute, the think tank group, and plays the role of the control tower of the group's businesses. The management of Samsung Electronics Co. Ltd., considers the actual management strategies and the tactics, referring to the advice of the structural adjustment headquarters (South Korean Economic Newspaper, 2003, p. 93). However, the ratio of net profit to sales was low at this time, though sales had expanded certainly. Samsung's administration is the same as the administration of the political system of South Korea, which is managed by the president in Samcheong-dong (Executive Office of the President) and each ministry agency below the Minister of State (Prime Minister). The source of the political dispensation in South Korea was Syngman Rhee.

Lee Kun-hee came up with the slogan "Let's change it!" in 1993. He said, "Let's change everything except the wife and the child". In this way he increased the capital to 3.6 trillion won, sales to 72.4 trillion won, ordinary profit to 3.54 trillion won, exports to 3.61 billion dollars and the number of employees to 260,000 in 1996. However, the Asian monetary crisis started in May 1997. In the Samsung Group, 59 enterprise companies were reduced to 45 companies, 167,000 full-time employees were downsized to 113,000 people; in other words 54,000 people and 32% were cut. A thorough "selection and concentration" strategy was undertaken. It was the electric and the electronics system enterprises (especially Samsung Electronics Co. Ltd.), the finance and the trade system enterprises (chiefly Samsung Life and Samsung Product) and the service system enterprises (Everland and Shilla Hotel) that were chiefly selected (Hong, 2003, p. 181).

The Samsung Group was able to decrease the debt ratio from 366% (1997) to 197% (1999) and then to 166% (2000) and 124% (2002) by this restructuring. The 2.3 trillion won in mutual debt security (cross-debt guarantees) between the group enterprises (1997) became almost 0 (1999) (Fukuda *et al.*, 2005, p. 43). Thus, even if it was temporary, Samsung surpassed Sony in the above-mentioned aggregate market value. Anyway, the South Korean style of management has disappeared from South Korea since the IMF crisis, and the global standard for management has become the norm. The global standard for management is a system that values the stockholder (after 2002, 50% or more of the stockholders of Samsung Electronics Co. Ltd. are foreigners or institutional investors in foreign countries), changes the domination structure of the enterprise, improves the transparency of accounting, changes the personnel system into a meritocracy, introduces a performance-related salary system, and slices the melon through qualified stock options, etc.

The global standard-oriented management in Samsung was practised more strongly by the leadership of Lee Kun-hee than the other financial cliques. Lee Kun-hee started the global standard-oriented management before the Asian monetary crisis.

References

Chosun Newspaper. http://japanese.chosun.com/.

Fukuda, Keisuke *et al.* (2005). Shock from South Korean management, *Weekly Toyo Keizai*, February 26, pp. 30–47 (in Japanese).

Hong, Ha-sang (2003). The man who established Samsung–Management History of Lee Kun-hee, Syokan Miyamoto (trans.), Nihonkeizai Newspaper (in Japanese).

Kimura, Kan (2003). *Birth of Authoritarian System in South Korea*, Kyoto: Minerva (in Japanese).

Kobayashi, Hideo (2001). *Asia after World War II and Japanese Companies*, Tokyo: Iwanami Shoten (in Japanese).

Lee, Keun (2000). Corporate governance and growth of Zaibatsu in South Korea, *Viewpoint to Asia*, December, pp. 97–122 (in Japanese).

National History Textbook about South Korea for Senior High School (ed.) (2003). *South Korean History*, Takeshi Otsuki (trans.), Tokyo: Akashi Shoten (in Japanese).

Samsung Japan. http://www.samsung.com/jp/.

South Korean Economic Newspaper (ed.) (2002). *Samsung Electronics Co., Ltd.*, Keisuke Fukuda (trans.), Tokyo: Keizai Shinpo Co. (in Japanese).

South Korean Fair Trade Commission. http://www.ftc.go.kr/eng/.

Yanagihara, Isao (2003). Samsung in South Korea, in Ikuo Iwasaki (ed.), *Entrepreneurs in Asia*, Tokyo: Toyo Keizai Shinpo Co., pp. 9–44 (in Japanese).

Part 2

Management Control of an Inter-Firm Network

3

The Importance of Inter-Company SCM in Consolidated Group Companies and Management Accounting

Kazuki Hamada

Kwansei Gakuin University

1 Introduction

The management of company groups as well as that of individual companies is important in obtaining competitive advantages. If we classify Japanese company groups from the viewpoint of inter-company relationships, we can divide them into "vertical" groups and "horizontal" groups. In a vertical group, companies are closely linked to carry out a series of business processes such as purchasing, production, sales, distribution, and so on. The various operations are carried out by internal organizations and companies outside the parent company. A horizontal group consists of internal organizations and companies outside the parent company, which are managed as one body although the internal organizations do not have a direct relationship with the outside companies. However, if we examine the core company in a horizontal group in detail, we can observe vertical relationships, with the core company as the central figure. Consequently, a company group is mainly structured vertically, and we can consider a horizontal group as an aggregation of vertical groups. An industrial group consists of many horizontal groups.

Each company group in Japan consists of many non-independent companies, such as subsidiaries specialized only in production, subsidiaries specialized only in sales, and so on. These companies depend on other group companies in the execution of their duties, and each individual company acts as part of the supply chains. Therefore, it seems necessary for managers of the parent company to manage the internal organization of the parent company as well as that of the group companies fulfilling various duties as a chain. In other words, it is necessary to manage the supply chains for each product. Various kinds of information are needed for this type of management, and, in particular, profit information for each product is important. Therefore, it is crucial to obtain the correct cost information for each product, and a revamping of the cost accounting system is necessary.

In recent years, the restructuring of organizations by outsourcing has become popular in Japan, and now a supply chain (SC) does not consist only of group companies, but is worm-eaten. Therefore, supply chain management (SCM) is difficult to carry out by the group companies alone; it has become increasingly necessary to establish co-operative relationships with companies outside the group and to share information (Hamada, 2003). It seems difficult to share information with companies outside the group, and easier to share it among the group's own companies. In particular, the companies of a consolidated group share information easily because they must exchange accounting information regularly to prepare financial statements. Therefore, from the viewpoint of feasibility, in this chapter I point out the importance of SCM in the companies of a consolidated group and mainly consider what kinds of management accounting information have to be shared. In particular, I focus on the profit and cost information for products. However, information from companies outside the consolidated group is also needed to execute SCM perfectly, a matter which I will also address.

2 The Characteristics of Group Companies in Japan

In some Japanese company groups, the parent company created company subsidiaries through purchase. However, in many cases, the parent company separated portions of large-scale company resources by multiple diversified managements and business development in the vertical direction, and established subsidiaries in this way. Although the number of subsidiaries decreased slightly as a result of group reorganization starting with the latter half of the 1990s, there are many subsidiaries now. There are cases in which not only the parent company but also its subsidiaries are listed on the stock exchange.

The split-off business units are either autonomous divisions which have all of the functions of the parent company, or non-autonomous divisions which have only one function, such as production, sales and so on (Shimoya,

2006, Chapter 6). An autonomous division is a split-off division in its primary meaning, and is a profit center. In this case the split-off subsidiaries
are generally large-scale and some of them are listed on the stock exchange.
A non-autonomous division is a split-off consisting of a factory or a business
office. This type of split-off becomes a production subsidiary or a sales subsidiary, respectively. The function of production subsidiaries is to deliver
products to the parent company and the group's other companies. The
function of sales subsidiaries is to sell products of the group's other companies exclusively. Some of these non-autonomous subsidiaries are named
using only the name of the place and region in which they are located.
The service-related departments at the headquarters, such as the financial
department, the information processing department, the personnel department, and so on, are often split-off. These subsidiaries tend to be 100%
subsidiaries, and their scale is generally small.

Until now, the study of split-off companies has focused mainly on
autonomous subsidiaries, but there are many non-autonomous ones in
Japan. This is the predominant feature of subsidiaries in Japan, and it
is also why we have many subsidiaries. In this type of subsidiary, systematic relationships in terms of the division of labor are constituted under
the control of the parent company. Therefore, the subsidiary is expected
to play the role of a member of the parent company or the company
group.

The reason for splitting off a company is clearly to achieve decentralization, which is a means of clarifying responsibility and accelerating decision-
making. However, the degree of decentralization in a subsidiary is low
because it is controlled by the parent company and has little real authority.
Professor Masahiro Shimoya describes this peculiarity of Japanese company
groups as follows: "...the peculiarity that subsidiaries are centralized by a
parent company while being decentralized by being split-off, in other words,
the peculiarity that pursues the delicate balance between centralization and
decentralization of power" (Shimoya, 2006, p. 273).

When we consider group management in Japanese companies, it is necessary to take into account such relationships, and to clarify and manage
the flow of products between the parent company and its subsidiaries and
among the subsidiaries rather than manage production subsidiaries and
sales subsidiaries individually. In other words, SCM across the entire group
is needed, because operations are continuously carried out between the parent company and its subsidiaries and among the subsidiaries.

3   Usefulness of Segment Information and Its Use for Consolidated Group SCM

Segment information, especially information on products, production bases and sales markets, is useful when assessing the situation of a consolidated group in detail. Therefore, in consolidated group SCM, it is necessary to consider how to obtain segment information on the above three points and how to use it.

Two of the possible unification axes of useful segment information are the product axis and region axis (market axis). When we choose the product axis as the unification axis, information on each product regarding production bases and sales markets is particularly important for SCM. When we choose the sales market axis as the unification axis, information on each sales market regarding production bases and products is important.

Generally, companies belonging to the home electric appliance industry or the office machine industry, both of which deal with many kinds of products, are best served by adopting the product axis as their unification axis (Fujino, 2007, pp. 10–13). Traditionally in these industries, overseas subsidiaries acted on the responsibility of an international division, and the responsibility for the overseas company lay outside the scope of the parent company. Also, managers tailored their production strategies to the peculiarities of the host country mainly in the form of product strategies, because the overseas production ratio was low. However, it has now become necessary to capture the domestic markets and the overseas market as a whole and to manage them accordingly, because the export ratio has decreased and the overseas production ratio has increased in recent years. In some companies, the overseas divisions which were profit centers have been dissolved and transferred to product divisions. Even if overseas business divisions remain, they tend to subsist as sections in charge of overseas investment, technological cooperation and management support of overseas subsidiaries, namely as cost centers (Fujino, 2007, Chapter 1).

In order to manage such global production and sales activities optimally, it is necessary to carry out management based on the product axis whether management is executed in the home country or in foreign countries, and to grasp the market and consumer trends quickly. Therefore, a consolidated performance evaluation system for each product, such as the one in Fig. 1, is necessary. It is assumed in Fig. 1 that the headquarters comprises all of the companies' support departments, production and sales departments and business control departments, and that the profitability of each product is controlled by the business control department.

		Headquarters				
		Control Department 1			Control Department 2	- - - - - - - - -
		Product 1	Product 2	- - - - -	- - - - - - - - - - - - -	- - - - - - - - -
Head-quarters	Support Department	××	××	- - - - -	- - - - - - - - - - - - -	- - - - - - - - -
	Production Department	××	××	- - - - -	- - - - - - - - - - - - -	- - - - - - - - -
	Sales Department	××	.	- - - - -	- - - - - - - - - - - - -	- - - - - - - - -
Production Subsidiary A		××	.	- - - - -	- - - - - - - - - - - - -	- - - - - - - - -
Production SubsidiaryB		.	××	- - - - -	- - - - - - - - - - - - -	- - - - - - - - -
.		.	.	.	.	.
.		.	.	.	.	.
Sales Subsidiary (a)			××	- - - - -	- - - - - - - - - - - - -	- - - - - - - - -
Sales Subsidiary (b)		××	××	- - - - -	- - - - - - - - - - - - -	- - - - - - - - -
.		.	.	.	.	.
.		.	.	.	.	.
Total		××	××	- - - - -	- - - - - - - - - - - - -	- - - - - - - - -

(×× shows the amount.)

Fig. 1.   Performance evaluation system for each product.

		Sales Subsidiaries (Market Axis)				Total
		(a)	(b)	(c)	- - -	
	A	× ×	× ×	× ×	- - -	× ×
	B	× ×	× ×	× ×	- - -	× ×
Production	C	× ×	× ×	× ×	- - -	× ×
Subsidiaries	.	.	.	.	.	.
(Production Base	.	.	.	.	.	.
Axis)	.	.	.	.	.	.
	.	.	.	.	.	.
	.	.	.	.	.	.
Total		× ×	× ×	× ×	- - -	

(× × shows the amount.)

Fig. 2.   Evaluation matrix for each product: The relationship between the production subsidiaries and the sales subsidiaries.

In order to clarify the profit earning structure of the SC, the market axis and the production base axis must be added, as show in Fig. 2, and the structure of each product must be grasped. When organizing information as in Fig. 2, the appropriate number of production subsidiaries must be selected and the companies related to the selected production company must be partially consolidated, because in reality production subsidiaries have a multi-storey structure, as subsidiaries of subsidiaries. Because group activities in a company are carried out by an SC unit as mentioned in the introduction, to grasp the actual situation is important in management.

In contrast, in an automobile company, the market axis is most effective as the unification axis because there are not many kinds of products (Fujino, 2007, Chapter 8). But even if the market axis is selected as the unification axis, management by product and management by production base are needed to manage the SC by product in detail.

In either case, because there are many non-autonomous subsidiaries in Japan, it is necessary to look into profitability by product from the overall viewpoint of production and sales, and management of the SC in each market is necessary. If we do not look at the whole SC, there is a risk of inducing local optima. To prevent this, global SCM is required.

Takeshi Suzuki of the Toyota Motor Corporation summarizes the situation as follows:

> The parent company and most of the subsidiaries at Toyota are connected by the commercial flow. If both the supply side and the demand side aim at individual profit maximization, a conflict concerning price arises. To solve this problem, it is important to look at the overall business and for the parent company and its subsidiaries to attain a holistic optimum as one body (Suzuki, 2003).

In addition, he mentioned the following:

> The performance evaluation of the subsidiaries is not executed strictly. Because the subsidiaries are connected by the commercial flow and the parent company decides the purchase prices and the sales prices for the subsidiaries, it is almost impossible to increase the profit of the subsidiaries. In some cases, the parent company only requires strict cost management (Suzuki, 2003).

He points out that management must work toward the holistic optimum of the SC.

The Mazda Motor Corporation adopts a consolidated profit management system that focuses on SCM. The company started its MPI (Management Process Innovation) project in May 2004, whose purpose is to reform all the business management processes, especially the global consolidated profit management processes (Morimoto and Koike, 2008, Chapter 6). The problems which occur due to the defectiveness of the consolidated profit management process are as follows:

> (1) The common consolidated profit results by product for the whole company are not available; (2) the analysis and

evaluation of the comparison between the plans and the actual results in production and sales by product and in terms of profit are not sufficiently thorough; (3) the precision of the data for each product at the subsidiary level is low; (4) a system that yields data in a timely fashion is lacking; (5) the management of the development program is performed at the product planning and development stages, but the follow-up after mass production is insufficient; (6) the important indicators of performance increase with each department are not sufficiently well defined (Morimoto and Koike, 2008, p. 155).

In addition, it turns out that there are serious problems of "vertical separations" and "horizontal separations". (Please note that the words "vertical" and "horizontal" as they are used in this section of the chapter have a specific meaning and refer only to Mazda.) The former is the problem that management by financial numbers and spot management are not linked. The latter is the problem that production, sales, etc., are not sufficiently linked. Therefore, in order to utilize the consolidated profit management system more effectively, management by balanced scorecard was introduced to break down the vertical separation, and management based on three axes was implemented to resolve the horizontal separation (Morimoto and Koike, 2008, pp. 171–178). The three axes are the product axis, the market axis and the production base axis (entity axis), and management based on these three axes consists in the formulation of strategies, planning drafts and managing budget attainment in terms of those axes. Management based on the product axis is particularly important for horizontal linking, and the considerations from different viewpoints of three axes yield good conflicts.

To pursue the flow of the SC and compute the profit and loss for every product, cost information on the product must be obtained. However, in the case of trading by transfer among related companies, the common consolidated procedure is as follows: the profit and loss of each consolidated group company is summed up, the internal trades are eliminated, and each cost remains unrevised except that the unrealized profit is eliminated from the total amount. In this method, the profit per product can be calculated, and the cost per product can be computed by the inverse operation. But this method has the disadvantage that the cost structures are unknown because the cost structures per product are not revised. Therefore, the material costs and processing costs per product are not computed. This is an important problem and I will discuss this point further in the next section.

With regard to segment information, a new standard of segment accounting was introduced in financial accounting in April 2010 in Japan, and the "management approach", according to which the divisions used in business management are disclosed as segments, has been adopted (Nakata and Miura, 2008). It seems to be easier to prepare segment reports by this approach. This will affect SCM among consolidated group companies.

4 The Necessity of Costing by Bills of Materials in Consolidated Group Companies

4.1 *Two types of consolidated group costing*

Segment information is necessary for the profit and loss calculation for every product, so it is necessary to grasp the cost structures of every product. Cost information is shown in factory costs reports, but these reports are not included in the consolidated financial statements to be disclosed. Therefore, there are problems which need to be solved radically when calculating the consolidated cost for every product, for example, the proper construction of the information system.

There are two methods of calculating consolidated costs so that they show the cost structure of every product. Professor Kawano introduces and discusses them in some papers, so I summarize them here (Kawano and Yokota, 2003; Kawano, Fujiwara and Hiraga, 2008, pp. 130–136). In the first method, the amounts in the factory costs report for each product are added up, the amounts related to internal trade are deducted, and the consolidated factory costs report is written out. Therefore, it is necessary, for management purposes, to grasp the trade among related companies for each product and subdivide the cost items at the appropriate level. This method usually becomes extremely complicated in terms of classification and procedure. However, it has the advantage that few changes are needed in the calculation method because it follows the same path as the common consolidated procedure. In addition, in this method, cost items must be unified, but the cost accounting system need not be unified. This makes it easier to apply.

In the second method, the costs are piled up with these bills of materials by connecting them among related companies. This is the calculation method which uses the actual unit cost in the same way as standard costing, where the standard unit cost is decided and the standard cost is computed as (standard unit cost × production volume). In other words, the actual production cost is computed as follows. First, the material consumption prices, consumption volumes, wage rates and working hours are decided by using bills of materials, which means that all categories of costs are computed. Then, the actual unit cost is calculated by piling up those costs. Finally, the actual production cost is computed as (actual unit cost × production volume). This method is called "actual unit costing". However, this method is not approved in financial accounting.

The places and cost items that should be reduced become clear when using this method, because the correct consolidated costs for every product can be grasped and the costs can be piled up in line with the business flow. Sharp Corporation adopts this management method, which in Japanese is called "kobetu-saisan kanri" (Saji, 2001). Many other companies, such as Mazda and Toyota, also use this method. But it is necessary to unify the bills of materials of all related companies when this method is adopted (Kawano and Yokota, 2003; Kawano, Fujiwara and Hiraga, 2008, pp. 130–136). In addition, it is necessary to unify not only the cost items of related companies but also the cost accounting system itself. The second method is indispensable to the analysis of costs in detail. In the case of companies which produce and sell only in Japan, many companies adopt a unified cost accounting system. However, it is most important to unify the cost accounting system in global companies.

4.2 Importance of bills of materials for the computation of exact costs

Because bills of materials play an important role in actual unit costing, I now discuss the relationship between bills of materials and costing. A bill of materials is the complete list of parts which compose a product. It was originally used for design purposes, but is now used not only in the design and production departments but in many other departments as well. Besides a list of constituent parts, a bill of materials contains various kinds of information such as suppliers, costs, processes, etc. These bills can be classified into two types. One is the summary type, which simply lists all the parts needed to produce the final product, without arranging the data in a hierarchical structure. The other is the structural type, which shows the constitutive parts in a hierarchical structure, such as a parental relationship. The former is used in the design department, the purchase department, etc., whereas the latter is used in the production department, etc. Bills of materials are often exchanged in intra-company settings.

Costing according to bills of materials is executed by the production number or by ERP (MRP) (Monden, 1991, Chapter 6). In the former way of costing, the parts and materials bear the production number (number of the production order) of the final product, and the computation is executed based on this number. The bills of materials used for computing are basic lists that ignore the hierarchy of the constituent parts. The disadvantage of this method is that the production number is difficult to change if the plan of the final product is changed. In the latter way of costing, the parts at each level are separated from the production number of the final product, and the required quantity of parts at each level is calculated by using multi-stage bills of materials; thus, the production cost of a product is computed in stages, based on the constituent parts.

Toyota has considered bills of materials to be extremely important for management, and has created integrated bills of materials; with the help of these bills, Toyota has started to manage the activities of development, production and purchasing in a unified manner at 60 regional bases in 27 countries (Yotsukura, 2004, pp. 72–76). Originally, bills of materials were separated into types according to their purposes, and each department had a system based on sets of partial optima. But Toyota considered that the operation process needed for a total global optimum could not be implemented if the bills of materials were of different types. When integrated bills of materials are compiled, it is necessary to unify the production numbers shown in 250 columns from all over the world. The numbers include various kinds of information on 30,000 parts per car; for example, the name of the maker, the quality, the types of car in which the parts are used, etc. In Toyota's integrated bills of materials, the information necessary only for the design departments, purchase departments or production departments can be isolated. In addition, necessary information from the past can be isolated because the data are presented in a time series. If such bills are prepared, the precision of costing can be raised.

5 The Necessity of Information from Outside the Consolidated Group for Effective SCM

In the preparation of Toyota's integrated bills of materials which I mentioned in the previous section, not only consolidated group companies but also affiliated parts makers are involved. Up to this point, I focused on SCM among consolidated group companies. However, it is necessary to address the problems of SCM not only in terms of the consolidated group companies but also in terms of companies outside the group.

As outsourcing is quickly on the rise now, companies outside the group become grafted onto the SC of each product, and the SC becomes complicated. As a result, the profit of the total SC for every product is different from the consolidated profit for every product. Therefore, it is necessary to look into the profit of the whole chain in order to assess the profitability of the total SC of a product (Hamada, 2005; Minagawa, 2008). In other words, it is necessary to add the profit of the companies included in the chain other than the consolidated companies. In addition, the consolidated profit is different from the profit of the total chain, because only 80% constitutes the consolidated profit if 80% of the stocks of the consolidated subsidiaries are owned by the parent company (Muto, 2002, Chapter 2).

If we draw up the SC matrix in Fig. 3, which shows how the products are produced and sold among the parent company and its subsidiaries and how they are offered to the end-consumers, it becomes clear how subsidiaries are involved in various products (Ito and Sudo, 1999, p. 46). It can also be comprehended how a given consolidated group company contributes to the increase in the total profit by calculating the profit of each consolidated group company for every product. This way of organizing the information is helpful when deciding on the phasing out of products which do not contribute to the consolidated group profit and the expansion of products which contribute to its profit. It is also possible to judge which part of the business should be outsourced.

If we include companies other than the consolidated group companies in Fig. 3 and can calculate the profit contribution share of those companies, we can grasp the ratio of the combined profit of all the consolidated group companies to the profit of the whole SC and the contribution share of each consolidated company. In addition, we can find the spot in the SC which should be emphasized by connecting a detail analysis of that spot with an analysis of the profit pool. The profit pool is the total profit that is gained in the field of all businesses in the industrial value chain, and profit pool analysis can clarify in which field profit is gained. Based on profit pool analysis, those fields that the company group should enter in the future and where it should acquire and enlarge businesses can be grasped by viewing the entire SC matrix. It is necessary to carry out these analyses frequently, because the fields of business that potentially yield profit change quickly.

	Research Development	Purchase Production	Sales	Distribution	Service etc.
Product 1	Parent company	Production subsidiary A Production subsidiary B	Sales subsidiary (a)	Company outside the consolidated group	Subsidiary X
Product 2	Parent company	Production subsidiary B Company outside the consolidated group	Sales subsidiary (b) Sales subsidiary (c)	Subsidiary Y	Subsidiary X
Product 3	Subsidiary W	Production subsidiary A Production subsidiary B Company outside the consolidated group	Sales subsidiary (b) Company outside the consolidated group	Subsidiary Z	Subsidiary U
. .	. .	. .	. .	. .	. .

Fig. 3.   SC matrix for each product: Companies related to the SC.

Considering SCM as laying stress on the product (business) axis means considering the parent company and group companies transversely. It also means carrying out matrix management. The difficulties of matrix management are often pointed out, but they constitute a crucial problem which must be overcome. In addition, it is important to share information among departments, subsidiaries and group companies beyond subsidiaries in order to prevent problems, because each department and each subsidiary, as elements of the matrix, are buried inside the matrix individually and this increases the risk of fostering local optima (Izumitani, 2001, Chapter 6). When Toyota designs and produces automobiles and their parts in North America, Europe and Asia, parts information for the main 1,500 clients all over the world can be read in real time. In this way, the most suitable parts in terms of cost and quality can be purchased, and SCM becomes efficient.

6   Summary and Conclusions

In this chapter, I emphasized that it is necessary to carry out group management while considering the dependence on the parent company and group companies in the buying and selling of products in management to attain a global optimum, because in Japan, there are many non-independent subsidiaries which depend on the parent company and the group companies.

In addition, because the offshore production ratio is increasing in Japanese companies, it is important for multi-product production companies to carry out management based on the product axis, without distinguishing domestic subsidiaries from overseas subsidiaries. In the case of companies which produce few kinds of products, such as automobile companies, management based on the region axis is crucial. But it is also necessary to carry out management based on the product axis according to the area of operations. From this viewpoint, it seems that management based on the product axis is important in the management of group companies.

Management based on the product axis is connected with SCM, because management must be focused on product flows. The object range of SCM is large, but in this chapter I focused mainly on consolidated groups. Consolidated group SCM makes it easy to circulate information from individual companies of the consolidated groups and easy to foster cooperation among the group's companies in comparison with other cases. This is also the reason why consolidated group SCM is a core part of SCM. It is my belief that the most effective consolidated information in SCM is product segment information, especially profit information for every product connected with the production bases and sales markets, and it is the effective subdivision of the segments that makes it possible.

Cost information on every product is needed to compute the profit for every product, and therefore the bills of materials must be prepared accurately. In addition, correct information on the cost items constituting the product cost is necessary to perform cost management, and bills of materials are indispensable thereto. It is important to provide bills of materials which represent unified cost items and processing methods for the company group as a whole, including foreign group companies, since company activities are presently undergoing globalization.

I mainly discussed the SCM of consolidated groups in this chapter, but information from companies outside the consolidated group is also needed. The profit computation of the total SC is possible perfectly only after the information is acquired. Finally, it seems that the success of SCM depends on the extent to which the correct profit computation is executed for the SC.

References

Fujino, T. (2007). *Consolidated Management in Japanese Companies: Subsidiary Policies and Possession Policies in the 21st Century*, Tokyo: Zeimukeiri Kyokai (in Japanese).

Hamada, K. (2003). The importance of inter-company management and management accounting, in Monden, Y (ed.), *Organization Structure and Management Accounting*, Tokyo: Zeimukeiri Kyokai (in Japanese).

Hamada, K. (2005). Roles of management accounting for inter-company management: Management by financial and non-financial indicators in SCM and ECM, in Monden, Y (ed.), *Organization Design for Corporate Value and Management Accounting*, Tokyo: Zeimukeiri Kyokai, Chapter 26 (in Japanese).

Ito, R. and Suto, M. (1999). *Strategic Group Management: Rebuilding of Business Portfolio*, Tokyo: Toyo Keizai Shinposha (in Japanese).

Izumitani, Y. (2001). *If You Can Grasp Profit, You Can Grasp Companies: All of "Murata Matrix Management by Using Information"*, Tokyo: Nihon Keizai Shinbunsha (in Japanese).

Kawano, K., Fujiwara, Y. and Hiraga, R. (2008). *Practices of Reviewing Cost Accounting, By Which You Can Defeat Present Conditions and Establish Your Stable Company*, Tokyo: Chuo Keizaisha (in Japanese).

Kawano, H. and Yokota, Y. (2003). The construction and utilization of global cost accounting system, *Kigyo Kaikei*, 55(6) (in Japanese).

Minagawa, Y. (2008). *Management Accounting for Supply Chains*, Kyoto: Koyo Shobo (in Japanese).

Monden, Y. (1991). *Cost Management in Automobile Companies: Target Costing, Cost Improvement and Cost Accounting*, Tokyo: Dobunkan (in Japanese).

Morimoto, T. and Koike, R. (2008). *Consolidated Business Management and Techniques for Practice in the Days of Quarterly Disclosure: Three Axes Management for the Global Manufacturing Industry*, Tokyo: Zeimu Kenkyukai Shuppankyoku (in Japanese).

Muto, Y. (2002). *Seven New Common Senses for Group Management: From the Viewpoint of Investors to the Viewpoint of the Company*, Tokyo: Chuo Keizaisha (in Japanese).

Nakata, S. and Miura, N. (2008). *Practices of Consolidated Business Management by Using New Segment Accounting Standards: From Formulation of Budget to Smooth Introduction*, Tokyo: Chuo Keizaisha (in Japanese).

Saji, H. (2001). Methods of business management at Sharp Corporation, *Business Research*, April (in Japanese).

Shimoya, M. (2006). *The Days of Holding Company: Business Combinations in Japan*, Tokyo: Yuhikaku (in Japanese).

Suzuki, T. (2003). The promotion of management optimization in the whole Toyota Motor Corporation group, in Kigyo Kenkyukai (ed.), *An Ideal*

Type of Global and Group Management in the 21st Century: Strategies and Management Systems for Corporate Value Maximization in the Company Group (in Japanese), Tokyo: Kigyo Kaikei.

Yotsukura, M. (2004). *Engineering Chain Management: Production Revolution by Global Integrated Bills of Materials,* Tokyo: Shoeisha (in Japanese).

4

Profit Allocation Rules to Motivate Inter-Firm Network Partners to Reduce Overall Costs

Yoshiteru Minagawa
Nagoya Gakuin University

1 Introduction

The most important task for many companies is satisfying the needs of the end-users of their products and services as swiftly and accurately as possible. Cooperation with business partners is an important element of this task, making competition between inter-firm networks all the more intense. However, partners will not invest their funds only for the sole purpose of increasing the entire interest of their own network or improving the performances of their partners.

Allocating the joint profits of the entire network is an important part of making investments in the network's performance improvement attractive to partners. This study examines a method of allocating a network's overall joint profit that facilitates cost reduction and process innovation across the entire inter-firm network.

The study was inspired by the recent research studies on the management control of inter-firm networks. The development of cooperative inter-organizational relationships has become one of the most active academic research areas. This is expected given that the reach of business networks in practical business scenarios is expanding. For example, Monden (2009, 2010) proposes a new joint profit allocation scheme for inter-firm networks as an incentive for management control.

2   Increases in Supply Chain-versus-Supply Chain Competition

2.1   *Key functions and types of supply chains*

Firms establish various relationships with other firms and end-consumers. Such inter-firm relationships form the building blocks of a firm's business infrastructure. Therefore, building sustainable inter-firm relationships should be at the top of a firm's agenda. This study will shed light on managing supply chains.

Supply chains involve a variety of value-creating activities, from the sourcing of materials and services, passing through production phases, and finally arriving at the delivery of finished goods to end-customers. Supply chains carry out two different types of functions, as in Fisher (1997, p. 107) and Ross (1998, p. 12). First, certain partners in a supply chain have access to market demand and will share information on customer demand throughout the entire supply chain. Second, the supply chain will yield a swift and cost-effective movement of goods throughout the whole supply chain.

It is crucial to differentiate between internal and external networks when examining how to manage supply chains. Internal supply chains comprise all of a firm's organizational units responsible for all business operations. In contrast, an external supply chain is made up of legally independent entities. This study addresses external supply chains and argues that the member organizations of an external supply chain enter into an inter-firm link yet simultaneously seek their own specific interests.

Miles and Snow (1992) divide network organizations into three types: the stable network, internal network, and dynamic network. The application of the Miles and Snow typology to the whole organizational forms of supply chains creates the following three categories: First, supply chains equal to the stable network maintain long-term sustainable partnerships and cooperation among the participating firms. Second, the supply chains of the internal network place all supply chain functions inside the boundary of a focal firm. Third, the supply chains of the dynamic network are short-term inter-organizational links built to attain the strategic goals of certain projects.

Among supply chain strategies is the transformation of the organizational structure into the one best able to satisfy current consumer requirements. Therefore, the organizational form of a supply chain is dynamic. For example, developing and capturing new core competencies for firms' growth is one of a variety of driving forces that cause changes in the organizational structure of supply chains. Suppose, then, that a supply chain partner succeeded in accumulating the core capabilities for a certain supply chain function that unrelated firms (i.e., non-participants in the supply chain) had been responsible for carrying out, thus allowing the firm to perform the function more effectively and efficiently: in that case, the function may well shift to that partner. However, organizational transformations of supply chains are left out of this study. Rather, it examines the external supply chains made up of legally independent firms, such as parts producers, finished goods manufacturers, and retailers. This study's main research task is to find the best way to allocate the total joint profits of an external supply chain among its participants throughout the lifetime of the supply chain.

2.2 Enabling characteristics of supply chains to improve participants' performance

What motivates firms to build new supply chains or be part of existing ones? One of the goals firms expect to achieve by building new supply chains or participating in existing ones is to enjoy a sustainable competitive advantage, derived mainly through collaboration among its member organizations, each one of which expects to achieve its own individual objective.

How does entry into supply chains enable firms to increase their own individual profits? Agile supply chains naturally respond to market changes with optimum speed and thus allow participants to meet end-consumer requirements in a cost-effective way. Most industrial sectors routinely cope with drastic changes in end-consumers' preferences and requests. As a result, the need for manufacturers of finished goods and parts to satisfy consumers' needs for related finished goods swiftly and at lower costs has become their most challenging issue. Parts producers must effectively and efficiently meet consumer needs for finished goods assembled using their own parts. This strategic scenario also applies to retailers. Retailers must supply goods in the right quantity when consumers need them if they are to improve their performance. Retailers will not achieve sustainable growth if they fail to provide customer satisfaction.

Firms are facing a challenging business environment, marked by a shrinking product life cycle, and thus need to become more flexible and agile in responding to changes in demand for finished goods. Firms should choose to build or participate in supply chain networks to achieve higher levels of customer satisfaction. Supply chains can easily fulfill the following functions beneficial to the achievement of customer satisfaction. First, supply chains can share information regarding end-consumers among their partners, thereby swiftly responding to market changes. Second, focal firms in well-coordinated supply chains can reassign functions or roles to those partners who are best positioned to carry out those functions in the shortest time, at the lowest cost.

These capabilities allow supply chains partners to reduce the period of time between the moment customers place an order and the moment customers receive it. The achievement of faster time to market is currently the most significant success factor for the growth of firms. Supply chain functions enable effective and efficient completion of and satisfaction of consumer requirements. Firms are part of a supply chain aiming to achieve their own individual growth by employing its power to create higher levels of customer satisfaction.

It is clear that competition in today's business world is no longer strictly a company-versus-company matter but increasingly an supply-versus-supply matter. Supply chain-based competition is becoming increasingly fierce.

3 Functional Shiftability

Functional analysis is an important supply chain management practice which investigates all supply chain activities linked to customer demand and reassigns functional responsibilities to the participants who can perform them most effectively (LaLonde and Pohlen, 1996, p. 5).[1] The transfer of responsibility is referred to as "functional shiftability" (Mallen, 1973). Functional shiftability initiates long-term partnerships among supply chains and does not apply to arm's length relationship among unrelated firms. Functional shiftability can bring about reduced distribution costs and a shortened time to market.

Well-integrated supply chains can swiftly and effectively link all activities performed by upstream and downstream partners while meeting customer demand. The shortest time to market and the lowest total supply

---

[1]According to LaLonde and Pohlen (1996, p. 5), the capabilities provided by supply chain costing include the ability to determine the overall effectiveness of the supply chain, identify opportunities for further improvement or re-engineering, measure the performance of individual activities or processes, evaluate alternative supply chain structures or select supply chain partners, and evaluate the effects of technological improvements.

chain costs are achievable if all supply chain activities are carried out by those partners who are best positioned to conduct them. Additionally, a network-wide collaborative review of the way supply chain activities are performed by each partner and consequent systemic improvements can enhance the performance of the whole supply chain. Thus, transferring responsibilities for specific supply chain functions among partners is a valuable method of improving the performance of the supply chain, as is completing that transfer by ensuring that partners know how to carry out their activities.

Thus, functional shiftability and operational improvement throughout the entire supply chain are key to reducing total supply chain costs. However, functional shiftability in a supply chain is not easy to carry out. The establishment of a win-win relationship, in which all partners of a supply chain benefit from functional shiftability, is a critical success factor for functional shiftability. Transferring functional responsibility can bring about reductions in the supply chain's total costs. With a view to discussing the role of managerial accounting in supply chains, Dekker and Goor (2000) show through a case study that a decrease in the total amount of transportation costs and stock-keeping costs for the entire chain is achievable when the producer takes over part of the wholesaler's stock-keeping function.

However, partners given additional tasks to carry out through functional shiftability may see a rise in their own costs. No partners will perform additional tasks assigned to them by functional shiftability in the face of resultant liabilities.

A review of the literature reveals that previous studies concerning supply chain coordination involved the creation of managerial practices which gave partners an incentive to implement functional shiftability (e.g., Norek and Pohlen, 2001). Deliberating on this issue, this study theoretically and rationally examines the efficacy of the allocation of a supply chain's total joint profits among the partners as a means of building win-win relationships.

4 Supply Chain-versus-Supply Chain Competition and Supply Chain Cost Reduction

As mentioned, many industrial sectors have witnessed shrinking product life cycles and changing market needs. Building or joining well-coordinated supply chains with higher level of alliances among partners is one of the best ways for management to overcome modern challenges. In other words, becoming a significant partner of a well-coordinated supply chain will benefit a firm's performance as market changes become more drastic and rapid.

The strategic importance of joining the best selection of supply chains holds true across the entire value system, ranging from upstream to downstream industries. Thus, supply chain-versus-supply chain competition will surely intensify.

Whether a supply chain can outperform others relies largely upon how much inter-partner cost reduction is achievable. The joint profit of the whole supply chain is calculated as follows:

Joint profits of the entire supply chain

= the supply chain's earnings from supplying finished goods

to end-customers

− total costs incurred from carrying out activities

by the individual partners

The encouragement of cost reduction across a supply chain is one of the factors which determine the total joint profits of the whole supply chain. Therefore, focal firms in a supply chain must encourage supply chain-wide cost reduction, thereby increasing the total joint profit of the entire supply chain. However, few supply chain partners will likely strive to increase the total joint profits of the whole supply chain, since their own profits will not rise if they receive no rewards for helping to increase the total joint profits of the whole supply chain. Thus, it is important to allocate supply chain joint profits to resolve this motivational problem, in an amount determined by the amount of cost reduction across the whole supply chain, as experienced by all the partners.

How does the focal firm of a supply chain use the joint profits of the supply chain as an incentive for partners to reduce their own costs, thereby increasing the supply chain's joint profits? The objectives of allocating the joint profits of a supply chain are, chiefly, to invest in new product development and compensate for the losses incurred from price cuts imposed on the supply chain's existing end-goods.

As stressed above, enhanced network-wide cost reduction and the investment of the resultant profits in process innovation figure among the most important contributors to the sustainable growth of supply chains. We may divide technological innovations in the manufacturing sector into two types: process innovation and product innovation. Process innovation leads to an improvement in the efficiency of production processes, thereby resulting in cost reduction. Product innovation leads to the introduction of technically advanced products (Utterback and Abernathy, 1975).

However, cost reductions across a supply chain cannot be created automatically (Jarimo and Kulmala, 2008, p. 508). The effective resolution of this issue will be considered in the sections below.

5   A Selective Review of the Literature Relating to the Allocation of a Supply Chain's Joint Profits among its Participants

This study theoretically and rationally examines the best rules governing the allocation of a supply chain's joint profits among participants, with a view to encouraging them to promote cost reduction, thereby increasing the supply chain's joint profits. The section will review a selection of what the relevant literature proposes concerning the three critical research perspectives upon which this study is based.

The first perspective: Who benefits from cost reduction across whole networks?

Kajüter and Kulmala (2005, p. 189) state that the question of how to spend profits generated through network-wide cost cutting involves the question of compensation for losses suffered through cuts to the prices of goods supplied to end-consumers by the network.

Jarimo and Kulmala (2008) study methods of allocating the overall network-wide cost savings among all partners in such a way as to encourage continuous cost reduction in the network. They describe a case network consisting of a firm that manufactures and sells steel roofs and roof assemblers. The overall network-wide cost savings is one of the most important benefits which collaborative networks can realize (Jarimo and Kulmala, 2008, p. 508). The cost savings enjoyed by the partners of a network can be used to increase the profits of the network's member organizations and lower the price of finished goods supplied by the network (Jarimo and Kulmala, 2008). Jarimo and Kulmala emphasize that finished product price-cutting enjoys a greater share of the overall network cost savings when the price of the network's finished product is above that of the competitors' than when the price is below it.

Open-book accounting was successful in the network, resulting in the effective allocation of network-wide cost savings among the partners (Jarimo and Kulmala, 2008).

Jarimo and Kulmala (2008) present two profit-sharing rules obtained in networks with many subcontractors. First, the egalitarian rule yields an equal profit for all subcontractors. Second, the contribution allocation rule offers rewards only to network member organizations who contributed to the increased performance of the whole network. Implementing the two types of profit-sharing rule in the allocation of cost savings among supply chain partners gives rise to two categories: one providing equal profits to each partner and the other rewarding only innovators.

Dudek (2003, Chapter 6) examines the allocation of overall cost savings realized across a supply chain among the partners based on their costs.

The second perspective: What type of reward system is the most effective?

Román (2009) examined the effects of a team-based incentive plan on business performance using data from several production units of a manufacturing factory. The firm restructured an original compensation plan comprising base pay, an individual attendance bonus, and a piece-rate bonus, since it was hardly effective in enhancing inter-team cooperation. According to Román, the firm's manager recognized that the original pay scheme helped motivate employees to work harder and earn higher bonus pay but could not motivate employees to collaborate in raising the combined performance of all the teams in the factory. Consequently, the firm instituted a two-tier incentive plan, comprising a team-incentive level and a plant-incentive one. The team-based bonus scheme rewarded each worker with a daily fixed cash bonus only if the respective team attained its pre-assigned goal; the plant-based scheme provided a cash bonus to all of the teams when they attained a plant-wide performance target.

Román (2009) emphasizes that one key task required of all teams who wished to gain the plant-based bonus was that of coordinating efforts through an alignment of incentives among all the team members. Thus, the plant-based pay was conducive to making the members of every team want to work harder toward the achievement of a high factory-wide performance.

The firm studied by Román (2009) adopted new management systems, including the distribution of performance reports among the teams, a mechanism designed to promote information sharing, and rules governing punishment for shirking and uncooperativeness.

The third perspective: What financial benefits from the business activities of an overall network should be allocated to the network's member organizations in order to encourage cooperation across the network?

The third perspective is an element of cooperative incentive systems. Chwolka and Simons (2003) conducted a comparative study on the performance of revenue-sharing schemes with profit-sharing and transfer-pricing in a buyer-seller relationship.

A supply chain's total profit reveals the overall financial outcome of its business activities. It should be noticed that the introduction of a comprehensive joint profit-based incentive system in a supply chain requires truthful and reliable costs (Chwolka and Simons, 2003, p. 66).

Monden (2009, 2010) proposes an inter-firm organizational management system based on "incentive price" with a view to allocating network-wide joint profits and thus enhancing inter-firm cooperation. The incentive prices are attached to transactions between the member organizations of a network, and they ensure the allocation of network-wide joint profits on the basis of the contribution made by each member organization to synergy effects.

6   A Method of Allocating Joint Profits Conducive to Facilitating Cost Reduction in Supply Chains

This section will consider the best way to allocate a supply chain's joint profits among the partners in order to encourage cost reductions across the whole supply chain. This study never empirically inquires into but rather theoretically and rationally examines the rule of supply chain joint profit allocation that is most conducive to facilitating inter-partner cost reduction. The remainder of the study will indicate how significantly beneficial for the encouragement of inter-partner cost reduction the method of supply chain joint profit allocation presented in this study is.

Outlined below is the best method of allocating a supply chain's joint profits among the participants presented in the study.

The first step is to conduct collaborative activity-based costing and activity analyses across supply chains based on partnerships among the partners. Then the firm must determine which of the partners is best positioned to perform each of the supply chain functions while drawing from the data on inter-partner activity-based costing and taking the perspective of functional shiftability.[2]

It is important to implement inter-firm activity-based costing before the business year begins, based on activity analyses across a supply chain,

---

[2]Cokins (2001, p. 30) emphasizes that activity-based costing (ABC) allows supply chain managers to evaluate alternative supply chain networks and structure.

with a view to expanding the potential for continuous cost reduction at every level of the supply chain. Network-wide activity-based costing driven by activity analyses enables partners to make distinctions between value-added and non-value-added activities across a network and gain a clear understanding of how much cost is incurred by the chain's members. The power of inter-firm activity-based costing with activity analysis in a supply chain allows the partners to conduct a collaborative investigation of functional shiftability across the supply chain.

In addition, collaborative supply chain-wide activity-based costing generally makes activity costs incurred throughout the supply chain open to all the partners. Thus, the application of inter-partner activity-based costing achieves cost transparency in supply chains through information sharing. Cost transparency in supply chains helps build a shared understanding of how activities performed by each partner affect the total costs and joint profits of the entire supply chain, thereby resulting in the optimization of all operations across the supply chain.

The second step occurs after a firm has determined the best performer for each activity carried out in the supply chain: the firm must now determine the standard activity cost required for the highest level of performance for each activity across the supply chain. It is mandatory here that the standard activity cost be determined collaboratively across a supply chain to reduce the risk of opportunistic standard cost setting by self-interested partners.

The third step is the execution of cost reduction by supply chain partners during the business year. All of the participants of a supply chain are expected to engage in cost reduction throughout the course of the year.

The fourth step is the calculation of supply chain joint profits at the end of the business year. As shown above, the joint profits of the entire supply chain is calculated by subtracting the total costs incurred for the activities conducted by the individual partners from the revenue earned by supplying finished goods to end-customers.

The fifth step is the allocation of the joint profits among the supply chain's participants. This study theoretically and rationally examines the important rules for sharing the supply chain's joint profits among the partners as a way of prompting partners to increase the joint profits of the whole supply chain through cost reduction. Three theoretically important objectives of allocating joint profits throughout the supply chain are illustrated below. The following discussion is based on Jarimo and Kulmala (2008) and Dudek (2003).

First, it is crucial for a supply chain whose finished goods are more expensive than those of its competitor to use a certain amount of its supply chain joint profits to compensate for losses resulting from price reductions on its finished goods (Jarimo and Kulmala, 2008). This allocation scheme occurs as follows. Price cutting causes losses through decreasing sales, other business conditions being constant: sales equal the product's selling price times quantity sold. It is thus essential to allocate a predetermined amount (α) of the supply chain's joint profits earned during the year equally among the partners. The equal share of the joint profits individual partners receive enables them to cover losses they suffered from the price cutting.

As Jarimo and Kulmala (2008) state, those supply chains whose finished products are priced lower than those of their competitors never need to apply the above-mentioned method of profit allocation: in this case, $\alpha = 0$.

Second, it is important to allocate an amount (β) of the total joint profits in a supply chain to all of its partners according to the ratio of their total standard cost. Based on Dudek (2003), allocating joint profits based on the ratio of firms' total standard cost gives each partner an identical percent profit of total standard cost. Consequently, the allocation of a supply chain's joint profits among the partners according to the ratio of standard cost meets fair allocation rules.

The supply chain joint profit allocation rule, based on firms' standard cost, grants each partner an equal percent profit of the per-unit standard cost, thereby strengthening the incentives for all partners to cooperate in increasing the supply chain's joint profits. Accordingly, the allocation of a supply chain's joint profits among its partners based on their standard cost can facilitate information sharing about cost reduction among all the partners, since such network-wide reciprocal transfers of cost-cutting know-how result in increased joint profits for the whole supply chain, leading to a proportional increase in its individual partners' shares of the joint profit. Furthermore, this allocation of a supply chain's joint profits enables the promotion of functional shiftability across the entire supply chain.

It should be noted here that operational inefficiencies in firms incur higher costs when firms use actual cost (instead of standard cost) as a base for allocating profit: the higher the cost incurred by the firm, the higher the share of the joint profits.[3] The allocation of the supply chain's joint profits

---

[3]Rese (2006) states that the allocation of network-wide revenue among the partners based on their actual cost rewards the most inefficient partner.

based on the partners' actual cost does not motivate them to improve the joint profits of the entire supply chain; it leads, on the contrary, to increased operational inefficiencies throughout the supply chain. This issue can be overcome by applying a standard cost-based profit allocation.

Third, it is crucial to grant an equal reward among the supply chain partners who generated process innovation and thus reduced the amount of the standard cost. Process innovation leads to higher levels of operational efficiency in firms, resulting in reduced total supply chain costs. Rewards to process innovators are calculated as a certain fraction of balanced joint profits (joint profits $-\alpha -\beta$) divided by the number of process innovators.

The third type of allocation of a supply chain's joint profits never rewards partners unconditionally. Under this allocation scheme, rewards are rendered solely to those partners who have contributed significantly to supply chain growth through cost reduction.

7   The Effectiveness of the Joint Profit Allocation Presented in the Study

The literature review makes clear that there are two main ways of allocating the joint profits of the entire supply chain among its partners (Jap, 2001). The first is the equal allocation of joint profits among all partners. The second is the allocation of a supply chain's joint profits in an amount proportional to the degree each partner contributed to an increase in the supply chain's joint profits.

This study draws on Jarimo and Kulmala (2008) in its illustration of a mixed type of joint profit allocation, consisting of an equal allocation and an allocation of a supply chain's joint profits according to the degree of the member's contribution to the enhanced joint profits of the supply chain as a whole. The power of this integrated profit allocation will be demonstrated below.

Suppose that the amount of joint profits in a supply chain is the sum of α, β, and γ. First, we consider the price-cutting of goods supplied by the supply chain to end-consumers, particularly when the price of the supply chain's goods is higher than those of its competitors. It is essential that the year after the supply chain's focal firm cuts its price, it allocates a fraction (α) of the year's supply chain joint profits equally among all the partners. That is, each of the partners receives an identical amount of profit, calculated as α divided by the total number of participating firms. The joint profit allocation scheme allows each partner to cover losses from price cutting.

Second, it is important to allocate a certain fraction (β) of a supply chain's joint profits to the individual partners according to the ratio of their standard cost and thus motivate them to work harder to realize cost reduction. Under this profit allocation, all partners receive an identical percent profit of their own total standard cost. Consequently, the more the supply chain's joint profits increase, the more each partner's shares of the joint profits increase. Therefore, the supply chain joint profit allocation scheme enables partners to strengthen their incentive to work harder on cost reduction in the entire supply chain. The impact of this change is one of the most significant driving forces for the promotion of knowledge sharing on cost reduction and functional shiftability across the supply chain.

Third, the focal firms of supply chains should reward only those partners who have succeeded in creating process innovation using γ. The third profit allocation scheme can facilitate the network-wide efforts of the participants to improve operational efficiency.

How can the multiple-tier joint profit allocation this study has illustrated contribute positively to the enhancement of incentive alignment across a supply chain? This study has explained the effects of the allocation of supply chain joint profits, outlining two specific schemes of supply chain joint profit allocation: one granting each partner an equal percent profit of individual partners' standard cost and the other rewarding process innovators only. This joint profit allocation facilitates the supply chain-wide transfer of knowledge and practices concerning cost reduction among partners and further strengthens their incentive to create process innovation.

The integrated joint profit allocation presented in this study strongly affects the financial performance of each partner. Consequently, the allocation method closely connects the total joint profits of a supply chain to the individual partners' growing profits. This leads, in turn, to enhanced integration and cooperation across the supply chains.

8 Conclusion

This study considered a method of allocating the joint profits of a supply chain among the participants to facilitate cost reduction across the chain. The study illustrated an integrated allocation based on two schemes. The allocation schemes closely connect the total joint profits of a supply chain to its partners' financial performance, thereby facilitating cost reduction across the supply chain.

The study provided no numerical guidance regarding how much of the joint profits should be allocated to each objective. Examining the optimal amount of profit to allocate to the various objectives may be an element of my future research.

References

Chwolka, A. and Simons, D. (2003). Impacts of revenue sharing, profit sharing, and transfer pricing on quality-improving investments, *European Accounting Review*, 12(1), 47–76.

Cokins, G. (2001). Measuring costs across the supply chain, *Cost Engineering*, 43(10), 25–31.

Dekker, H.C. and Goor, A.R.V. (2000). Supply chain management and management accounting: A case study of activity-based costing, *International Journal of Logistics: Research and Applications*, 3(1), 41–52.

Dudek, G. (2003). *Collaborative Planning in Supply Chains*, Berlin: Springer.

Fisher, M.L. (1997). What is the right supply chain for your product? *Harvard Business Review*, March–April, 105–116.

Jap, S.D. (2001). Pie sharing in complex collaboration contexts, *Journal of Marketing Research*, 38, 86–99.

Jarimo, T. and Kulmala, H.I. (2008). Incentive profit-sharing rules joined with open-book accounting in SME networks, *Production Planning & Control*, 19(5), 508–517.

Kajüter, P. and Kulmala, H.I. (2005). Open-book accounting in networks: Potential achievements and reasons for failures, *Management Accounting Research*, 16, 179–204.

LaLonde, B.J. and Pohlen, T.L. (1996). Issues in supply chain costing, *International Journal of Logistics Management*, 7(1), 1–12.

Mallen, B. (1973). Functional spin-off: A key to anticipating change in distribution structure, *Journal of Marketing*, 37, 18–25.

Miles, R.E. and Snow, C. (1992). Causes of failure in network organizations, *California Management Review*, 34(4), 53–72.

Monden, Y. (2009). *Inter-firm Management Control Systems Based on "Incentive Price": A "Profit-Allocation" Scheme for Inter-Firm Cooperation*, Tokyo: Zeimu Keiri Kyokai.

Monden, Y. (2010). Concept of incentive price for motivating inter-firm cooperation, in Hamada, K. (ed.), *Business Group Management in Japan*, Singapore: World Scientific, pp. 193–208.

Norek, C.D. and Pohlen, T.L. (2001). Cost knowledge: A foundation for improving supply chain relationships, *International Journal of Logistics Management*, 12(1), 37–50.

Rese, M. (2006). Successful and sustainable business partnerships: How to select the right partners, *Industrial Marketing Management*, 35, 72–82.

Román, F.J. (2009). An analysis of changes to a team-based incentive plan and its effects on productivity, product quality, and absenteeism, *Accounting, Organizations and Society*, 34, 589–618.

Ross, D.F. (1998). *Competing Through Supply Chain Management: Creating Market-Winning Strategies Through Supply Chain Partnerships*, New York: Chapman & Hall.

Utterback, J.M. and Abernathy, W.J. (1975). A dynamic model of process and product innovation, *OMEGA*, 3(6), 639–656.

5

The Role of Intangible Assets in Allocating the Inter-Firm Profit of a Global Consolidated Business: International Transfer Pricing

Yasuhiro Monden

University of Tsukuba

1 Introduction

This chapter will investigate how to use intangible assets as the allocation base for allocating the joint profit earned by inter-firm collaborations in a global consolidated business group. In other words, the amount of intangible assets will be used as a measure of each firm's contribution to the joint profit.

The author's intention is to interpret this allocation method from the viewpoint of cooperative game theory as well as to investigate the method for measuring intangible assets.

This method was originally developed in tax law for international transfer pricing when goods are transferred between two countries, and it has been called the *residual profit allocation method*. However, this method can be used as a technique for fairly allocating joint profits among firms that belong to a global consolidated business group, apart from taxation matters. It can be utilized even as a managerial accounting method for fairly evaluating the managers of each firm.

This residual profit allocation method of international transfer pricing will be explained in the Sections 2–4, and is summarized below:

Step 1: Measuring the profit as allocation object;
Step 2: Measuring the basic profit;
Step 3: Measuring and allocating the residual profit;
Step 4: Measuring the profit after allocation.

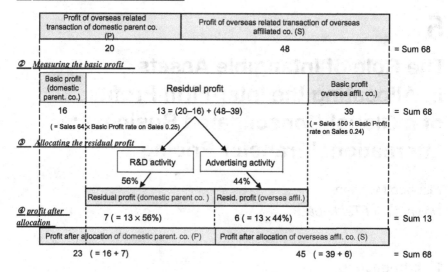

Fig. 1. Summary of the residual profit allocation method (unit: 100 million yen). *Source:* Japan National Tax Administration Agency (2007), p. 69. Revised and numerical figures changed by author.

Now, let us briefly examine the steps of the residual profit allocation method.

Step 1, Measuring the profit as allocation object, in Fig. 1 indicates the calculation of the operating profit earned by parent company P in Japan which sold the merchandise (production resource) to its overseas subsidiary company. In the example of Fig. 1, a profit of 20 (unit: 100 million yen) is calculated. At the same time, subsidiary company S in the overseas country should measure the operating profit that it earned through processing the production resource imported from company P and selling the final product to the customers in company S's country. That amounts to 48 in Fig. 1.

Step 2, Measuring the basic profit, means calculating the operating profits of companies P and S by assuming that each company independently earns its profit through dealing with some third-party company in the market. In other words, the profit of each company is not earned with the cooperation of the other company P or S. Therefore, we assume the third-party company is operating at almost the minimum level of the operating profit rate on sales in the industry in question, because this company has no significant know-how (intangible assets) at all. Both companies P and

S should find such an independent third-party company, and they should assume that they have each dealt with such a company. As a result, it follows that company P's independent profit is 16 and company S's independent profit is 39. Subtracting these independent profits from the operating profits of 20 and 48, respectively, jointly or cooperatively earned by companies P and S together, the difference will be $(20 - 16) + (48 - 39) = 13$. This sum of 13 is the *synergy effect* (complementarities) of cooperation between companies P and S, utilizing their parent and subsidiary relationships.

Next, step 3, allocation of the residual profit, indicates the allocation of this synergy effect of 13 (i.e., the total amount of residual profits) to companies P and S. The allocation base should be the contribution grade measure that can express how each company (P and S) has contributed to creating the synergy effect of 13. This measure is the amount of intangible assets (or know-how) that each company holds. We can identify the merchandise development technology and manufacturing technology as intangible assets of parent company P that should be transferred to company S. Let us call these technologies R&D know-how. Also, as intangible assets of subsidiary company S, we can assume that this company has sales know-how such as marketing technology and a sales network. If we use as a measure of R&D know-how the disbursement amount, 19, for the R&D development of company P, and also use as a measure of sales know-how the amount of sales expenses 15, then the synergy effect of 13 will be allocated to each company as follows:

Since $19 : 15 = 56\% : 44\%$,

$13 \times 0.56 = 7$, which is allocated to company P;

$13 \times 0.44 = 6$, which is allocated to company S.

Finally as step 4, calculation of the profit after allocation, let us sum the basic profit and allocated residual profit of companies P and S, respectively. Then it follows that the profit after allocation of company $P = 23$ $(= 16+7)$, and the profit after allocation of company $S = 45$ $(= 39 + 6)$.

2   Step 1: Measuring the Joint Profit as Allocation Object

The object of international transfer price tax is confined to the transaction conducted between the parent company P and its overseas subsidiary company S within a consolidated business group. Company P is a Japanese domestic company and company S is its overseas subsidiary. The profit as allocation object refers to the profits of each of these companies measured under a given transfer price between the companies. In this section, let us examine how the profits of companies P and S will be calculated.

2.1 Example of assumed conditions

First, let us look at some concrete examples of global consolidated business companies which are carrying out resource transactions encompassing two countries (i.e., Japan and country X) to see how they are transferring their products between two countries and what economic effects appear as a result of their cooperation.

Transaction between Japanese parent company and its overseas subsidiary company

As depicted in Fig. 2, the Japanese company P is manufacturing and selling product A in Japan. This company has acquired a subsidiary company

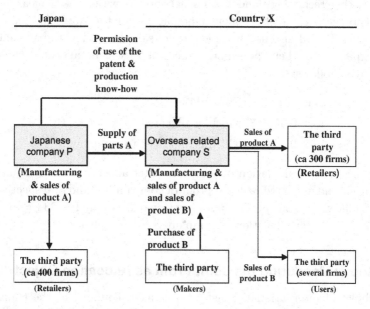

Fig. 2. Transaction relationships between the Japanese company and the affiliated overseas company.
Source: Adapted from Japan National Tax Administration Agency (2007b), p. 55.

from company C in country X. This acquired company is now called company S and is currently manufacturing and selling product A in country X. Company S is a 100%-owned subsidiary company of company P.

Company S is also purchasing product B from third-party company C, which does not belong to the company P group, and selling it to customers in country X.

The internal organization of company P consists of (1) the manufacturing department (plant) for producing parts A and product A, (2) the R&D department which develops its products and manufacturing technologies, (3) the domestic sales department for product A, and (4) the general administrative departments.

Intangible assets of domestic company P and its overseas transactions

Company P is providing parts A to be utilized for product A to company S. (Parts A contain the unique technology of company P.) At the same time, company P is providing the manufacturing patent and know-how about product A to company S. The cost of the patent and know-how is compensated for by the payment of royalties to company P.

The function and intangible assets of overseas company S

Company S has acquired a high reputation for its product A due to its unique marketing activities and its widely spread network of retailers, which made it possible for company S to achieve a large market share. Such a sales network is what the predecessor company C held as an intangible asset before company S entered country X.

Synergy effect of the intangible assets of companies P and S

The highly valued brand and recognition of product A in market X has been created by both the unique engineering function of company P (i.e., intangible assets of company P) and the sales capability of company S (i.e., intangible assets of company S). Thus, the sales and profit of product A are based on the synergy effect of the intangible assets of both companies.

2.2   *Measuring the profit as allocation object from the income statements of companies P and S*

The income statements of companies P and S include not only the overseas transactions, but also the domestic transactions in Japan and country X, respectively.

Thus, in order to measure only the profit as allocation object out of the income statements of companies P and S, we have to pick out only the overseas transactions and their profits from the income statements of both company P and S. These overseas transaction profits are the profit as allocation object, to which the residual profit allocation method can be applied.

The summarized income as a result of exploiting the overseas transactions and their profits will be as shown in Fig. 3.

Thus, the operating profit of the parts A division of company P is measured as 20, while the operating profit of the product A division of company S is measured as 48.

Income Related to Overseas Transactions between Companies P & S

Income Statement of Parts A Business of Company P

Sale of parts A	64
Royalties received	5
Total sales revenue	69
Cost of sale of parts A	−25
Cost of goods sold	−25
Gross margin of sales	44
Sales expense of parts A	−2
Allocated R&D costs	−19
Allocated admin. costs	−3
Total sales & admin. costs	24
Operating income	20

Income Statement of Product A Business of Company S

Sales of product A	150
Sales revenues	150
Purchased parts A costs	−64
Royalty paid	−5
Other costs of product A	−10
Total cost of goods sold	−79
Gross margin of sales	71
Sales expense of product A	−15
Allocated admin. costs	−8
Total sales & admin. costs	−23
Operating income	48

Fig. 3.   Income related to the overseas transactions between companies P and S (unit: 100 million yen).

3 Step 2: Measuring the Basic Profit

3.1 *Selection of a comparable target company that has no significant intangible assets*

When companies P and S earn income from overseas transactions, both of them are utilizing significant intangible assets, which are the original sources of their extra income as earned through their consolidated business group. Thus, in order to fairly grasp the extra income that they earn cooperatively through overseas transactions, we have to measure the basic profit beforehand, which is the profit to be gained from the basic activities without utilizing their significant intangible assets.

For this purpose we need to apply the so-called *arm's length price*, which is not the actual transfer price used within the global consolidated business group in question, but the price that will be used for the transaction between the independent firms. This is a principle of international transfer pricing.

The basic profit that will be calculated by applying the arm's length price is equivalent to the individual profit in cooperative game theory: the profit which will be gained as an independent company without making a coalition with any other company. This is the profit to be considered as an opportunity cost that should be sacrificed when the independent company in question participates in a certain business group.

To measure this basic profit, we have to investigate a company that does not hold any significant intangible assets that are held by companies P and S. Such a comparative target company should be selected from those which are similar in terms of the industry code, treated products, transaction stage (retail or wholesale, etc.), overseas sales amount, sales scale, facilities (tangible fixed assets), and number of employees, etc.

In the case of companies P and S, first we have to find the same parts A manufacturing and sales company in the same industry, and also must find the same product A manufacturing and sales company in the same industry.

Among them, we have to exclude companies that have significant intangible assets. The amount of R&D costs or marketing costs will determine whether or not significant intangible assets exist.

Most firms have some grade of intangible assets, but it cannot be said that they hold significant intangible assets if they have merely an ordinary level of marketing activities, such as ordinary sales networks. The judgment criterion must be whether they have a relatively lower level of operating profit rate on sales or ROI compared to other companies in the same industry.

3.2   *Profit measure used in calculating basic profits*

As stated above, the comparable target company has relatively lower figures in terms of ROI or operating profit rate on sales in the industry in question. Let us call this measure the basic profit rate in the industry in question.

The basic profits of the overseas transactions for companies P and S is calculated as follows:

Returning to the numerical examples of Fig. 3, we see the actual operating profit rate on sales of companies P and S:

The operating profit rate on overseas transaction sales for company P

= operating profit 20 ÷ sales 64 = 0.31.

The operating profit rate on overseas related transaction sales for company S

= operating profit 48 ÷ sales 150 = 0.32.

Suppose that the basic operating profit rate on overseas transaction sales for the comparable target companies in the same industries as companies P and S, respectively, is as follows: The basic operating profit rate on sales of the comparable company for company P = 25%, and the basic operating profit rate on sales of the comparable company for company S = 26%.

Then,

the basic profit of company P = actual amount of sales of the company P 64 × *basic* operating profit rate on sales 25% = 16;
the basic profit of company S = actual amount of sales of the company S 150 × *basic* operating profit rate on sales 26% = 39.

3.3   *Measuring the residual profit of companies P and S*

As a result, it follows that

the residual profit of the overseas transactions of company P

= profit as allocation object 20 − basic profit 16 = 4;

the residual profit of the overseas transactions of company S

= profit as allocation object 48 − basic profit 39 = 9.

Thus, the residual profit as a sum of both companies = $4 + 9 = 13$.[1]

4 Step 3: Allocation of the Residual Profit Based on the Expense of the Intangible Assets

Because the allocation criteria for the residual profit to the domestic parent company P and the overseas subsidiary company S is the ratio of the contribution by the significant intangible asset to the creation of the residual

---

[1]As a general case, let us suppose that parent company P, located in Japan, produces intermediate products (i.e., parts A, B, and C, etc.) and transfers these parts to the subsidiary companies A, B, and C, all located overseas. Thus, this global business group is operating three businesses at the same time: Pa, Pb, and Pc. In this case, the author wishes to show how a general method of determining the transfer prices of each part works separately.

First, let us measure the sub-consolidated profits, R_{Pa+A}, R_{Pb+B}, and R_{Pc+C}, of each business segment of the parent company P separately, which entails the transfer of parts A, B, and C, respectively. In order for the parent company to allocate these sub-consolidated profits, R_{Pa+A}, R_{Pb+B}, and R_{Pc+C}, to the parent company and the overseas subsidiary companies, they have to determine the fair international transfer prices of parts A, B, and C separately.

According to the residual profit allocation method that was dealt with in this chapter, the parent company P first has to measure the basic profits, R_{Pa}, R_{Pb}, and R_{Pc}, of the parent. These profits are kind of an arm's length measure of firm profits for each business. On the other hand, the overseas subsidiary companies also measure the basic profits R_A, R_B, and R_C, respectively. These profits are also kind of an arm's length measure of firm profits for each subsidiary company.

Then, the residual profit of each business segment (i.e., the synergy effect of each segment) will be measured with the following formula. In the case of the business segment Pa,

$$\text{Residual profit of business Pa} = R_{Pa+A} - (R_{Pa} + R_A).$$

This residual profit will be allocated to the parent P and the subsidiary A, based on the ratio of the intangible asset I_{Pa}, that was utilized by the parent in developing part a, and intangible asset I_A, which was used by subsidiary A in manufacturing and selling product A.

The same procedure will be applied and repeated when some new part d is developed and transferred to the overseas subsidiary company D, which will further process and sell the new product D in the overseas country in question.

profit, this allocation base of the residual profit should be the value of the intangible asset. Thus we will examine various methods of measuring the intangible asset.

4.1   *Measurement methods of intangible assets*

In order to measure the degree of contribution by the intangible asset to the creation of income, it is not necessarily required to measure the absolute value of the intangible assets; it is sufficient to measure only the ratio of the relative value of the intangible assets of the domestic company and the overseas related company.[2]

Therefore, it is recognized to use the historical acquisition cost of the significant intangible assets, or the amount of expenses disbursed for developing the assets, as a solid allocation base ('Notice of the special action law of tax' in Japan, 66-4(4)-5). Let us examine this notice in detail.

4.1.1   *Method of measuring the absolute value of intangible assets*

As a method of measuring the absolute value of intangible assets, the so-called income approach that will be used in evaluating the business value can be applied. The discounted cash flow (DCF) method of the income approach uses the sum of the present values of estimated future cash flows that a certain intangible asset, such as a patent, will provide.

---

[2]However, according to the National Tax Administration Agency (2007a, b), measuring and using the *absolute value* of intangible assets is not denied, but using the *relative value* is merely permitted. However, the reason why only the measurement of historical costs or periodical outlay expenses are considered practical techniques is the objectivity in measurement, although some subjectivity still enters into the estimation of the duration period of the effects. On the other hand, the DCF method relies heavily on estimation data in measuring the absolute value.

It is true that if only the ratio between the intangible assets of both companies is measured, the allocation of the residual profit is well achieved. However, the author does not believe that the ratio of *absolute values* of intangible assets is equivalent to the ratio of *relative values*, because the ratio of market prices is not the same as the ratio of historical costs.

4.1.2 *Method of measuring the relative value of intangible assets*

To measure the relative value of intangible assets, we can use either the historical cost (i.e., book value of investment) of the intangible assets or the annual cash disbursement for the intangible assets.

4.1.2.1 The historical cost of the intangible asset

The historical cost of the intangible asset means the investment amount of the intangible asset. This amount is the residual balance of the deferred asset, which has been depreciated in accordance with the decrease in the value as time elapses. Such a treatment is possible even if the total investment amount for R&D is treated as a lump-sum expense according to the financial accounting standard, and the amount will be a deferred asset for the purpose of the residual profit allocation method.

However, in order to treat the cash outlays for an intangible asset as a deferred asset, the amount of cash disbursement for development and maintenance of an individual patent and individual engineering technologies, etc., must be identified for each project.

Further, since the development of an intangible asset requires continuous investments for a longer period of time, the cash outlay data for this longer period must be available for the individual project.

In addition, we have to estimate the duration period of the intangible asset in question in order to estimate its annual depreciation cost. When the cash outlay is treated as a deferred or intangible asset, it is necessary to depreciate it based on the estimated duration period. For this purpose, we have to estimate how the effect of cash outlay in this period will continue in the succeeding periods. The behavior pattern of this effect is called a lag pattern. The value of the intangible asset will first increase as time elapses, and decrease in the aftermath (see Tokunaga, 2007, p. 118).

For example, the lag pattern of the effects of R&D costs (formally called experimental and research expenses), which are the cash outlay for continuously developing new products or new production technologies, is the bell-shaped type, so that the effect will be gradually increased in the first half of the duration between the initial cash outlay and the end of development, but it will gradually decline in the aftermath.

The advertising costs, however, will have an effect immediately after the outlay, but the effect will very soon disappear.

In such ways, the duration period of intangible assets that are treated as deferred assets will be estimated by the individual company in question based on their past experience of the lifetime of effects or the period of the R&D project in question.

4.1.2.2   Annual cash disbursement or expense for developing and maintaining the intangible asset

There are many cases in which it is difficult to identify the cash outlay for the patent and the manufacturing know-how developed and maintained through R&D activities for each individual patent or know-how, respectively. In such cases, the tax rule admits the use of the amount of cash outlay in each period as the relative value of the intangible asset. The tax authority guideline is as follows:

2-1: If the amount of annual expense for making the intangible asset is relatively stable every year, then it is reasonable to use the yearly amount of the expense as an allocation base.

2-2: If the amount of annual expense for making the intangible asset varies largely every year, then the following method can be utilized.

 (a) A method of using the average amount of cash outlay for the reasonable span of periods.
 (b) A method of using the average amount of cash outlay during the duration periods of the effect.

2-3: Even though the amount of contribution factors (i.e., intangible asset as allocation base) is small compared to the amount of residual profit, the residual income allocation method for international transfer pricing is valid.

In summary, from the practical point of view, it is best to use the following expenses to create the intangible asset as an allocation base of the residual profit.

(1) For an intangible asset that contributes to production function, such as a patent or manufacturing know-how, use the expenses related to the R&D department and the manufacturing department.

(2) For an intangible asset that contributes to the marketing function, such as a commodity brand, patent, sales network, and stable customer list, use the expenses related to the advertising department, promotion department, and marketing department.

(3) For an intangible asset that contributes to strategic decisions and management control functions, such as finding strategic business domains,

risk management, capital procurement, and sales policy, use the expenses related to the corporate planning department, finance department, and sales department.

Every company has some intangible assets. Thus, the expenses that appear in the R&D department, sales department, and general administrative department raised in (1), (2), and (3) will accrue in any company, though their amounts may differ. However, an individual company belonging to the network of a global business group will partake in the most powerful function of its own. This powerful function is supported by the company's most significant intangible asset, and thus the cost of its creation could be a reasonable allocation base of the joint profit earned simultaneously by both parties (companies P and S).

4.2 *Application of the method to the numerical example*

Finally, let us review the whole procedure of the residual profit allocation method, which was summarized in Fig. 1. Also, according to the numerical example of Fig. 3, the allocation base and its numerical figures are as follows:

R&D expense of the overseas transactions by company P = 19.

(This figure 19 is not the total amount of company P's R&D costs, but the amount that company P has paid for the overseas parts A business.)

Sales expense of the overseas transactions by company S = 15.

(Again, this amount is not the total amount of company S's sales costs, but the amount that company S has paid for the overseas product A business.)

Therefore, the ratio of intangible assets of both companies is 19 : 15 = 56% : 44%.

With this ratio, the total amount of residual profit, 13, which was calculated at the end of Section 3.3, will be allocated to companies P and S. This procedure was described when we examined the allocation of the residual profit in step 3 of Fig. 1.

5   Conclusion: Game Theoretic Scheme of the Residual Profit Allocation Method

Finally, we will formalize the profit allocation based on the residual profit allocation method. The formula will be as follows. We will use companies P and S that appeared in the case study of this chapter.

Synergy effect = total amount of residual profits

= (extra profit of company P that exceeds its basic profit)

+ (extra profit of company S that exceeds its basic profit).

Allocated profit to company P

= (synergy effect)

$$\times \frac{\text{value of intangible asset of company P}}{\text{sum of the values of intangible assets of companies P and S}}$$

+ (basic profit of company P).

Allocated profit to company S

= (synergy effect)

$$\times \frac{\text{value of intangible asset of company S}}{\text{sum of the values of intangible assets of companies P and S}}$$

+ (basic profit of company S).

Here, the value of the intangible assets of each company is measured as either its absolute value, applying the DCF method to the future cash flows caused by the intangible asset, or its relative value, applying the amount of expenses for developing and maintaining the intangible asset.

This formula will satisfy the condition of individual rationality of the cooperative game. Because the partial coalition among multiple firms within the companies of the consolidated business group will not happen due to the governance of the capital ownership of the central parent company, the allocation of profits that merely satisfies individual rationality will be stable, and all participating companies will be satisfied to participate in the current business group.[3]

---

[3] An analogy between the allocation methods of the residual profit and the synergy of M&A:

Finally, apart from the taxation purpose of international transfer pricing, the author wishes to emphasize that the managers of individual companies that belong to the global consolidated business group wish to be fairly evaluated based on the amount of profit that they earn themselves. (This will be especially true when their rewards, or bonuses, are determined in proportion to the amount of profit they earn.)

From this viewpoint, it would be a good incentive to motivate the manager of each participating company if the parent company in the group allocates the profits among companies in the global business group. Profit allocation based on the residual profit allocation method shown above will be useful, because it will satisfy the condition of individual rationality of the cooperative game.

References

Miyamoto, K. (1983). *Foundation of International Management Accounting*, Tokyo: Chuoh-keizaisha.

Monden, Y. (1989). Profit allocation by cumulative opportunity cost method, *Journal of Japan Industrial Management Association*, 40(4), 211–217 (in Japanese).

Monden, Y. (2010). Acquisition price as an incentive Price of M&A, in Hamada, K. (ed.), *Business Group Management in Japan*, Singapore: World Scientific Pub. Co.

Monden, Y. (2011). From Adam Smith's Division of Labor to Network Organization, in Monden, Y. (ed.), *Management of Inter-Firm Network*, Singapore: World Scientific Pub. Co.

Monden, Y. and Koh, S. (1988). Profit allocation based on goal programming and moriarity method (1) and (2), *Accounting* (Kaikei), 134(6), 58–69, 135(4), 92–102 (in Japanese).

Moriarity, S. (1975a). Another approach to allocating joint costs, *The Accounting Review*, 50(4), 791–795.

To allocate the present value of the synergy effect of both merger-participating companies, the author proposed in another chapter to use the standalone stockholders' value of each company before the press release for the merger (see Monden, 2010, 2011). On the other hand, if we use the market price of investment for intangible assets as an allocation base of residual profits in global consolidated companies, the idea is entirely equivalent to the synergy allocation of M&A. The calculation formula of acquisition price in M&A and the calculation formula of international transfer price in this chapter are the same in their logic.

Moriarity, S. (1975b). Another approach to allocating joint costs: A reply, *The Accounting Review*, 51(3), 686–687.

Mouritsen, J. and Thrane, S. (2006). Accounting, network complementarities and the development of inter-organizational relations, *Accounting, Organizations and Society*, 31, 241–275.

National Tax Administration Agency (1986). *Special Action Law on Tax*, Article 66 (Taxation on the transaction with the related overseas company) (in Japanese).

National Tax Administration Agency (2007a). On partial revision of "Guideline of International Transfer Pricing", June 25 (in Japanese).

National Tax Administration Agency (2007b). Reference cases for applications of international transfer pricing, June 25 (in Japanese).

Nishiyama, Y. (2007). Selection of international transfer pricing between arms-length firms, *Zeikei Tsushin*, 62(13), 70–86 (in Japanese).

Shubik, M. (1962). Incentives, decentralized control, the assignment of joint costs and internal pricing, *Management Science*, 8(3), 325–343.

Tokunaga, M. (2007). Applications of international transfer pricing — 3: Residual profit allocation method, *Zeikei Tsushin*, 62(13), 110–125 (in Japanese).

Ueno, K. (2007). On the revision of "Guideline of International Transfer Pricing" and "Guideline of International Transfer Pricing Related to Consolidated Company," *International Taxation*, 26(6) (in Japanese).

6

Exploratory Research in Cooperative Action for SMEs: The Possibilities of Applying Qualitative Comparative Analysis

Satoshi Arimoto
Niigata University

1 Introduction

In Japan, the competitiveness of small and medium business enterprises (SMEs) is considered to be one of the best sources of competition in the Japanese economy as a whole. The keiretsu business style dominant in the Japanese manufacturing industry has existed for a long time, and was created by combining the Japanese management style with a variety of other elements. However, the difficulties that SMEs face in today's business environment are very well-known. In the current circumstances, many SMEs are vulnerable while they wait for the recovery of the global and Japanese economies. In fact, many companies are exploring a variety of new opportunities. Much of the relevant literature stresses the importance of cooperative action among SMEs as a way out.

In the academic field of management accounting, clarifying what the function of accounting information is as inter-organizational collaboration is becoming an important concern. The main purpose of this chapter is to identify how Japanese SMEs arrange and conduct such cooperative action and how useful numerical information like accounting information will be to undertake such action. For this purpose, I would like to give a summary of the results of a questionnaire on the status of cooperative action among SMEs in Japan. The purpose of the questionnaire was to investigate to what extent Japanese SMEs have recognized the need for cooperative action and how they conduct such action. In this chapter, I intend to present a brief analysis of how important accounting information is when SMEs conduct cooperative actions. Because of the restriction of samples, I will attempt to use qualitative comparative analysis to classify some cases. I would also like to mention the possibility of future research using this approach.

2   Features of Cooperative Action among SMEs

Establishing ways in which the provision of accounting information can assist in setting up cooperative action between organizations has been an important area of current research in management accounting. However, regarding cooperative action between SMEs, there are not many previous studies. We first need to ask what requirements will be focused on when analyzing the cooperative action of SMEs.

First, the SMEs are responsible for a small number of business processes as compared to large companies. Moreover, because of company size or constraints on resources, SMEs are expected to face a severely competitive environment. Large corporate businesses, when building up their competitiveness, have shown that it is possible to combine a number of business processes. However, SMEs are expected to be relatively difficult to differentiate in the way they combine business processes. Therefore, SMEs need to be actively seeking partnerships or establishing patterns of cooperative action with other companies. In these circumstances, I will set out the following characteristics to reveal the nature of cooperative action between SMEs.

The first feature of cooperative action between SMEs is concerned with creating effective levels of management and organization across a range of small businesses. In many studies that have been carried out into intercompany collaborations and alliances, the researchers have aimed to clarify how cooperation can be organized in a vertical direction with strategies such as developing a so-called buyer-supplier relationship. In contrast, cooperative action between SMEs was intended to improve the quality of a particular business process (value-added products) or to expand the capacity of the process. Thus, in terms of horizontal cooperation, different perspectives are necessary.

The second feature — namely, the rules for participating in cooperative action — tends to be quite modest. Between large companies, a working alliance is usually necessary to maintain relationships, and various techniques may be used for this purpose, such as an agreement for an alliance or a capital tie-up. Similar schemes may be used by SMEs. Compared to large companies, a number of SMEs seem to have been managing cooperative action in a moderate and effective way for some time.

The third feature indicates that the SMEs need to have an effective cooperative strategy. Because of the bursting of the economic bubble or some aspects of the conversion to Japanese-style management, most of the SMEs face a severe situation in that it is difficult for them to survive only on the back of their own businesses. In response to the questionnaire item on what percentage of sales is brought about through cooperative action, most of the companies indicated that the proportion is less than 20%. This implies that their own businesses are prioritized and that cooperative action is a relatively new supporting method.

Lastly, while SMEs have been doing business in particular local areas on a limited scale, a partnership of companies is considered to have a different character. For example, it may emphasize technical cooperation through cooperative action using certain trades, or it may emphasize scale expansion through cooperative action within a local area. We need to note how the cooperative action has been built up, how it has developed, and what reasons it may have to end its cooperative relationship at some point.

For the above reasons, in analyzing SME cooperative action, the existence of another point of view is considered important.

3 Previous Research on Management Control of Inter-Company Cooperation

As for the analysis of cooperation between companies, we need to ask what approach should be considered for the fields of management and accounting. With regard to this, we will need to review some previous research.

Many researchers who carry out analyses of which management methods are used to manage certain transactions often rely on the concept of transaction cost economics. Hagedoorn *et al.* (2000) pointed out that the methods of analysis of inter-company cooperation can be classified into the transaction cost economics approach, the corporate strategy approach, and the organization theory approach.

Langfield-Smith and Smith (2003) analyzed the issue of management control and trust in outsourcing relationships. In this case study, control patterns in outsourcing have been shown to be divided into market-based patterns, bureaucratic patterns and trust-based patterns. These classifications were based on three factors: transaction characteristics, transaction environment, and transaction partners. Such ideas, especially of transaction characteristics and the transaction environment, were based on a perspective derived from transaction cost economics. This study has demonstrated the relationship between transaction characteristics and control mechanisms. Depending on transaction cost economics perspectives, the control mechanism was highly related to task programmability, output measurability, asset specificity, and repetition of transactions. Of course, it is too simple to think that the control mechanism is decided only by transaction characteristics or just by the transaction environment. Control mechanisms are very complex and need to be flexible. So, we should consider control mechanisms to be determined by an aggregate of such factors. For accounting research, in developing an aggregate of such factors, we need to find out how work accounting information is organized. In this case, numerical information is more useful in situations with high task programmability, high output measurability, low asset specificity, and high repetition of transactions. In short, this means that a company can predict outcomes or contingencies. In this situation, the control mechanism is likely to be in a market-based pattern. If a company cannot easily predict outcomes or contingencies, its control mechanism is likely to shift to a bureaucratic pattern or a trust-based pattern. In order to achieve effective cooperative action, SMEs have to incorporate a positive attitude towards diversity. It is essential to realize that this mechanism is determined by an aggregate of such factors.

Kamminga and van der Meer-Kooistra (2007) analyzed management control in joint venture cases. They demonstrated that joint venture control could be based on transaction unit or relationships. By following the progress of a single case, this research showed that a control mechanism could change through environmental change. In particular, the growing complexity of the joint venture made it more difficult to observe outcomes or performances. Subsequently, the focus of control shifted to how inputs were cast rather than outputs. Thus it was shown that the control mechanism was determined not by each transaction but the ability of companies to build relationships based on trust.

In my research, I have discovered that SMEs which cooperate to achieve diversity, whether they are in the same local area or not, or in the same business or not, have a very useful commonality.

The common element of the research described here is that the sources all try to explain that it is possible to carry out a kind of numerical control. When outsourcing, the growing difficulties of achieving numerical control mean that another mechanism, such as the building of trust, is required. In joint venture research, in situations with the possibility of numerical control, this can be woven into the contract. However, in assessing the difficulties of numerical control, contracts tend to shift to being incomplete. These conclusions help us to understand the cooperative actions of SMEs.

4 Summary of Questionnaire Survey

As confirmed earlier, the questionnaire regarding cooperative action in SMEs was conducted from the perspective of the previous studies. The title of the survey is "Investigation of inter-firm cooperative action of business processes of SMEs in manufacturing". I sent the questionnaire out in July 2009, and collected answers until mid-September. I used the Nikkei Telecom database, and sent 997 questionnaires to SMEs involved in manufacturing across the nation. I chose the companies based on the Japanese definition of SMEs. These companies were of various sizes, as to produce a valid rational economic analysis, SMEs should be of a certain size. So I chose those with larger numbers of employees. Valid responses came back from 111 companies, and the recovery rate was 11.1%.

After having done this I attempted to see how popular the management practices of cooperative action between SMEs are. The results produced some surprises. Currently, 52 companies are linked to 100 firms actually carrying out cooperative actions. More than 60% of the companies were considering taking such a course, including some that had done so in the past. Among these companies, regarding the question of whether to continue the cooperative action, 95% answered yes.

Among the companies that answered, only five were not considering cooperative action. Asked whether cooperative management practices were going to be important in the future, 53.8% of the companies answered yes. Regardless of whether cooperative action between companies had been implemented, we can see that SME owners have a great interest in cooperative action. Further studies are needed in this area, using analytical methods. This research can be predicted to be fruitful.

5   Exploratory Research Using Qualitative Comparative Analysis

5.1   *Implications of applying qualitative comparative ● analysis to the survey*

There are many SMEs that currently implement cooperative action. I was able to effectively sample 34 companies, which is not a statistically sufficient number of samples. It is debatable as to how many samples are necessary when trying to produce effective results to stimulate a useful debate. In particular, deciding on the kinds of dependent variable that should be used has been a difficult problem for me. Because most SMEs are privately owned, there are constraints in obtaining financial data. So, deciding on which variables should be used to judge the success of cooperative actions can be a vexing problem.

In order to produce some significant results I will apply the approach of qualitative comparative analysis (QCA) with Boolean algebra to the results of my questionnaire. QCA is a method of extracting causal relationships in complex data by using the concept of set theory and Boolean algebra. It was first proposed by Ragin (1987).

Yamashita *et al.* (2001) point out that QCA is suitable for intermediate sample numbers that are too small for statistical analysis but too large for case studies. It is suitable for a number of samples that traditional social sciences find difficult to treat. Through using this method, it is possible to identify causal relationships, including a variety of complex interactions.

In this chapter, by applying this approach, my aim is to try to extract features that represent success stories. In this analysis, I will replace each question with two values, 0 or 1. Such a method is called a crisp-set QCA (csQCA). For a brief description of this analytical technique, please refer to the Appendix.

In analyzing the 34 SMEs' cooperative action stories, I reckoned that the success of cases is demonstrated when companies can retain the desired effect that was assumed before the start of the cooperative action. Thus the purpose of the analysis is to find the commonalities in companies that can contribute to targeted transactions.

It is true that the definition of success may be reconsidered. For example, after the start of cooperative action, some companies will feel effects that were not expected in advance. Such companies, in order to maintain their success, will create various effects. If these companies can feel the significance of cooperative action as a result, these cases may be said to be successful cases. So, the success stories to be analyzed in this chapter represent just one aspect of the success of SME cooperative action.

In the area of management accounting research, the type of research that applies a QCA approach is relatively new. Because it is not large companies but SMEs which are being analyzed, and because the method of analysis is relatively new, this research can be said to be exploratory.

5.2 *Basic scenario and variables*

The basic idea of this analysis follows the following two questions. With regard to the pre-arranged stages before cooperative action starts, the first question is "What is an attribute of a transaction?" and the second, "What does important information constitute?" The aim of the analysis is to show how the combination of these variables can lead to successful cases. The variables are explained in Table 1.

Of course, SME cooperative action is not simple. I recognize the importance of other attribute variables. However, many variables make using condensed formula very complex. In this chapter, I will try to focus on ways in which companies may already have partnerships.

Next, I will try to understand the information needed to conduct cooperative action among SMEs from two viewpoints. One is through public or private accounting information, while the other is focused on numerical information or non-numerical information. This idea derives from

Table 1. Explanatory variable 1: Attributes.

| Name | Meaning | Meaning of the Two Values | |
		1	0
tra	Are there other pre-existing business relationships with partnership companies or not?	There are some business relationships	There is no business relationship
loc	Location of partnership companies	Same local area	Other local area or foreign company
cob	Category of business of partnership companies	Same category	Other category

earlier studies which have applied a transaction cost economics approach, especially a numerical or non-numerical one.

The question used in my survey is "What information did you emphasize at the start of cooperative action? Please rank the following".

A. Public accounting information
B. Public non-accounting information
C. Non-public accounting information
D. Non-public non-accounting information

I translated this rank into a certain point. One variable means whether a company did emphasize public information. I call this variable bpi (beforehand public information). Comparing the points of answer $A + B$ and the points of $C + D$, if $A + B < C + D$, the variable is regarded to be of value 1. This means this company has emphasized public information more. Further, if $A + B > C + D$, bpi is regarded to be of value 0. This means that the company has emphasized non-public information more.

The other variable indicates when a company did emphasize accounting information. I call this variable bai (beforehand accounting information). Comparing the points of answer $A + C$ and the points of $B + D$, if $A + C < B + D$, the variable is regarded to be of value 1. This means that this company has emphasized accounting information more. In addition, if $A + C > B + D$, bai is regarded to be of value 0, which means that this company has emphasized non-accounting information more.

Using these explanatory variables, I will try to discover what combination of these variables in successful cases would consist of. Dependent variables are known as Be (beforehand effect). Be indicates that the company can sustain the effects expected before the start of cooperative action. Interpretation of this variable is very difficult, and there is something very arbitrary about it.

First, I asked what effects were expected before the start of cooperative action. There are various choices, like maintaining existing businesses, cost reduction, accessing technology that your company does not have, and so on. However, due to simplification, the choice did not matter in my analysis. Next, I asked whether the effect continues today. The choices are divided into five levels. Above average cases are regarded to have value 1. This means that the company can feel and retain the effects expected. Below average cases are regarded to have value 0. This means that a company cannot feel or retain the effects expected. I must say that this interpretation is very arbitrary. This point must be reconsidered in future research.

5.3 *QCA analysis*

I will now present the QCA analysis. The software I use is fs/QCA version 2.5.

$$\text{Model: Be} = \text{f(tra, cpb, loc, bpi, bai)}$$

It is necessary to ask what the commonality is that can feel and keep effects that are expected before the start of the cooperative action of SMEs. The existence of the dependent variable Be = 1 means that a company can feel the effects expected; Be = 0 means that the company cannot feel the effects expected.

Number of cases: 0 terms: 10; 1 terms: 5

Minimum sum-of-products form

$$= \text{tra}^*\text{cob}^*\text{loc}^*\text{bpi}^*\text{bai} + \text{TRA}^*\text{cob}^*\text{LOC}^*\text{bpi}^*\text{bai}$$

$$+ \text{TRA}^*\text{cob}^*\text{loc}^*\text{BPI}^*\text{bai} + \text{TRA}^*\text{COB}^*\text{loc}^*\text{bpi}^*\text{BAI}$$

$$+ \text{TRA}^*\text{COB}^*\text{LOC}^*\text{BPI}^*\text{bai}$$

I tried to analyze 34 cases. However, in this model, 15 cases (0 terms: 10; 1 terms: 5) are shown in a reduction formula. This means that given the same mix of variables, some companies can feel the expected effects, whereas others cannot feel these effects. In these cases, this analysis leads to the conclusion that there are contradictions. Among the 34 cases, contradiction cases are excluded.

Variables in capitals in the formula mean 1, and variables in lowercase mean 0. This formula means that among 15 cases there are five cases that can feel and keep the effects expected (Be = 1). In these five cases, the formula is condensed, and as a result there are five items. There seems to be no point because in five Be = 1 terms there is no commonality. However, as mentioned before, the contradiction cases are already excluded. The mix of variables in these five cases leads surely to 1 in my survey, and this result is very meaningful.

I believe that there are two interesting points in the condensed formula. First, in four of the five cases, the company conducted cooperative action with a partner with which there was already a business relationship (tra = 1). Second, in cases of cooperative action with other business categories (cob = 0), the company tended not to emphasize accounting information (bai = 0).

These interpretations are of great interest. First, SME cooperative action with no business relationship may be difficult. In other words, it can be said that an SME has a certain difficulty in selecting new companies to build cooperative action with. This is one reason that most SMEs have considerable constraints on management resources, and their information gathering capacity for human resources is restricted.

Second, it is very important to state that the companies which conduct cooperative action with other categories of business tend not to emphasize accounting information. There seems to be more uncertainty in this case, in comparison to those companies which can be placed in similar categories. Accounting information is often said to be objective, but a little intensive. So, cooperative action with other categories of business seems to need more qualitative information. This implication is consistent with previous studies. However, this does not mean that accounting information is not useful for cooperative action with other categories of business. This only suggests that there is more useful information than numerical information to be found. To achieve success, SMEs need to access qualitative information, such as technological information.

If I now try to switch 0 and 1 in the variable Be, I can see more implications.

$$\text{Model: Be} = f(\text{tra, cpb, loc, bpi, bai})$$

It is necessary to ask what the commonality is that cannot feel and keep effects that are expected before the start of the SMEs' cooperative action. If the dependent variable Be = 1, that company cannot feel the expected effects, and if Be = 0 this means that company can feel the expected effects.

Number of cases: 0 terms: 5; 1 terms: 1

Minimum sum-of-products form

$$= \text{TRA*BPI*BAI} + \text{tra*COB*loc*bai} + \text{tra*COB*loc*bpi}$$
$$+ \text{cob*loc*BPI*BAI} + \text{TRA*COB*LOC*BAI}$$
$$+ \text{tra*cob*LOC*BPI*bai}$$

In this model, there are ten cases that cannot experience the expected effects, and these ten cases are condensed into six patterns. As mentioned before, contradictions are already excluded. These six patterns form the commonality that indicates that cooperative actions are not proceeding as expected.

The characteristics are as follows: The first and fifth terms of the formula show, in cases with partnerships, that there is a business relationship already (tra = 1) and when they emphasize numerical information (bai = 1), the company cannot feel the expected effects. This is consistent with the result that is shown in the previous model. Next, the second, third, and sixth terms in the formula show, in cases of partnership, that there was no previous business relationship (tra = 0), and that the company cannot continue to be affected by the effects expected even if the partnership company is in the same industry category (cob = 1) or in the same local area (loc = 1). Furthermore, the first, fourth, and sixth terms in the formula show that, in cases where a company cannot experience the effects expected, it tends to emphasize accounting information (bai = 1). In comparison to the results of the previous model, this is extremely interesting.

5.4 *Overall interpretation*

From the above, the following tendencies can be observed in the results from my questionnaire. First, many of the successful cooperative actions that a company can experience are in cases where those companies have a business relationship already. On the other hand, companies that have no business relationship may not produce the expected results. Second, the cooperative actions between SMEs in different categories need not only numerical information or accounting information but also qualitative information. Third, among the cases that emphasize public information or numerical information, the SMEs cannot conduct cooperative action as planned.

This analysis shows that the success of SMEs is not so simple. If one company faces severe economic conditions, and tries to coordinate any cooperative action without much effort, SMEs cannot achieve so much. Even among companies in the same local area or the same industry category, this tendency is the same. For successful cooperative action, SMEs must make considerable preparations and effort.

6 Conclusion and Possibilities for Future Research

This analysis has intended to discover commonalities among the 34 cases. Certainly, the implications from what had already been established seem to be consistent with previous studies, and some implications seem to be due to certain peculiarities of particular SMEs. At this stage, in order to simplify the analysis, I will try to analyze the variables in as simple a way as possible. More detailed analysis with more variables needs to be done. However, I think it is important here to analyze some of the variables applied to transaction cost economics studies, such as uncertainty and transaction frequency.

The fundamental problem of this approach is that the answers to the questionnaire are replaced by two values (1 or 0). In the process of this change, arbitrary intervention is inevitable. For example, the variable Be is considered to be an indicator of the success of cooperative action. Some cooperative action aims to justify cost reductions. In such a case accounting information is very useful in coordinating cooperative action. In other words, numerical control may be more powerful. On the other hand, like technical cooperation or trial manufacture cooperation, if cooperative action can be called a "one-shot deal", numerical control may be very difficult. Thus, my arbitrary decision, regardless of its aims, is that, if the expected effect is obtained, the cooperative action will be judged as a success. Normally, it is necessary to fully examine such aims.

Furthermore, the success of cooperative action can be brought about by experiencing effects that are not expected in advance. In such cases, the planning of an arrangement is more important than what happens before the arrangement itself is made. By continuing a cooperative relationship, trust between companies can be built up. In this case, without a change in the information, the transaction may work.

I must recognize that there are a lot of problems to be considered. However, through this approach, we can see certain tendencies of SMEs toward cooperative action. Therefore, I believe that this research is significant.

Appendix: A Brief Interpretation of the Boolean Algebra Approach (QCA)

This approach was designed by Ragin (1987) as a case study of comparative quality. I would like to briefly introduce the features and operational procedures. To do so, I want to examine an example that has been featured in Kanomata *et al.* (2001). This supposes that there are four cases as follows:

	a	b	c	Y
Case 1	1	1	1	1
Case 2	1	0	1	0
Case 3	1	1	0	1
Case 4	0	1	0	0

Variables a, b, c are explanatory variables and variable Y is a dependent variable. This table is called a truth table. It shows a causal relationship between the occurrence of the three explanatory variables that leads to the occurrence of the dependent variable Y. 1 means yes, and 0 means no. So, case 1 means that all the explanatory variables a, b, and c are the result of occurrences, and that the dependent variable Y occurs. Further, case 2 indicates that when the results of explanatory variables a and c occur and the variable b does not occur, the dependent variable Y does not occur.

These cases can be represented in the form of a formula. This formula is called the standard sum-of-products formula:

$$Y = ABC + ABc.$$

The cases in which the variable Y does occur are case 1 and case 3. Each variable in capital letters means 1 and each in small letters means 0. Thus, case 1 can be expressed as ABC and case 3 can be expressed as ABc.

Boolean minimization rules are based on two basic principles:

$$\text{Absorption: } A + AB = A$$

$$\text{Reduction: } AB + Ab = A(B + b) = A.$$

According to this principle, $Y = ABC + ABc$ can be summarized as follows:

$$Y = ABC + ABc = AB(C + c) = AB.$$

In the four cases in this example, the variable Y occurs in cases 1 and 3. Furthermore, compared to cases 1 and 3, variables a and b occur. However, despite the occurrence of variable c, variable Y always occurs. This means the occurrence of variable Y is not dependent on the occurrence of variable c. Hence, in these four cases, the factor necessary for the occurrence of dependent variable Y is variable a (yes) and variable b (yes).

In my analysis, through these basic ideas, I will try to clarify which factors are essential for the occurrence of the dependent variable Be.

References

Anderson, S.W. and Dekker, H.C. (2005). Management control for market transactions: The relationship between transaction characteristics, incomplete contract design, and subsequent performance, *Management Science*, 51(12), 1734–1752.

Byrne, D. and Ragim, C.C. (2009). *The SAGE Handbook of Case-Based Methods*, London: Sage Publications Ltd.

Dekker, H.C. (2004). Control of inter-organizational relationships: Evidence on appropriate concerns and coordination requirements, *Accounting, Organizations and Society*, 29(1), 27–49.

Dekker, H.C. (2008). Partner selection and governance design in inter-firm relationships, *Accounting, Organizations and Society*, 33, 915–941.

Hagedoorn, J., Link, A.N. and Vonortas, N.S. (2001). Research partnerships, *Research Policy*, 29(4–5), 567–586.

Kamminga, P.E. and van der Meer-Kooistra, J. (2007). Management control patterns in joint venture relationships: A model and an exploratory study, *Accounting, Organizations and Society*, 32(1–2), 131–154.

Kanomata, N., Nomiya, D. and Hasegawa, K. (2001). *Qualitative Comparative Analysis*, Kyoto: Minerva Shobo Ltd. (in Japanese).

Langfield-Smith, K. and Smith, D. (2003). Management control systems and trust in outsourcing relationships, *Management Accounting Research*, 14(3), 281–307.

Oz, Ozlem (2004). Using Boolean- and fuzzy-logic based methods to analyze multiple case study evidence in management research, *Journal of Management Inquiry*, 13(2), 166–179.

Ragin, C.C. (1987). *The Comparative Method: Moving Beyond Qualitative and Quantitive Strategies*, Berkeley: University of California Press.

Speklé, R.F. (2001). Explaining management control structure variety: A transaction cost economics perspective, *Accounting, Organizations and Society*, 26, 419–441.

Tomkins, C. (2001). Interdependencies, trust and information in relationships, alliances and networks, *Accounting, Organizations and Society*, 26, 161–191.

van den Abbeck, A., Roodhooft, F. and Warlop, L. (2009). The effect of cost information on buyer-supplier negotiations in different power settings, *Accounting, Organizations and Society*, 34, 245–266.

Yamashita, T., Kono, Y. and Shimada, M. (2001). A case-oriented study using the combination of qualitative comparative analysis and fuzzy reasoning, *Journal of Japan Society for Fuzzy Theory and Systems*, 13(3), 334–339 (in Japanese).

7

Performance Measurement of an Inter-Firm Network from the Viewpoint of Reduction of Total Lead Time for Investment Recovery

Shino Hiiragi
Aichi Institute of Technology

1 Introduction

In the examination of inter-firm network issues, one must focus on both the specific problems of single companies and the collaborative problems between such entities. This chapter treats one of these inter-firm problems, one that affects capital efficiency in the whole network, namely, the efficiency of investment recovery.

It proposes as a model a network with a manufacturing company as its core component. The analysis is carried out from the following macro/micro viewpoints:

1. A deliberation on the entire corporate management is carried out first. Is the total capital placed in the company or the inter-firm network efficiently recovered? While placing priority on this total optimization viewpoint, an examination is made of management control challenges and the index of the whole network.
2. At this point, a concrete instance is analyzed. In each organization, the management control challenges and the control index are examined, in order to achieve total optimization.

2 The Overall Challenge of Investment Recovery Efficiency in an Inter-Firm Network

In this section, the overall challenge of investment recovery efficiency in an inter-firm network is studied. First, it looks at the investment recovery efficiency that is common to a single company, the network company, and the inter-firm network. In addition, the cooperation problem in an inter-firm network is examined.

2.1 *The structure homogeneity of production spot challenges and the overall challenges faced by the company*

The investment recovery efficiency is broken down into two factors: the rate of the recovery quantity and the rate of the speed of recovery. It is thereby formulated as follows:

Investment recovery efficiency

= profit margin on sales × capital turnover ratio

= (margin/sales) × (sales/capital)

When capital and sales are considered to be uniform, the right-hand side of the definitional identity, the profit margin on sales, is changed by the amount of the surplus recovery. In comparison, the capital turnover ratio works directly with the turnover period and is influenced by the speed of recovery.

The guarantee of quality, a constant basic premise, ranks among the leading quality, cost, delivery (QCD) production concerns of the manufacturing company. Its next priorities are cost and lead time reductions. These are the production spot challenges of the products, which concern outputs, and they must be treated homogeneously as part of the overall challenges faced by the company in the process of seeking investment recovery efficiency (Fig. 1).

The business challenges faced by the company in seeking sustainability are summarized as how speedily, through the minimum input and in the greatest amount, the investment placed should be recovered. In the lower part of Fig. 1, this perspective very much resembles the QCD spot challenge of how products of good quality and low cost are quickly produced. In both cases, the maximum removal of waste and the greatest increase of output for input, of productivity, are essential.

In the past, the profit rate has mainly attracted attention in the recovery of investment. Scholars have pointed to the importance of lead time reduction associated with collection period reduction, but no convincing arguments on this issue have been advanced. In this section, it is taken up and explored.

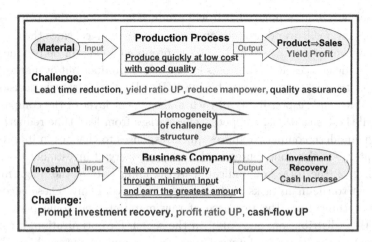

Fig. 1.   The homogeneity of company challenges and production spot QCD challenges.

2.2   Lead time reduction in each facet of the business, as the strategic challenge of the company

The business activity of the manufacturing company is distributed as illustrated in Fig. 2. In the first stage, the firm develops its business and product

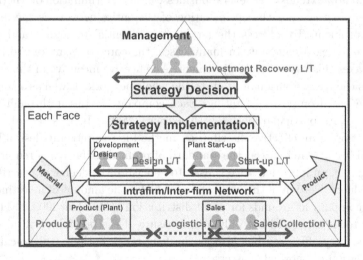

Fig. 2.   Lead time (L/T) in each facet of the manufacturing company.

strategies, which determine what it will produce for its potential customers. At this point, facility and production strategies are in place, since these processes concentrate on where and how the proposed good will be produced. They include choices at the business level, such as product-out or market-in and make-to-stock or business to business (B to B). Such strategic decisions are the duty and responsibility of each management layer of the company.

In all these situations, competitiveness arises from lead time reduction, since the modern company requires quick responses to changes in its product strategy; it also contributes to the early recovery of investment.

In Fig. 2, the total flow indicated in the lower part of the diagram is equivalent to the main tasks of the manufacturing company. These encompass everything from the purchase of raw materials and some parts, to production, distribution, and sales. In the search for optimization, a company seeks to enhance its internal organization and its external collaboration with associated firms in the inter-firm network. The last objective poses a cooperation challenge within a network seeking investment recovery efficiency.

2.3   *The total index of management control in an inter-firm network*

The total flow extends over several businesses; the determination of whether each company acts for the optimization of the entire network is the most crucial problem. To address the latter, it is essential to understand the incentive for each company. In many cases, the core company of the network makes this control and adjustment. An effective incentive in this case includes the redistribution of profit to the whole network, as well as a transfer price based on cost accounting. Each company devises it through the conduct of its particular business (Kurokawa, 2008). In this regard, the construction of an effective distribution method is theoretically desirable.

To this end, the index as the standard of profit distribution is required. For example, an incentive price is used to "measure the degree of contribution to the realization of the unification profit for the amount of investment of each company as grounds for profit distribution" (Monden, 2009, p. 115). This factor is evaluated not only as a measure of the possibility of investment recovery efficiency but also as the long-range outlook, the so-called accumulation of knowledge assets.

An effective index of the challenge of total lead time reduction in the inter-firm network is proposed. Cash flows are quoted in the index to enable the external analysis of financial statements. This procedure is formulated by indirect and indicative methods, as follows (Monden, 2011):

$$\text{JIT cash flows} = \text{operating income} -(+) \text{ inventory increase (decrease)} \tag{1}$$

$$\text{JIT cash flows} = \text{sales amount} - \text{amount of purchased direct materials}$$
$$- \text{ all of the cash-paid processing costs} \tag{2}$$

This index gives the incentive for inventory and lead time reduction for all consolidated companies (Monden, 2011). These have high utilization, since their calculation from financial numerical values is easy. When a network is consolidated, these very effectively give the total index of the overall corporate management.

3 A Concrete Instance of the Lead Time Reduction Challenge in an Inter-Firm Network

As a concrete instance of the inter-firm network challenges presented in the preceding section, automobile manufacturing company X and automobile dealers A and B, all located in the sales network of X, are examined through financial analysis and interviews. In the former, attention is paid to the issue of inventory when the economy fluctuated rapidly after 2008. Furthermore, an interview with the former financial affairs officer, Mr. C, of company A, reveals the problems of operating the retail business. In terms of analysis, it highlights the improvements in the production spot. Specifically, the manufacturer and the retail store, each a separate entity in the inter-firm network, take part in a back and forth process.

3.1 *The cooperation challenge among the companies in an inter-firm network: Financial analysis*

The financial panic started with the subprime loan crisis in the United States in 2007, an event that had a serious influence on the real economy. As of 2010, the economy has not yet attained full-scale recovery. In Japan, the negative impact on export industries was marked, with the auto industry experiencing one of the most dramatic contractions. The serious downturns of excellent companies created serious general economic and social difficulties (Hiiragi, 2009b). The gigantic fixed cost burden and the sudden increase in inventories were the fundamental problems of the automobile sector.

This section addresses especially the second of these issues. In the productive system of Japan, manufacturing improvement is represented by the Toyota Production System (TPS), which is firmly established. It has been said that the inventory level of the auto industry of Japan exerted a strong prohibitive power in all situations. In addition, some issues were possibly unresolved in the cooperation spots of production and sales.

Studies of the manufacturing inter-firm network have pointed out the importance of cooperation toward total optimization. Many studies exist on the relationship between a manufacturer and its suppliers (Fujimoto *et al.*, 1998; Kurokawa, 2008; Liker and Chei, 2004; Maguire and Peacock, 1998; Nishiguchi, 1998; Shiomi, 1985), but few between it and its dealers. Of the latter, research has centered on the monthly and daily production schedules of the maker, on the basis of the exchange of information between it and its dealers (Asanuma, 1994; Kurokawa, 2008; Monden, 1983, 2011; Ogawa, 1994; Okamoto, 1995; Tomino, 2003, 2004, 2010).

According to these inquiries, three facets of the production schedule, which have affected the monthly, ten-day, and daily orders of automobile manufacturers in Japanese domestic production since the 1990s in Japan, are currently the most flexible areas of cooperation between the points of production and sale. Offshore production has not experienced a parallel evolution. Build-to-order as the most evolved form has not yet been realized (Holweg and Pil, 2004; Iyer *et al.*, 2009). It is essential to realize that the information input of monthly orders does not automatically translate into real, actual commands. This observation is made for the following reason:

> To reach an equilibrium, an adjustment has to be made monthly between the total demand that the distribution side of the network transmits to the planning centre and the total production capacity available.... Since production capacities cannot be very quickly increased or decreased, the distribution side is expected to absorb the burden for this adjustment to a non-negligible degree (Asanuma, 1994, p. 138).

With this expectation of the sales side, the other expectation is analyzed as follows:

> I spotlighted the following two factors as critical elements of the organizational skill required on the part of the core firm to achieve a flexible production system: (1) leveling the production schedule to the detailed specifications level, and (2) making of sustainable monthly production plans (Asanuma, 1994, p. 148).

There are two kinds of functions demanded of the maker, the core company. The first is the ability to adjust production to a demand change and the second is the ability to design, coordinate, and lead the entire company in order to create an effective plan in collaboration with the dealers.

In this regard, car manufacturer company X and the affiliated companies A and B are analyzed. Company X had more than 5,000 stores of 400 companies in its sales network as of December 2009. Company A is a retail business that is part of the network and a wholly owned subsidiary of company X. Company B is an independent local dealer with a long business relationship with the manufacturer. It is one of the largest dealers, with more than 60 stores, and it has approximately 10 times the sales of company A.

Figure 3 shows the change in the inventory profit rate and the inventory turnover for X, A, and B during five accounting periods from 2006 to 2010. The change in the inventory turnover in the economic recession period attracts attention. From 2008 through 2009, the inventory turnover of the manufacturer, company X, markedly dropped, but it rose for the dealers, companies A and B.

Figure 4 shows changes in the sales and inventories of companies X, A, and B based on the numerical value of 100 in 2006. The sales of X declined greatly, but its inventory did not change very much. In comparison, the

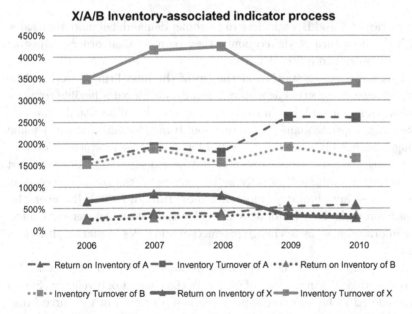

Fig. 3.   An indicator of the inventories of the automobile maker and dealers.
Source: The financial statements of companies X, A, and B.

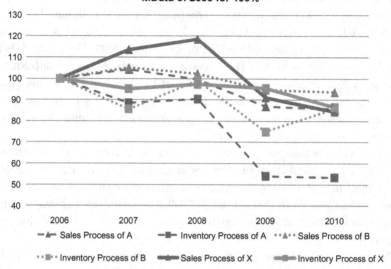

Fig. 4.   The change in sales and inventories of the automobile maker and dealers. *Source*: The financial statements of companies X, A, and B.

inventories of A and B, each close to customer demand, fell more than sales. With the downturn of the economy, they reduced their orders, adjusting their inventories to reflect demand.

This finding suggests that at the tip of the inter-firm network, where the customer is directly encountered, retailers achieved a flexible response to changes in demand, but in the core company, this alteration did not provoke an appropriate management reaction. It may be said that the demand change was quickly sensed at the retail but not at the production level.

Among the two functions pointed out previously, the ability to adjust production is evaluated globally as the source of the competitiveness of the Japanese auto industry (Fujimoto, 2007; Hiiragi, 2009a). However, this situation reveals the need for a greater enhancement of management control over information so as to change production schedules as market situations change.

The possibility that the corporate scale affects the production control is also estimated. When the rate of decline in the amount of inventory (Fig. 4) is considered to be an expression of the power of each of the three firms, this power becomes weaker in the order of A, B and X, moving from the company with the smallest amount of inventory to that with the largest. It is estimated that inventory control during the demand slump period becomes more difficult as the quantity of handling increases. It is indicated that the collective control and adjustment of the demand by the main office were not necessarily effective. The demand corresponding to each locality is needed.

It is also interesting to note that the inventories of B increased immediately in the next year. The same tendency is evident in 2008, and one can say that it is a reflection of the aggressive policy of B. The adoption of an offensive policy will be analyzed in the future.

3.2 The challenges at the final stage of an inter-firm network: The interview

What kind of concrete problem exists at the edge of the network? To clarify this issue, the internal problems of the dealer with lead time reduction are analyzed in an interview with Mr. C of company A (January 2010).

Figure 5 shows a flow of sale duties and accounts of the automobile dealer company A. In this flow, the order of a car by a customer is posted

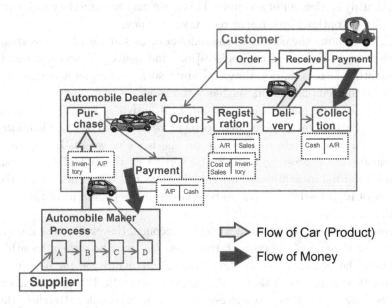

Fig. 5.   The flow of sale duties and accounts of automobile dealer company A.

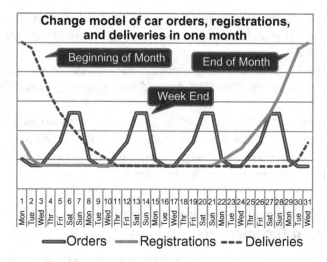

Fig. 6. The change model of the number of car orders, registrations, and deliveries in one month of company A.

under the sales of company A. It assumes that the bill is paid after the car is delivered to the customer. Company A, as other Japanese companies, relies on a monthly settlement of accounts. This cycle may become the checkpoint for achieving optimal investment recovery efficiency.

Figure 6 shows the change in the number of cars at each business stage of company A, such as order, registration, and delivery. Various seasonal and monthly factors do not always produce such a wave, so it is modeled in a state that emphasizes its tendency to change.

The sales staff engages in daily business activities in order to reach a target. This target receives management review each week. Therefore, the order number tends to fluctuate on the basis of weeks. In contrast, the registration processing tends to be settled at the end of the month because the total monthly sales are calculated at this time. As a result, the delivery of registered cars tends to be focused at the beginning of the next month.

Automobiles are produced in a cycle of seconds. However, at the dealer, which is at the end of the process, these become stock because of monthly handling. The lead time to collecting payment on an order at the beginning of a month is longer than that at the end of the month. If the registration work is done continuously in succession or in more, smaller stretches, the lead time is reduced for investment recovery.

For the quantity of future investment recovery to increase, the sales staff must concentrate on the business activity of orders. The attainment of this balance is the challenge in the sales spot. Can the improvement technique in the production spot be used? A business activity can carry out its main activity, and others be given supporting work, so as to find the most suitable combination of resources. Another idea is for the sales staff to concentrate on its main function, while registration is handed over to other employees. However, the basic measure remains the review of the monthly settlement of accounts.

The production/sales lead time of the whole inter-firm network can be reduced to ten days at most. Such a change allows for the efficient recovery of investment. From the point of view of cash management, when investment is recovered progressively, smaller investment sums are needed at any one time than if it is collected once a month, a very large benefit. In one trial, another company Y has started making efforts to speed up the registration process (Tomino, 2010, p. 10).

A real case is hard to work out, since the payment to the maker must be changed at the same time, but if the total cycle of the fund flow is changed to every week from every month and the period becomes a quarter, the quantity of necessary investment is theoretically obtained in a quarter. Such timing would be of great value to a business.

3.3 The management index in each facet of an inter-firm network

In Section 1, JIT cash flows as the total index for control was evaluated. In this section, the index for the daily management control is examined. Therefore, external financial data is not used; rather, data internal to the company are employed.

As pointed out in Section 1, real company activity takes place in a variety of situations. Lead time reduction should be realized in all these situations, in order to increase the firm's competitiveness. Naturally, it must be reduced during development, design, and factory setup. In this case, the basic index is the time taken for this purpose.

In comparison, a substitute index exists for each situation in the flow of the main duties of manufacturing, since the product really flows through a material process, and this movement is not always smooth. The stock quantities show the amount of available resources. Lead times and the stock changes are not linked, but the stock quantities in the daily process become the effective index of management in the lead time of the production spot. In this section, the example of the slippage between the maker and the dealers is also to be analyzed from this viewpoint.

It must be stated again that a non-financial affairs index is more important than a financial one in daily on-site management. With this observation in mind, the necessity of converting the money accounts and financing indexes to the equivalent monetary value is more evident. From the viewpoint of investment recovery, it is desirable that the index be established by the amount of money involved.

In this regard, the money flow rate, the pace at which money comes and goes, is evaluated, since it treats investment flow both by its amount and its speed (Preiss and Ray, 2000a,b). However, this concept is not typical, so it is difficult to diffuse and fix it in the production spot.

On the other hand, the J-cost Theory integrates cost and lead time and makes it a basic index of the J-cost (Tanaka, 2004, 2008, 2009). Its rough numerical profit is divided by the J-cost for the profitability index. The J-cost is calculated with a QCD numerical value, called the cost and lead time available in the production spot, so its introduction and practical use are easy. It has the function of visualization. The J-cost theory is evaluated in these terms.

There is a limit to catching profit in non-compound interest, both in the money flow rate and the J-cost theory. Efficiency can be judged by these factors in every cycle and in each facet, so their practical applicability to daily spot management is high. However, they require basic data collection and calculation; as a result, more labor time must be devoted to these tasks. The interlocking movement with an IT system, such as FOA (Oku, 2010), is an effective method of approaching this problem.

4 Conclusion

In this chapter, the total lead time for investment recovery was analyzed. First, in Section 1, the importance of total lead time reduction as a strategy for business competitiveness in the inter-firm network was emphasized and studied from the viewpoint of total optimization.

In the next section, the main business flow of the manufacturing company was shown, and the problems of the final stage were discussed. In particular, the analysis emphasized that the collection of funds after delivery must be framed within the context of investment recovery efficiency in the whole inter-firm network.

Finally, the necessity and importance of synchronizing the settlement of accounts for each network stage, as well as payment collection from the customer at the final stage, are highlighted. The settlement of accounts should be considered from the perspective of the entire process of manufacturing. Besides, synchronization is necessary in the whole inter-firm network, as well as in a single company.

Digitizing information as a management control index is necessary. This step should be combined with a fair performance evaluation of company activity, in order to ensure future growth and competitiveness. To this end, accounting should fulfill the function of the bridge principle (Takeda, 2006; Hiiragi, 2010a), which links business competitiveness to a performance evaluation. Accounting must be a compass of corporate management, including every business aspect, from the financial to the non-financial, so as to identify the right course for that company.

References

Asanuma, B. (1994). Co-ordination between production and distribution in a globalizing network of firms: Assessing flexibility achieved in the Japanese automobile industry, in M. Aoki, R. Dore. (eds.), *The Japanese Firm: Sources of Competitive Strength*, Oxford: Oxford University Press.

Fujimoto, T., Nishiguchi, T. and Ito, H. (eds.), (1998). *Readings on Supplier Systems*, Tokyo: Yuhikaku (in Japanese).

Fujimoto, T. (2007). *Competing to Be Really, Really Good: The Behind-the-Scenes Drama of Capability-Building Competition in the Automobile Industry*, Tokyo: I-House Press.

Hiiragi, S. (2009a). Accounting suitable for the Toyota Production System: Feasibility of the fair performance evaluation, Doctor of Business Administration and Computer Science 2009, No. 7, Aichi Institute of Technology (in Japanese).

Hiiragi, S. (2009b). Return to the original spirit of Toyota Production System — in terms of the efficiency of investment recovery, *The Journal of Ohara Institute for Social Research*, No. 608, 17–31 (in Japanese).

Hiiragi, S. (2010a). Accounting to make effective use of "Genba Power" — for the fair performance evaluation and implementation of total management control, *Journal of the Society for Social Management Systems*. SMS10–102.

Holweg, M. and Pil, F.K. (2004). *The Second Century: Reconnecting Customer and Value Chain through Build-To-Order*, Cambridge, MA: MIT Press.

Iyer, A.V., Seshadri, S. and Vasher, R. (2009). Toyota supply chain management, McGrow-Hill.

Kurokawa, F. (2008). *Strategy of Automobile Industry in the 21st Century*, Tokyo: Zeimukeiri Kyokai (in Japanese).

Liker, J. and Chei, T.Y. (2004). Building deep supplier relationships, *Harvard Business Review*, Dec, 104–113.

Maguire, N.G. and Peacock, E. (1998). Evaluating the cost of lead-time on the supplier selection process: An ABC driven methodology, *Journal of Cost Management*, Nov/Dec, 27–28.

Monden, Y. (1983). *New Development of Toyota Production System*, Tokyo: Japan Management Association (in Japanese).

Monden, Y. (2009). *A Profit Allocation Pricing for Cooperation between the Companies*, Tokyo: Zeimukeiri-Kyokai (in Japanese).

Monden, Y. (2011). *Toyota Production System: An Integrated Approach to Just-in-time*, 4th Ed, Cambridge, MA: Taylor & Francis.

Nishiguchi, T. (1998). Innovation of the production system: Toyota Production System, in Itami, H., Kagono, T., Miyamoto, M. and Yonekura, S. (eds.), *Innovation and Technological Accumulation*, Tokyo: Yuhikaku, 56–89 (in Japanese).

Ogawa, E. (ed.) (1994). *A Study of the Toyota Production System*, Tokyo: Nikkei Inc. (in Japanese).

Okamoto, H. (1995). *Unification of Production and Sales in the Modern Company*, Tokyo: Shinhyoron (in Japanese).

Oku, M. (2010). Integrated manufacturing information system case series (1): An example of management (FOA concept) by field principles, MMRC Discussion Paper Series No. 308 (in Japanese).

Preiss, K. and Ray, M. (2000a). Time-based costing: Part 1: Costing for a dynamic business environment, *Journal of Corporate Accounting & Finance*, 11(5), 65–74.

Preiss, K. and Ray, M. (2000b). Time-based costing: Part 2: Scope and application, *Journal of Corporate Accounting & Finance*, 11(6), 47–56.

Shiomi, H. (1985). Production logistics structure: The case of Toyota, in K. Sakamoto (ed.), *Technological Innovation and Corporate Architecture*, Kyoto: Minerva-Shobo (in Japanese).

Takeda, R. (2006). The role of the "Bridge Principle" in the theory constitution: Accounting and the "Pajna-para-mita sutra," *Newsletter TKC*, Oct. (in Japanese).

Tanaka, M. (2004). The consideration of the new profitability evaluation system, J-cost, thinking of the time cost, *IE Review*, 45(1), 85–92 (in Japanese).

Tanaka, M. (2008). Accounting for the manufacturing improvement: The report of the practice of J-Cost Theory, MMRC Discussion Paper Series No. 208 (in Japanese).

Tanaka, M. (2009). *Management Accounting for the Continuous Improvement in Toyota Way*, Tokyo: Chukei Publishing Company (in Japanese).

Tomino, T. (2003). Build-to-order system of the automobile company (1): Integration of long and short planning cycle, *Meidai Shogaku Ronso*, 84(1) (in Japanese).

Tomino, T. (2004). Build-to-order system of the automobile company (2): Integration of long and short planning cycle, *Meidai Shogaku Ronso*, 86(2) (in Japanese).

Tomino, T. (2010). Nissan Production Way and build-to-order system: Comparative to the Toyota System, MMRC Discusion Paper Series No. 295 (in Japanese).

8

The Relationships between a Manufacturing Firm and a Customer Firm: The Situation in Japan

Junya Sakaguchi
Kansai University

1 Introduction

In recent years, the research field of inter-organizational management control, which addresses inter-firm relationships, has assumed a high profile globally (Caglio and Ditillo, 2008). In this field, researchers have studied a variety of topics, such as the selection of suppliers as business partners (Dekker, 2008), the design of management control structures as exemplified by contract conclusions with suppliers (Anderson and Dekker, 2005; Dekker, 2004, 2008; van der Meer-Kooistra and Vosselman, 2000), and collaboration with suppliers after designing management control structures (Cooper and Slagmulder, 2004; Mahama, 2006). Meanwhile, Japanese academic circles in the management accounting field have also published a range of papers dealing with literature reviews introducing related research trends in Europe and North America (Kobayashi, 2004; Kubota *et al.*, 2008), a literature review regarding the trust developed in inter-organizational relationships (Oura, 2006), and demonstrative researches focusing on collaboration between buyers and suppliers (Kubota, 2001; Sakaguchi, 2004, 2009).

Conventionally, as typified in the research into buyer-supplier relationships, researches in the field of inter-organizational management control that address inter-firm relationships have maintained a primary emphasis directed toward the upper stream in supply chains. Not much attention has been directed toward the lower stream in supply chains; comprehensive researches have yet to be conducted regarding what kind of business relationships a specific company has with its customer firms. It is true that in the field of management accounting, a number of researches have been conducted with a focus on customer relationship management. However, in many cases, it has been assumed that the research into customer relationship management discusses B-to-C transactions, that is, transactions between businesses and general consumers. Accordingly, adequate research emphasis has not been placed on B-to-B transactions, or business-to-business transactions, despite the fact that they occupy a significant segment of the real economy. In this context, discussing the management of relationships with customer "firms" is particularly important, because it is expected to contribute not only to further advancement in research in the field of inter-organizational management control that focuses on inter-firm relationships, but also to research advancement in other areas of customer relationship-oriented management, as well as to an improvement in practices in business operations conducive to better relationships with customer firms.

In this respect, this research attempts to identify the actual situation regarding the management of business relationships with customer firms, on the basis of a questionnaire survey conducted for Japanese companies in the basic materials industries.

This research is structured as follows: First, the whole picture regarding Japanese companies' management of business relationships with their customer firms is defined, on the basis of the questionnaire survey results. Specifically, this management is divided into two aspects, (1) the business relationships with customer firms and (2) the practices for customer firm management, and is characterized separately from these two aspects. Second, sample companies are categorized into four groups according to their sales and other financial variables, and these groups are characterized separately in terms of the management of business relationships with their customer firms. Finally, the author summarizes this research and clarifies several issues that need to be addressed in the future.

2 Whole Picture Regarding the Management of Business Relationships with Customer Firms

2.1 *Sample and measurement scale*

The questionnaire survey used in this research was conducted primarily among sales managers or directors of 318 listed companies on the First Section of the Tokyo Stock Exchange, which are categorized into the basic materials industries — including pulp and paper, chemicals,

Table 1.   Sample for this research.

Industry	Total Number	Number of Respondent Companies
Pulp and paper	12	2
Chemicals	120	22
Pharmaceuticals	35	1
Oil and coal products	11	3
Rubber products	12	2
Glass and ceramics products	29	4
Iron and steel	35	3
Non-ferrous metals	27	9
Metal products	37	8
Total	318	54 (16.981%)

Source: Author's tabulation.

pharmaceuticals, oil and coal products, rubber products, glass and ceramics products, iron and steel, non-ferrous metals, and metal products — in which B-to-B transactions are widely conducted. The survey was conducted from July 18 through August 8 in 2008. This survey sample is relevant in light of the purpose of this research, namely examining the management of business relationships with customer firms.

The number of companies that returned questionnaire sheets totaled 54, and the response rate was 16.981% (54/318 companies). Table 1 outlines the response status of the survey sheets. Since these 54 respondents answered all the questions relevant to this research, the submitted answers were all analyzed in this research.

The survey questions used in this research concerning business relationship management (11 questions in total) are divided into the following two categories: (1) *business relationships with customer firms* and (2) *practices for customer firm management*. Category (1) focuses on what types of business relationships the sample companies have formed with their customer firms. This category comprises two parts: (1-1) development of *bargaining power* (two question items, $\alpha = 0.954$), which addresses what level of bargaining power the sample companies have with their customer firms; and (1-2) development of *trust* (two question items, $\alpha = 0.836$), which addresses what level of trust the sample companies have in their customer firms. The two question items regarding (1-1) development of bargaining power intend to clarify how small the number of similar products is and how small the number of comparable products is. The two question items for (1-2) development of trust inquire about cooperative behaviors and fair and honest behaviors.

Another category, (2) practices for customer firm management, focuses on how the sample companies specifically manage and maintain transactions with their customer firms. This category comprises two parts: (2-1) *information sharing and problem solving* (four question items, $\alpha = 0.849$), which addresses the level of closeness and frequency in collaboration between the sample companies and their customer firms; and (2-2) *management employing accounting information* (three question items, $\alpha = 0.869$), which addresses the accounting information-based management regarding business relations with their customer firms. The four question items regarding (2-1) information sharing and problem solving intend to reveal the collaboration status, asking about sharing of information, sharing of events and changes, sharing of problems and joint problem-solving. The three question items for (2-2) management employing accounting information intended to reveal the transaction management status, inquire about the setting of target prices, price evaluation prior to transactions and price maintenance after transactions.

For all of the question items, this questionnaire adopted a five-point Likert scale that includes the choices of "1: Strongly disagree", "3: Neutral" and "5: Strongly agree". The questions in this survey were developed on the basis of prior researches concerning management accounting and other related disciplines (Anderson and Dekker, 2005; Asanuma, 1997; Kato, 1993; Mahama, 2006; Nishiguchi, 1994; Sako, 1992).

2.2 *Whole picture of business relationship management*

Out of all the questions related to business relationship management, the author first examines the answers to the questions regarding (1) business relationships with customer firms. These questions focus on what types of business relationships the sample companies have formed with their customer firms, in terms of the development of bargaining power and trust. As indicated in Table 2 below, with respect to the questions regarding (1-1) development of bargaining power, the averages of the answers stand at approximately 3, and the standard deviations, which indicate the dispersion in answer, are approximately 1. This shows that the level of bargaining power with customer firms varies among sample companies. Meanwhile, with respect to the questions regarding (1-2) development of trust, the

Table 2.　Relationships with customer firms.

	n	Mean	S.D.
1-1 Development of bargaining power	**54**	**3.07**	**0.992**
How small the number of similar products is	54	3.11	1.003
How small the number of comparable products is	54	3.04	1.027
1-2 Development of trust	**54**	**3.35**	**0.572**
Cooperative behaviors	54	3.41	0.567
Fair and honest behaviors	54	3.30	0.662

Source: Author's tabulation.

averages of the answers slightly exceed 3, and the standard deviations in the answers are relatively small. This suggests that, in general, Japanese companies develop a relationship of trust to some extent, not only with their supplier firms positioned in the upper stream in supply chains, but also with their customer firms in the lower stream in supply chains. However, given the fact that the answers indicating the level of trust in customer firms average at a level slightly over 3, and that the dispersions in the answers are relatively small, it can be said that while Japanese companies tend to develop a certain level of relationship of trust with their customer firms, this tendency is not as noticeable as indicated in many prior research findings that define the business relationships among Japanese companies as being trust-based.

Next, out of the questions related to business relationship management, the author examines the answers to the questions regarding (2) practices for customer firm management. These questions address how the sample companies specifically manage and maintain transactions with their customer firms, focusing on the closeness in collaboration with their customer firms and the employment of accounting information in management practices. As indicated in Table 3 below, with respect to the questions regarding (2-1) information sharing and problem solving, the averages of the answers are nearly 4, a relatively high value, and the standard deviations stand below 1. This suggests that many Japanese companies share with their customer firms knowledge about transaction-related information and events as necessary, as well as about problems to be solved, and that they also cooperate with their customer firms in finding optimal solutions to the shared problems. These findings, showing Japanese companies' active collaboration with their business partners, are consistent with those observed in previous

Table 3.   Practices for customer firm management.

	n	Mean	S.D.
2-1 Information sharing and problem solving	**54**	**3.92**	**0.637**
Information sharing	54	3.81	0.754
Events and changes sharing	54	3.94	0.712
Problems sharing	54	3.94	0.856
Joint problem-solving	54	3.98	0.739
2-2 Management employing accounting information	**54**	**4.14**	**0.784**
Setting of target prices	54	4.15	0.960
Price evaluation prior to transactions	54	4.00	0.991
Price maintenance after transactions	54	4.26	0.650

Source: Author's tabulation.

researches that focused on the relationship with supplier firms (Nishiguchi, 1994). Meanwhile, with respect to the questions regarding (2-2) management employing accounting information, the averages of the answers are relatively high, standing at or exceeding 4, and the standard deviations stand below 1. This suggests that many Japanese companies tend to set target prices even when transacting with their customer firms and make continuous efforts to maintain these set prices. Notably, the results show that the sample companies make active efforts, particularly in maintaining the set prices after transactions. These findings regarding the accounting information-based business relationship management are also consistent with those obtained in previous researches (Asanuma, 1997; Kato, 1993). Moreover, the findings in this research also suggest that accounting information is actively employed in managing and maintaining inter-firm business relationships, and that the inter-firm relationship constitutes an important research theme in management accounting, one of the research fields of accounting, as suggested by prior researches (Dekker, 2003).

As described above, the whole picture of the business relationship management among Japanese companies has been examined on the basis of survey results. The observations can be summarized as follows:

(1) Business relationships with customer firms: The level of bargaining power development over customer firms varies according to individual companies. While Japanese companies tend to develop a relationship of trust to a certain level with their customer firms, this tendency is not

sufficiently evident to define the business relationships among Japanese companies as being trust-based.

(2) Practices for customer firm management: Many Japanese companies actively engage in close collaborations with their customer firms, such as sharing knowledge about diverse information and events and cooperating in resolving shared problems. Management practices employing accounting information, such as setting target prices and making continuous efforts to maintain the set prices, are frequently conducted by many Japanese companies.

However, the above-mentioned characterizations regarding the Japanese companies' management of business relationships with their customer firms are general. Therefore, further analysis is necessary to provide more useful insights for practices in business operations. In this respect, the next section examines in further detail the Japanese companies' management of business relationships with their customer firms, by means of categorizing sample companies into four groups and comparing the answers indicated in each group.

3 Business Relationship Management in Each Group

3.1 *Categorization into four groups*

To provide useful insights into practices in business operations, this section categorizes the sample companies into four groups, and attempts comparison in further detail between these groups' respective answers. Specifically, based on recent results of annual sales and operating profit margin (OPM), the sample companies were classified into the following four groups: The first group comprises the companies characterized by high sales and high OPM (14 companies). This group maintains higher levels in both sales and OPM and, accordingly, a relatively large amount of profit. Therefore, this group is referred to as (I) *the ideal type*. The second group consists of the companies characterized by low sales and high OPM (13 companies). Since this group particularly emphasizes maintaining higher levels of OPM, it is referred to as (II) *the profitability-oriented type*. The third group comprises the companies characterized by low sales and low OPM (14 companies). This group's sales and OPM stand at lower levels, and accordingly, its profit amount is relatively small. Therefore, this group is named (III) *the troubled type*. The fourth group

Table 4.   Categorization by sales and OPM.

II. Profitability-oriented type (13 companies)	I. Ideal type (14 companies)	high
III. Troubled type (14 companies)	IV. Sales-oriented type (13 companies)	low

OPM

| low | Sales | high |

Source: Author's tabulation.

comprises the companies characterized by high sales and low OPM (13 companies). Since this group particularly emphasizes maintaining higher levels of sales, it is referred to as (IV) *the sales-oriented type*. Table 4 shows these four groups and the number of sample companies classified into each group.

3.2   *Business relationship management in each group*

Out of the questions related to business relationship management, the author first examines the answers to the questions regarding (1) business relationships with customer firms. As indicated in Table 5, the averages of the answers to the questions regarding (1-1) development of bargaining power and (1-2) development of trust are both relatively high in (II) the profitability-oriented type. This suggests that the companies categorized as this type tend to have a higher level of bargaining power with their customer firms, and that they tend to trust their customer firms in the security of such bargaining power.

To be more specific, the result regarding the item (1-1) development of bargaining power shows a significant difference between (II) the profitability-oriented type and (IV) the sales-oriented type ($t = 1.782$, 10% level, two-tailed). Regarding the item (1-2) development of trust, the result shows a significant difference between (I) the ideal type and (II) the profitability-oriented type ($t = -1.919$, 10% level, two-tailed). These results suggest that in comparison with the companies categorized as (II) the profitability-oriented type, the companies categorized as (IV) the sales-oriented type tend to be in a relatively weak position against their customer firms. The results also imply that the companies classified as (I) the ideal type display a relatively low tendency to trust their customer firms, and that they tend to manage and maintain business relationships with their customer firms in a prudent manner, by actively engaging in the practices for customer firm management as described in the following paragraphs.

Next, out of the questions related to business relationship management, the author examines the answers to the questions regarding (2) practices for customer firm management. As indicated in Table 5, the averages of the answers to the questions regarding (2-1) information sharing and problem solving and (2-2) management employing accounting information are both relatively high in (I) the ideal type. This suggests that the companies classified as this type have a higher tendency to share important transaction-related information and to cooperate in solving shared problems with their customer firms, and that these type (I) companies are more active in setting target prices and making efforts to maintain these set prices.

To be more specific, the result regarding the item (2-1) information sharing and problem solving shows a significant difference between (I) the ideal type and (II) the profitability-oriented type ($t = 2.059$, 10% level, two-tailed), and also between (I) the ideal type and (III) the troubled type ($t = 2.003$, 10% level, two-tailed). This result implies that in comparison with the companies categorized as (I) the ideal type, the companies classified as (II) the profitability-oriented type and (III) the troubled type are less active in engaging in information sharing and collaborative practices with their customer firms, and that these type (II) and (III) companies tend to be less responsive to diverse needs from their customer firms. Meanwhile, concerning the result of the item (2-2) management employing accounting information, a significant difference is not seen between (I) the ideal type and each of the other groups.

As described above, the survey results were analyzed on the basis of four-group categorization, to examine each group's characteristics in business relationship management. The observations can be summarized as follows:

I. Ideal type: While displaying a relatively low tendency to develop a relationship of trust with their customer firms, the type (I) companies are relatively active in information sharing and joint problem-solving with their customer firms, as well as in management practices employing accounting information.

Table 5. Business relationship management in each group.

	I. Ideal Type	II. Profitability-oriented Type	III. Troubled Type	IV. Sales-oriented Type
1. Business relationships with customer firms				
1-1 Development of bargaining power	3.04	3.46	3.00	2.81
	(0.970)	(0.803)	(1.109)	(1.052)
1-2 Development of trust	3.14	3.54	3.36	3.38
	(0.413)	(0.628)	(0.569)	(0.650)
2. Practices for customer firm management				
2-1 Information sharing and problem solving	4.20	3.65	3.77	4.06
	(0.582)	(0.767)	(0.550)	(0.542)
2-2 Management employing accounting information	4.33	3.79	4.29	4.10
	(0.996)	(0.856)	(0.583)	(0.583)

(The upper rows indicate "mean", and the lower rows indicate "S.D".)
Source: Author's tabulation.

II. Profitability-oriented type: These companies tend to have a higher level of bargaining power with their customer firms, and they tend to develop a relationship of trust with their customer firms in the security of such bargaining power. Meanwhile, these type (II) companies tend to place less emphasis on information sharing and joint problem-solving with their customer firms.

III. Troubled type: These companies tend to place less emphasis on information sharing and joint problem-solving with their customer firms

IV. Sales-oriented type: These companies tend to have a relatively weak bargaining power with their customer firms.

4   Summary and Future Research Opportunities

This research has identified the actual situation regarding the Japanese companies' management of business relationships with their customer firms, based on the results of the questionnaire survey conducted among companies in the basic materials industries. As a result of the analysis, several findings have been obtained concerning the whole picture of the management of business relationships with customer firms. Regarding the business relationship with customer firms, it was observed that the level of bargaining power development with customer firms varied according to individual Japanese companies, and that while there was a tendency to develop a relationship of trust to a certain level with their customer firms, this tendency was not sufficiently evident to define the business relationships among Japanese companies as being trust-based. Moreover, regarding the practices for customer firm management, it was observed that many Japanese companies actively engaged in close collaborations with their customer firms, such as sharing of knowledge about diverse information and events and cooperation in resolving shared problems, and it was also observed that management practices employing accounting information, such as setting target prices and making continuous efforts to maintain the set prices, were frequently conducted by many Japanese companies. Some findings are similar to those obtained in previous researches that focused on the relationship with supplier firms.

Furthermore, additional findings were obtained regarding business relationship management that were analyzed based on group categorization according to sales and other financial variables. Regarding the business relationship with customer firms, it was observed that the group emphasizing profitability tended to have a higher level of bargaining power with their customer firms, and that this group tended to trust their customer firms in the security of such bargaining power. With respect to the practices for customer firm management, it was observed that the group emphasizing both sales and profitability had a higher tendency to share with their customer firms important transaction-related information and cooperate in solving shared problems, and that this group was more active in setting target prices and making efforts to maintain these set prices.

The findings obtained in this research are expected to provide two contributions to practices in business operations. One comprises the insights into the actual situation concerning the management of business relationships with customer firms. Conventionally, in the research field of inter-organizational management control that addresses inter-firm relationships, researches have not fully been conducted with a focus on the relationship with customer firms. In this context, it is notable that this research has contributed to identifying the actual situation regarding the management of business relationships with customer firms, on the basis of the survey results. Another contribution of this research is related to the role of accounting information-based management in conducting business relationship management. As suggested by the survey results, accounting information-based management does not, by itself, enable companies to achieve remarkable results. Whether or not such results can be secured seems to largely depend on other contextual factors, such as management practices and relationships with business partners, including close collaborations with these partners. Therefore, mere active use of accounting information is not adequate; it will be necessary to consider how accounting information should be used in combination with other management practices, and how such combination of practices should be designed in consideration of various conditions regarding business partners and transaction arrangements. It is also notable that this research has contributed to identifying the issues to which attention needs to be paid when engaging in practices in business operations.

However, since the questionnaire and the response analysis method employed in this research are primitive, additional questionnaire surveys should be conducted in order to explore this research even further. Moreover, a crucial task will be to collect case examples of individual companies. Through these efforts, knowledge will be further accumulated regarding the management of business relationships with customer firms, one of the critical themes in surviving business competition.

References

Anderson, S.W. and Dekker, H.C. (2005). Management control for market transactions: The relation between transaction characteristics, incomplete contract design, and subsequent performance, *Management Science*, 51(12), 1734–1752.

Asanuma, B. (1997). *Organizations of Japanese Firms: The Mechanisms of Innovative Adaptations*, Tokyo: Toyo-keizai (in Japanese).

Caglio, A. and Ditillo, A. (2008). A review and discussion of management control in inter-firm relationships. Achievements and future directions, *Accounting, Organizations and Society*, 33(7/8), 865–898.

Cooper, R. and Slagmulder, R. (2004). Interorganizational cost management and relational context, *Accounting, Organizations and Society*, 29(1), 1–26.

Dekker, H.C. (2003). Value chain analysis in interfirm relationships: A field study, *Management Accounting Research*, 14(1), 1–23.

Dekker, H.C. (2004). Control of inter-organizational relationships: Evidence on appropriation concerns and coordination requirements, *Accounting, Organizations and Society*, 29(1), 27–49.

Dekker, H.C. (2008). Partner selection and governance design in inter-firm relationships, *Accounting, Organizations and Society*, 33(7/8), 915–941.

Kato, Y. (1993). *Target Costing: Strategic Cost Management*, Tokyo: Nihon-keizai Shinbunsha (in Japanese).

Kubota, Y. (2001). Interorganizational interactive control systems in target cost management, *Genkakeisan Kenkyu*, 25(2), 10–18 (in Japanese).

Kubota, Y., Oura, K. and Nishii, T. (2008). Interorganizational management accounting: A review and implications for future research, *Kokumin-keizai Zassi*, 198(1), 113–131 (in Japanese).

Kobayashi, T. (2004). Management accounting for managing inter-firm relations, *Kigyo-kaikei*, 56(1), 4–11 (in Japanese).

Mahama, H. (2006). Management control systems, cooperation and performance in strategic supply relationships: A survey in the mines, *Management Accounting Research*, 17(3), 315–339.

Nishiguchi, T. (1994). *Strategic Industrial Sourcing: The Japanese Advantage*, New York: Oxford University Press.

Oura, K. (2006). Trust and control beyond organizational boundaries, *Genkakeisan Kenkyu*, 28(2), 63–71 (in Japanese).

Sakaguchi, J. (2004). Buyer-supplier collaborations in manufacturing firms: Evidence from Japan, *Genkakeisan Kenkyu*, 28(2), 47–56 (in Japanese).

Sakaguchi, J. (2009). Inter-organizational collaborations and part/material characteristics, *Genkakeisan Kenkyu*, 33(1), 41–53 (in Japanese).

Sako, M. (1992). *Price, Quality and Trust: Inter-firm Relations in Britain and Japan*, Cambridge: Cambridge University Press.

van der Meer-Kooistra, J. and Vosselman, E.G.J. (2000). Management control of interfirm transactional relationships: The case of industrial renovation and maintenance, *Accounting, Organizations and Society*, 25(1), 51–77.

Part 3

Task Control of Production, Sales and Physical Distribution in an Inter-fi m Network

9

Green Economies and Green Processes, and Their Implications for Supply Chains

Henry Aigbedo
Oakland University

1   Introduction

Sustainability and environmental responsibility (greening) have been on the radar of many organizations in recent years. They have become even more important because of the roles governments around the globe are playing, especially with respect to mandates and guidelines under which organizations should operate. The 1997 Kyoto Accord conducted under the auspices of the United Nations, and to which many countries are signatories, provided an impetus for countries to make efforts to reduce greenhouse gases and stem the hazardous effect of climate change. If a government mandates a certain standard, then companies are bound to operate under those standards. Japan and many countries in Europe such as Iceland and Switzerland have been in the forefront of promoting green initiatives more than the United States. Mandates are not necessarily the same even in a given country. For example, the state of California has more stringent emission standards than other states. Such standards prohibit the selling and operation in California of certain equipment such as lawn mowers that use internal combustion engines with certain specifications, whereas those types of equipment can be sold elsewhere in the United States and also in other countries.

Soon after taking over office in January 2009, the United States president, Barack Obama, signed two executive orders that are geared towards improving the fuel efficiency of American cars. While this singular act portrays his administration's commitment to greening, it also doubles as a major initiative to reduce US dependence on foreign oil, which is often considered to have ramifications that include the war against terrorism.

Even though the green concept is widely talked about in government and business circles, it appears that there is no consensus on what it really entails. Broadly speaking, however, most agree on certain general aspects such as energy conservation; that is, requiring the use of less energy and moving more in the direction of renewable sources of energy such as solar energy, wind energy, and geothermal energy as opposed to non-renewable sources such as fossil fuels. Some also talk about the need to reduce pollution and stem climate change, which have implications for preserving the ecosystem for future generations.

We can discuss the importance of green initiatives by examining it from a regulatory perspective, a social responsibility perspective, and from a business profitability perspective. As has been observed above, the regulatory perspective is something that companies cannot escape from as that sets a precondition for whether or not they can operate or sell their products in certain countries or regions. However, to some extent, one could say that depending on the circumstances, there can be reprieve based on the dominant political ideology at any particular point in time. For example, in the United States, the Democratic Party sees greening as a major policy issue whereas the Republican Party does not think of it in the same way. Since support by the US president and legislation by the US Congress are necessary, the direction of greening in the US will depend on who occupies the White House as well as the balance of power in the US Congress at any given point in time. The issue of social responsibility above has proved to be challenging, largely because there appears not to be general consensus among scientists and political pundits about the effect of human activity on climate change, for example. Does going green have positive impacts on the profitability of businesses? There are a growing number of executives in major companies that are beginning to look at this as a business initiative that can, in fact, bring about better financial outcomes for their companies. A clear example of this is Wal-Mart CEO's assertion recently about their green targets. This will involve Wal-Mart's employees as well as its approximately 100,000 suppliers around the globe (e.g., Larson, 2009).

The methodology I have adopted for this chapter involves framework development and a review of the literature; including traditional peer-reviewed academic journals, newspapers and magazines, news reports, company reports, as well as information gleaned from company websites. What

I intend to do in this chapter is to provide some unified frameworks that look at green initiatives from the perspective of multiple stakeholders as well as how companies and supply chains can walk the fine line of addressing the concerns of these stakeholders through their operations. The remaining sections are organized as follows. First, I provide a review of the extant literature on some frameworks that have been developed by other researchers as they pertain to green principles. Thereafter, I describe characteristics of companies and countries that are considered to be in the forefront of promoting a green culture. Next, I provide frameworks to describe the relationship between greening and the well-known and successful paradigm of lean, and also to describe the link between several stakeholders and green initiatives. Through yet another framework that relates to how greening can have an impact on businesses, I then proceed to discuss the implications of greening for supply chains. Finally, I provide some concluding remarks.

2 Literature Review

Orsato (2006) proposes a two-dimensional framework to describe environmental strategies that can be used by business organizations. This framework which has competitive advantage (differentiation and lower cost) in one dimension and competitive focus (organizational processes and products/services) in the other dimension leads to four competitive environmental strategies; namely eco-efficiency, beyond compliance leadership, eco-branding, and environmental cost leadership.

Nidumolu *et al.* (2009) discuss the importance of sustainability and its relationship with innovation. Using examples of several companies the authors have studied, they propose that companies need to be proactive in anticipating future government regulations. They suggest that such a framework provides competitive advantage for those organizations. They also observe that sustainability implies the ability of companies to continue to operate successfully, and that it is either sometimes considered as an alternative term for greening or as a broader umbrella that encompasses it.

The attitude of business organizations with respect to sustainability is the focus of an extensive study by Berns *et al.* (2009). The study, which covered several industries, included information gleaned from MIT scholars in a wide range of subject areas, corporate leaders and CEOs in several companies around the world. It also comprised responses from a survey of respondents who were corporate executives and managers. One of their key findings is that most people agreed that sustainability is going to have a significant impact on how companies compete, going forward. Furthermore, the study showed that in spite of the global economic downturn, companies are putting greater corporate focus on sustainability.

The Boston Consulting Group carried out a study on consumer attitudes as they relate to green products. Hopkins (2009) summarizes some key findings from that study. For example, they found that price is not the most significant factor inhibiting consumers from considering the purchase of green products. Rather, a large percentage of those who do not purchase green products act that way either because they are unaware of green products, do not know where to find them, or think that green product options are not enough. Another important finding is that the percentage of consumers who are willing to pay a premium for purchasing green products (at least 10% more money) depends on the type of product and the perceived benefits. In other words, consumers tend to be more willing to pay a premium for goods such as plug-in products (e.g., washing machines, refrigerators, and consumer electronics) as compared to disposable products (e.g., paper products and garbage bags). Furthermore, even within each product category, the percentage of consumers willing to pay a premium varies significantly. For example, in the ingestible products category, while about 16% are willing to pay a premium of at least 10% more for dry and canned food, more than twice of these consumers are willing to pay same premium for fresh meats.

Unruh and Etterson (2010) provide a prescription for managers thinking of how to operate in the green arena, especially as it pertains to existing standards or certifications relating to greenness. They provide a two-dimensional framework comprising four quadrants: Co-opt, Define, Adopt, and Break Away, each representing a strategy that the organization can choose to adopt based on their particular circumstances. These quadrants are derived from two dimensions: one dimension indicates whether or not the organization's capabilities in terms of implementing green initiatives are high or low; and the other dimension represents whether the standards that already exist in the industry to which the organization belongs are low or high.

Hoffman *et al.* (2008) summarizes discussions of business leaders, company executives, and thought leaders in academia, among others, on some key issues surrounding green strategy and practices. These discussions were hosted by *Harvard Business Review*. It highlights the importance that greening will have in setting the pace for companies' success not only now, but well into the future. Furthermore, it suggests that the aspect that generated the most discussion related to the challenges in the development and management of standards as they pertain to relationships with suppliers. Bishop *et al.* (2008) is a detailed chronicle of six different aspects of the discussions highlighted in Hoffman *et al.* (2008).

3   Leading Green Companies

Several organizations around the world are considered leaders in the pursuit and implementation of green initiatives. This is based on assessments of thought leaders in academia, opinions of business executives, as well as a comprehensive assessment methodology that includes some of the aforementioned sources of data. *Newsweek*'s recent ranking of the top 100 green companies has IBM, Hewlett-Packard, Johnson & Johnson, Sony, and GlaxoSmithKline occupying the top 5 spots in that order. *Newsweek*'s methodology involves ranking these companies on the basis of a Green Score, which is derived from three component scores: Environmental Impact Score, Green Policies Score, and Reputation Survey score. This Green Score was obtained from the three components identified above by giving them weights of 45%, 45%, and 10%, respectively [More details of the rankings and the methodology are available from Newsweek (2010)]. Toyota (No. 17), Wal-Mart (No. 39), and General Electric (No. 47) in this *Newsweek* ranking are among those that have also been identified from other sources as leaders in this arena. I will briefly describe highlights of the characteristics of some of the companies in the top 5 spots as well as those of Toyota and Wal-Mart in order to provide a broader span of industry representation.

IBM views sustainability in a strategic way and as a company they set annual goals, which they strive hard to achieve. In addition to helping clients from around the globe to build systems to foster sustainability goals, they have been in the forefront of ensuring that this is pursued in their own internal systems as well. Notable achievements include saving over 5.1 billion kilowatts of electricity over the period 1990–2009, consequently leading to a reduction of CO_2 emissions of the order of 3.4 million tons. Also, about 76% of their hazardous wastes in 2009 were recycled (Palmisano, 2010).

For more than 10 years Hewlett-Packard (HP) has been working on producing energy-efficient computer hardware that reduces energy consumption and thereby minimizing negative impacts on the environment. They have also designed systems that dynamically adjust the allocation of power to cool equipment, thereby also reducing energy consumption by up to 40%. As part of their efforts, they have several hundred cooling and power-related patents (HP, 2010). HP's approach to sustainability includes several dimensions, one of which is their elaborate recycling program that essentially ensures that 100% of their equipment is recyclable — this includes metals, plastics, as well as toxic materials such as mercury (Fortune, 2007).

Sony considers sustainability as one of the most important issue facing humanity in the 21st century. They have been involved in this for well over a decade and have grown in their quest to become a leader in sustainability. A major highlight of their approach relates to procurement practices. During supplier selection, an audit is conducted to ascertain that they qualify as green partners under Sony's Green Partner Environmental Quality Approval Program. The company strives to make use of products with the "eco" mark — this applies to products that they use for manufacturing as well as other items such as stationery.

In the automotive sector, Toyota Motor Corporation has been a leading proponent of environmental responsibility. A hallmark of Toyota's drive in this arena is the launching of the first hybrid vehicle, the Prius, which opened the door to many other automotive manufacturers that have come out with or are planning similar types of cars. Toyota's hybrid offering has expanded to seven vehicle types including the Lexus brand. In fact, almost 75% of all hybrids sold in the United States are made by Toyota. Another dimension of Toyota's quest in this sphere is a new type of plastic known as ecological plastic, which has been shown to emit less CO_2 when compared to those made from petroleum products.

Fortune Magazine's 2010 ranking of the world's largest corporation in terms of revenue has Wal-Mart, the giant retailer, on top. Although in relative terms Wal-Mart is still in its infancy in the green pursuit, the size of the company is indicative of the enormous benefits that can be derived from its efforts in this direction if properly pursued. Highlights of some of Wal-Mart's efforts in this area include use of solar and wind power as sources of energy, use of smart packaging as well as adopting methods to minimize travel distances for their trucks so as to reduce fuel consumption.

4 Leading Green Countries

A Yale University research report (Yale Center for Environmental Law & Policy, 2010) ranks countries on green initiatives based on environmental performance indices (EPI). The EPI is obtained by using weights for several constituent factors under the broad categories of ecosystem vitality (e.g., climate change, agriculture, fisheries, forestry, etc.) and environmental health (environmental burden of disease, air pollution impact on humans, water impact on humans). The top five countries are Iceland (93.5), Switzerland (89.1), Costa Rica (86.4), Sweden (86.0), and Norway (81.1). Table 1 provides highlights of the top three countries' scorecard on environmental responsibility.

Table 1. A summary of key characteristics of leading green countries.

Country	Highlights
Iceland	(1) It derives 80% of its energy needs from renewable energy — primarily geothermal and waterfall (aided by its geography)
	(2) Government has put in place incentives that encourage people to use non-traditional energy to power their cars
	(3) Technical knowhow on geothermal energy is being harnessed for sale to other countries
Switzerland	(1) It recently instituted a stimulus package to facilitate reduction of energy consumption and greenhouse gases in several areas, including renovation of old buildings in the country
	(2) It has established rigorous standards to ensure that the country continues to progress in its green quest
	(3) About 60% of the country's energy needs is from renewable sources
Costa Rica	(1) More than 90% of the country's energy supply is from renewable sources
	(2) Reforestation policies over the past 30 years has led to more than 50% of the country being covered by trees as compared to 20% in 1980
	(3) Government instituted a carbon tax policy in 1997 and the proceeds are used to pay farmers not to chop down trees

5   Relationship between Lean and Green

Lean manufacturing, which is often used in the West as a synonym for the Toyota Production System, has been around for several decades now. Undoubtedly, it has changed the competitive landscape for many businesses, extending well beyond the automotive industry from where it has its roots. Industries where it has been successfully applied include the hospitality industry, healthcare sector, aerospace, transportation, and retail, to mention a few. It is well known that lean production principles largely focus on the elimination of waste in production systems (e.g., Monden, 1983, 1998; Koufteros *et al.*, 1998; Aigbedo, 2000; and Liker, 2004). A careful examination shows that implementation of lean principles can foster the achievement of green and sustainability objectives. Figure 1 provides a framework that shows the relationship between key aspects with which lean is concerned and their relationship to the implementation of green initiatives.

Making defect-free products is essential to the successful implementation of a lean system. When products need to be reworked, oftentimes more raw materials or parts may need to be used, which further tasks the environment. This is in addition to more energy used to run equipment for

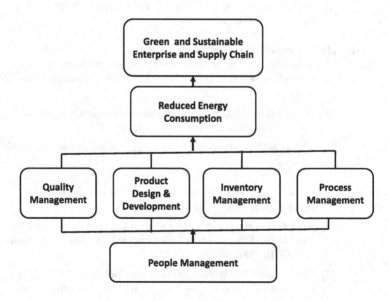

Fig. 1.   A conceptual framework for the lean-green relationship.

the rework. Sending scrapped products or parts to landfills have their own negative environmental consequences.

Simplification and improvement of processes within the plant and between supplier and OEM plants often lead to reduction in distances travelled. Such reductions in movement and transportation lead to less energy consumption, which is good for sustainability. For example, Golicic *et al.* (2010) chronicles how many Fortune 500 companies such as Home Depot, Federal Express, and Whirlpool are working to curtail the negative impact of transportation on the environment.

Inventory management, another key aspect of lean principles, requires the maintenance of only the required items in the required quantities. Overproduction invariably leads to unnecessary storage space and multiple handling of parts and products. Clearly, therefore, practice of lean principles in this respect will obviate the need to build large storage spaces, which consumes resources including energy and also eliminates the need to heat and provide lighting for such facilities.

Lean product design and development can be considered to comprise the "soft" and "hard" parts. While the former relates to the effective and efficient management of the processes involved in product design and development, the latter is concerned with the components of the product. The improvement of processes in product design and development leads to the same benefits for lean processes outlined earlier. In the latter case, use of common platforms across multiple product lines, for example, can lead to reduced resource needs and ultimately reduction in energy use. Furthermore, proper design at the outset with a cradle-to-grave mentality makes it possible to carry out recycling and remanufacturing activities which are overall beneficial to the planet and to society.

The node at the base of Fig. 1 (people management), which in the Toyota Production System is referred to as respect for humanity, can be considered a key foundation for achieving success in lean as well as green implementation. In other words, employees' opinions and suggestions in all the other areas have to be valued and incorporated into processes and products.

6 Green Stakeholders

Figure 2 provides a conceptual view of the relationship between the implementation of green processes and the various associated stakeholders. First, we examine the government link. Governments in most

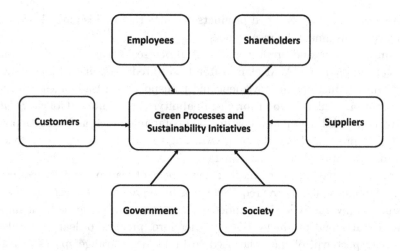

Fig. 2.   Greening and the various stakeholders.

countries — especially democratic ones — are instituted primarily to protect the interests of the citizenry and to foster prosperity. The latter part of this role is captured in the remarks of Swiss President Doris Leuthard who recently (April 2010) noted that "Countries that embrace a long-term policy towards clean technology will be the winners in the future market". With respect to the former, legislations and regulatory policies are put in place to assure the safety and health of the people. For example, recently the United States Environmental Protection Agency (US EPA) instituted mandatory reporting of the emission of greenhouse gases in some focused sectors of the US economy (EPA, 2009). This includes power plants, production facilities (such as automotive plants, steel processing plants, and aluminum processing plants), and the transportation sector. The six key greenhouse gases in the atmosphere which are considered to have a negative impact on public health as well as the welfare of current and future generations are carbon dioxide (CO_2), methane (CH_4), nitrous oxide (N_2O), hydrofluorocarbons (HFCs), perfluorocarbons (PFCs), and sulfur hexafluoride (SF_6). Fuel efficiency rules under the Corporate Average Fuel Economy (CAFE) standards have until now been focused on passenger cars in the United States. However, in October 2010, the US EPA is instituting new fuel efficiency rules for trucks and buses aimed at cutting fuel consumption and emissions of the order of 10–20% by 2018. Although this class of vehicles comprises only 4% of vehicles in the US, it uses about 20% of the fuel. In parallel, research is continuing, aiming at having hybrid versions of trucks, and this move is anticipated to reduce fuel consumption by as much as 35% by 2020 (Thomas, 2010).

Society does have a stake in green implementation. This ties in closely with that of the government which (in most countries) are put in place to protect the interest of the citizens. For example, pollution from industrial wastes can lead to many unintended consequences like health hazards and degradation of agricultural yield. The British Petroleum (BP) oil spill that occurred in the Gulf of Mexico during the summer of 2010 heightened environmental awareness among citizens and residents of the United States about the gravity of the need for companies to be environmentally responsible. Based on reports in the media so far, it seems too early still to be able to assess the full impact of the spill on ocean creatures, such as fish and shrimp, and the ecosystem in general.

Green implementation is important to customers and attitudes differ, depending on several factors such as country, type of product, and the relative value placed on its costs and benefits. There are customers who will almost pay any amount of money to support green — but apparently this is still a very small fraction of the customer base.

Shareholders typically look at organizational performance from profitability and return on investments perspectives. Therefore, going green will be well received by this constituent if it helps achieve these goals.

Almost all organizations rely on input parts and raw materials for making their products or providing valuable services to customers. Therefore, it goes without saying that true green implementation cannot be achieved without cooperation from the supplier base. It is easy to see how this extends to several companies when dealing with complex supply chains with several links and levels.

How can organizations leverage their employee base in the successful pursuit of green implementation? It is important to get their *buy-in*, to see how it will lead to the betterment of the company and by extension their own personal enhancement. There is a need to recognize possible resistance to change either because of fear that such change could bring about negative personal circumstances even if it is positive for the organization. For example, depending on the case, some managers and employees may resist green implementation because of the fear of possibly losing their jobs. Perhaps it might be useful to help employees relate by discussing comparisons with certain other successful initiatives that have been implemented in the said organization.

7 Implications of Greening for Supply Chains

In the foregoing discussions, we have examined two key aspects of green-ing; namely, one that relates to economies or essentially to governments of countries and another that relates to companies. What I would like to do here is to assess the impacts of these two interrelated dimensions, and to highlight issues that managers need to consider in order to ensure that their supply chains deliver the value that is desirable.

Figure 3 is a useful framework to present this aforementioned assess-ment. Government policies that have been laid out in a given country are boundary conditions and they are therefore not directly represented in the framework. If a company decides to establish green processes or to pursue sustainability as a goal, what are the driving forces? It goes without saying that the issue of profitability cannot be thrown into the wind. As Goldratt and Cox (2004) succinctly points out, the goal of any business organization is to make money. Improving process efficiencies through elim-ination of redundancies and waste leads to cost reduction which has pos-itive benefits for the organization. Furthermore, consumers who see the benefit of greening, especially from a non-monetary perspective, will hold the implementing company in high regard. This will lead to better repu-tation and goodwill. Some of such consumers will prefer to buy products from those companies, thus leading to a larger customer base and improved revenue stream. On the other hand, however, there is some cost associated

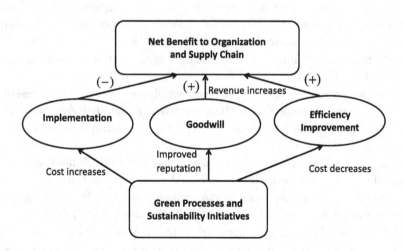

Fig. 3.   Impacts of green processes and sustainability initiatives.

with implementation. In some cases, expensive equipment may need to be procured (as in the case of building wind farms to generate electricity) or upfront cost may need to be incurred for process assessments and improvements. How do all these benefits and costs compare for the organization or supply chain? It is a well-known fact that not all businesses operate with a long-term view of their initiatives. How long is management prepared to wait to see the financial reward from implementation?

The complexity of supply chains tends to increase with the complexity of the associated final product. For example, the aerospace supply chain is far more complex when compared to the supply chain for a simple product such as a telephone set. This means that a company that is truly serious about greening its supply chain has to first fully understand the length and breadth of the chain. It is insufficient to mandate that direct suppliers show evidence that they are green or working toward that end — it needs to extend to all suppliers at the various tiers. As a matter of fact, there has been movement in the direction of companies (e.g., Wal-Mart) working to be able to assign indices to their products based on the extent to which green activities have been incorporated throughout the supply chain. This is no doubt a daunting undertaking. Furthermore, due to the global network of suppliers that form most complex supply chains, it is obvious that suppliers will come from various countries that have different policies and requirements as they pertain to greening. How, for example, will a company's management deal with a situation where the sole supplier available for a crucial part is not committed to greening? This may perhaps be so by virtue of the policies of its home country government as well as the fact that it has so much clout that it feels it can still operate successfully without the business from the company in question. No doubt, the power play under such circumstances can be extremely challenging. Furthermore, as Lee and Klassen (2008) and Thun and Muller (2010) observe, some suppliers may be willing to go green but are simply incapable of doing so because of the extra financial burden that it places on them.

As is typical for companies that are aggressively pursuing lean initiatives, and in our context here green initiatives as well, process improvements can lead to reduction in employee requirement. Larger companies are often able to move displaced workers to other areas of need. This can be difficult for smaller firms which tend to plan ahead for this by augmenting their workforce with temporary workers. While this generally works well to some extent, the framework is not without its challenges, e.g., less commitment, lower morale, and lower quality output.

8 Conclusion

Everyone does not necessarily agree on a precise definition of what being green means or entails. Nevertheless, one thing that is certain is that there is a lot more discussion about greening and implementation of green initiatives today than there was about 10 years ago. Applications have ranged from simple areas such as recycling of newspapers, cans, and drink bottles, to more elaborate aspects such as remanufacturing of intricate parts like automotive transmissions as well as replacement of non-renewable sources of energy by renewable sources such as wind, solar, and geothermal energy.

Ironically, while technological advancement is itself helping to facilitate greening (many activities such as keeping of records, e.g., patients' hospital records, publication of journals and books, and even communication, are now conducted electronically), maintaining those storage systems often require more energy than otherwise would be the case.

In this chapter, we set out to address the role of economies and processes in achieving greenness in supply chains. We provided several unifying frameworks that help managers to understand the stakeholders as well as how various components interact in determining the impact of green initiatives on supply chains. This will enable executives and managers to see the ramifications of greening and therefore properly plan for their organizations. Given the continued growth in world population as well as technological advancement that will lead to more energy use, it is very easy to predict that before long greening will become an imperative for all businesses. Those businesses that are proactive in moving in that direction will certainly be better placed relative to their competitors.

References

Aigbedo, H. (2000). Just-in-time and its cost reduction framework, in Yasuhiro Monden (ed.), *Japanese Cost Management*, London: Imperial College Press.

Berns, M., Townend, A., Khayat, Z., Balagopal, B., Reeves, M., Hopkins, M. and Kruschwitz, N. (2009). The business of sustainability, *MIT Sloan Management Review*, 51, 19–26.

Bishop, S., Walker, B., Hoffman, A., Woody, J., Rose, S., Samuelson, J., Khurana, R. and Nohria, N. (2008). Six critical conversations about business and the environment, *Harvard Business Review*, Spring, 1–88.

EPA (US Environmental Protection Agency) (2009). Regulatory plan and semiannual regulatory agenda, *Federal Register*, 74(233) (http://www. epa.gov/lawsregs/documents/regagendabook-fall09.pdf).

Fortune (2007) 10 green giants (http://money.cnn.com/galleries/ 2007/fortune/0703/gallery.green_giants.fortune/10.html, accessed on October 27, 2010).

Gifford, D. (1997). The value of going green, *Harvard Business Review*, 75(5), 11–12.

Goldratt, E. and Cox, J. (2004). *The Goal: A Process of Ongoing Improvement*, Great Barrington, MA: North River Press.

Golicic, S., Boerstler, C. and Ellram, L. (2010). "Greening" transportation in the supply chain, *MIT Sloan Management Review*, 51(2), 46–55.

Gross, D. (2008). Iceland's green man: How a tiny island nation weaned itself off fossil fuels and took the lead in alternative energy, *Newsweek*, April 26 (http://www.newsweek.com/2008/04/26/iceland-s-green-man.html, accessed on October 28, 2010).

Hoffman, A., Woody, J., Samuelson, J., Bishop, S., Khurana, R., Nohria, N., Rose, S. and Walker, B. (2008). The Green Conversation: Takeaways from HBR's discussion about leadership and the environment, *Harvard Business Review*, September, 1–4.

Hopkins, M. (2009). What the green consumer wants, *MIT Sloan Management Review*, 50, 87–89.

HP (2010). Data center power and cooling, Hewlett Packard Company website (http://www.hpl.hp.com/research/about/power_cooling.html, accessed on October 27, 2010).

Koufteros, X., Vonderembse, M. and Doll, W. (1998). Developing measures of time-based manufacturing, *Journal of Operations Management*. 16(1), 21–41.

Larson, A. (2009). Green supply chains, Darden Case No. UVA-ENT-0136, University of Virginia.

Lee, S. and Klassen, R. (2008). Drivers and enablers that foster environmental management capabilities in small and medium-sized suppliers in supply chains, *Production and Operations Management*, 17(6), 573–586.

Liker, J. (2004). The Toyota Way: 14 management principles from the world's greatest manufacturer, New York: McGraw-Hill Publishers.

McCrea, B. (2010). Why "green" equals good business, *Supply Chain Management Review*, 14(2).

Monden, Y. (1983). *Toyota Production System: A Practical Approach to Production Management*, Norcross, Georgia: Industrial Engineering and Management Press.

Monden, Y. (1998). *Toyota Production System: An Integrated Approach to Just-In-Time*, Georgia: Engineering and Management Press.

Newsweek (2010). Green rankings — Global companies, October 18 (http://www.newsweek.com/2010/10/18/green-rankings-global-companies.html, accessed on October 22, 2010).

Nidumolu, R., Prahalad, C. and Rangaswami, M. (2009). Why sustainability is now the key driver of innovation, *Harvard Business Review*, September, 57–64.

Orsato, R. (2006). Competitive environmental strategies: When does it pay to be green?, *California Management Review*, 48(2).

Painter, J. (2010). Why Costa Rica scores well on the happiness index, *BBC News*, February 7 (http://news.bbc.co.uk/2/hi/americas/8498456.stm, accessed on October 29, 2010).

Palmisano, S.J. (2010). A smarter planet for a sustainable future, Text of a speech delivered at the IBM Summit, London, September 16.

Thomas, K. (2010). Government pushing more fuel efficiency for trucks, *Associated Press*, October 25.

Thun, J. and Muller, A. (2010). An empirical analysis of green supply chain management in the German automotive industry, *Business Strategy and the Environment*, 19, 119–132.

Unruh, G. and Etterson, R. (2010). Winning in the green frenzy, *Harvard Business Review*, November, 1–6.

Yale Center for Environmental Law & Policy (2010). Environmental Performance Index 2010 (http://epi.yale.edu/, accessed on October 29, 2010).

10

Issue of SCM for Japanese Companies and Their Efforts Toward Green Logistics

Yoshiyuki Nagasaka
Konan University

1 Introduction

The world is drastically changing course toward a recycling-based society. As such, supply chain management (SCM), with the aim of overall management of the flows of physical distribution, storage, information and money between companies, departments and customers in the course of merchandise production, physical distribution, sales, disposal and recycling, will play an increasingly important role. This chapter re-examines the significance of SCM in its "arterial" and "venous" capacities in the recycling-based society, focuses on green logistics for the purpose of examining the problems to be solved for environment-oriented management, and reviews some cases of related efforts made by Japanese companies.

2 Recycling-based Society and SCM

Various efforts to reduce CO_2 emissions are underway around the world. In 2009, the 15th Conference of the Parties (COP 15/MOP 5) was held in Copenhagen and overall goals were set: (1) holding down rising world temperature to less than two degrees centigrade, (2) greatly reducing global greenhouse gas emissions, and (3) stopping increases in CO_2 emissions as soon as possible. In Japan, the Basic Act on Global Warming Countermeasures was approved by the Cabinet in March 2010 and submitted to the Diet. The target specified in the bill is to reduce greenhouse gas emissions to 25% below the 1990 level by 2020, premised on the establishment of a fair and effective international framework by all major economies and agreement on their respective targets. This will be a costly accomplishment. In addition, a multifaceted approach through the industry-university-government cooperation is necessary.

The basic policy of waste and recycling has been established. For this cyclic type of industry system implementation, supply chain management (SCM) will play an increasingly important role. Namely, it is important for SCM to function well mainly in so-called arterial physical distribution, while reverse logistics management (RLM) functions well mainly in venous physical distribution. In every company, SCM is one of the key themes for embodying environmental management. It is with SCM that a company can quantitatively measure and evaluate its environmental load reduction and the degree of its contribution to the recycling society.

Zero emissions design (proposed by the United Nations University in 1994) is recognized in Japan, and various actions are being carried out by companies. In addition, the Basic Law for Establishing a Recycling-based Society has been enforced to promote the formation of a recycling society in Japan since 2000. According to Article 2 of the law, a "recycling-based society" means a society where the consumption of natural resources will be restrained and the environmental load will be reduced as much as possible, by preventing products from becoming waste, promoting appropriate recycling of products, and securing appropriate disposal of the recyclable resources not recycled.

ISO14000 certification acquisition activity (an international evaluation of environmental management) has already advanced in most Japanese companies.

Figure 1 shows a conceptual diagram of the recycling-based manufacturing system proposed by the Strategic Integrated Manufacturing System Society (SiGMA) of the Association of Kansai Industrial Engineering (Nakano, 2007). Natural resources such as iron ore, coal, quartz, crude oil and wood are collected; and coke, refined oil, resin, glass and pulp are manufactured. From these, steel sheets, plastic products, casting and forging products, press products, and electrical components are manufactured in the process system manufacturing industry. Furthermore, they are gathered by the assembly system manufacturing industry, and an end-product for the end-consumer is made. Eventually, these are discarded. Some parts are reused or recycled, and the other parts are disposed of. It is important that not only SCM (as arterial physical distribution) but also RLM (as venous physical distribution) is well implemented and carried out as shown in Fig. 1.

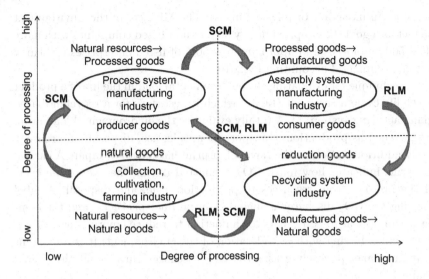

Fig. 1.   Conceptual diagram of recycling-based manufacturing system.

Reverse logistics was proposed in 1992 by James R. Stock based on results of research sponsored by the Council of Logistics Management (CLM) in the United States. It is a technical term related to logistics regarding product collection, resource saving, recycling (substitution of material, reuse of material, waste disposal), repair and reproduction of the product by dismantling the parts. In Japan, arterial and venous physical distribution were clearly distinguished from each other. However, most Japanese companies had used the term venous physical distribution to signify collection of damaged or outdated products, as well as container packaging, and had not used the term in connection with environmental issues. Reverse logistics is highlighted as a link (a ring) to circulate through physical distribution, and is different from venous physical distribution (JILS, 2009).

3   Visualization and Evaluation of Action on Green Issues

The Ministry of the Environment in Japan promotes a Reduce, Reuse and Recycle (3R) policy not only in people's daily lives but also in corporate activities. Furthermore, it publicized guidelines on introducing an environmental accounting system in May 2000 and has maintained them since. Japanese enterprises should quantitatively measure and recognize the costs and effects of environmental conservation in business activities as much as possible (in monetary or physical units). The Ministry of the Environment has set as a goal that approximately 30% of non-listed companies with more than 500 employees and approximately 50% of listed enterprises will carry out environmental accounting by 2010.

A technique for evaluating the environmental load in the life of a product is the life cycle assessment (LCA), which is necessary for a recycling-based manufacturing system. LCA totally evaluates the environmental load at all stages, such as production, transportation, sale, use, disposal, and reuse.

In addition, action on the carbon footprint has begun in Japan. A carbon footprint indicates how much CO_2 is emitted during the overall life cycle of the product from resources to production, sale, and disposal. A label showing the CO_2 discharge is included on product packages, and the company can appeal to consumers for an action to reduce environmental load. It promotes buying with consideration of the environment. It is important that the maker precisely grasps the CO_2 discharge throughout the supply chain.

It will be necessary for companies to disclose appropriate information in greater detail about the action on environmental problems to investors. In other words, in a recycling-based society, switchover of corporate strategy is necessary not only for earnings by value-added improvement through product manufacturing but also for environment harmoniousness.

The transportation sector produced approximately 20% of the carbon dioxide emissions in Japan in 2007. About half were from cars for private use, and approximately 35.5% were from physical distribution such as trucks. Measures for traffic systems, more efficient distribution, promotion of public transport, improvement of energy consumption of rail and aviation are promoted by considering the Kyoto Protocol of 2008.

Each company must be able to visualize CO_2 discharge to improve the efficiency of physical distribution. Three energy saving methods are recommended by the Ministry of the Environment in Japan. Namely, they are the fuel method, mileage method and ton-kilometer method according to the energy consumption calculation methods of shippers. For example,

$$CO_2 \text{ discharge} = \text{haul distance} \times \text{weight} \times \text{loading rate}$$
$$\times \text{ unit calorific value} \times CO_2 \text{ discharge coefficient}$$

by the ton-kilometer method. Several applications to accurately measure CO_2 discharge have been developed beyond the estimation level. At the Omron Corporation, a function for grasping movement distance, positional information, and running information of a vehicle including acceleration with a handheld PC and GPS function, a weight measurement function for ordinary operation of trucks, and a function to manage vehicle information by a device for reading plate numbers have been developed and applied to measure real CO_2 discharge by the ton-kilometer method.

Transportation modes from the viewpoint of CO_2 discharge can be approximately compared as follows:

$$\text{Truck : ship : rail} = 1 : 1/4 : 1/8.$$

It is called a modal shift to change to ship and rail from truck. If ship and rail are used, carriage lead time becomes longer than with truck, but the cost can be cut down in the case of a long distance. It is necessary to compare the fuel cost, overheads, and CO_2 discharge of the entire journey by truck with those where part of the journey has been replaced by rail and ship for quantitative verification. Which channel, port and station should be selected is also important for optimal transportation. The concrete energy conservation effect is calculated by the combination of transport methods and routes. There are many shipping enterprises that can reduce their emissions by more than 20–30% by such a re-examination. Based on the balance of cost cutting and CO_2 reduction, the approach by which CO_2 discharge decreases naturally with improved efficiency of transportation has taken first priority.

Comparison and benchmarking with other companies and establishments are important, too. Appropriate benchmarking is required according to business category.

4 Logistics and SCM

Logistics involves planning, operation and control of all processes of development, manufacturing, sales, consumption and recycling to satisfy the needs of the customer. It links the chains between organizations across a range of physical distribution activities. SCM enables the optimization of whole processes across companies and plays an important role in a recycling-based society.

The requirements for logistics that supports SCM mainly are getting severer and severer. The background is as follows: (1) Companies have to cope with individual customer needs quickly and precisely. (2) The strategy of JIT (just-in-time) spreads through production and distribution, and time competition is getting severer. (3) Globalization advances, and material procurement and product supply must be carried out in a world market. (4) With the progress of IT, production, distribution and sales can be closely harmonized by sharing the information quickly. (5) Consideration for the global environment has comes to be strongly demanded while deregulation advances.

All physical distribution functions mentioned below should be integrated and optimized for logistics.

(1) Procurement of physical distribution: Order for raw materials and transportation, safekeeping before being received. Recovery of physical distribution materials (container collection) is included.
(2) Physical distribution in the company: Finished products or half-completed goods are transported from the factory to distribution centers and other factories.
(3) Sales distribution: Transportation from the factory or the distribution center to a wholesale or a retail store.
(4) Venous physical distribution: Merchandise return of finished goods. Carriage of waste.

Physical distribution is individually processed for packing, cargo work, safekeeping, and transportation based on separate information. On the other hand, logistics is entirely optimal. For example, a benefit appears even if carrying costs are more expensive. Adjustment of production lots to reduce the stock in the warehouse is also effective.

It is important to consider the amount of objects such as materials and goods, place, movement and elapsed time chiefly for managing the process of the movement of objects. It is required to move only the necessary number of the object to the necessary place in the shortest time for the smallest cost when it is necessary. To keep the object in a certain place for a few days while it is being moved means that stock is being held. Therefore, the greatest problem of logistics is how much stock can be reduced for half-finished goods in the factory and storeroom, including finished goods in retail stores, even for raw materials and parts in the procurement stages. Thus, encyclopedic information management for procurement, manufacturing and sales, as well as the movement of objects, is necessary to fulfill customer requests.

Logistics becomes very important to the entire supply chain as well as to sections of companies. SCM is a method for optimizing the flow from procurement and production to supply by managing objects and information flow collectively for maximization of customer satisfaction. It is for optimization of the flow of goods (distribution), demand and business information (commercial distribution, information flow) and money flow. Logistics for the whole optimal supply chain is necessary. This may be called supply chain logistics. Conventionally, some companies do a lot of trading that compete mutually for risk hedging. However, some companies create a few trading companies to establish a much stronger collaborative relationship in the SCM.

The so-called green SCM is proposed for the environment while aiming for optimal quality, cost, delivery (QCD) (Utsumi, 2008). For green SCM, logistics management between the companies is particularly important. The purpose is to meet the requirements of the customer while minimizing the environment load in all supply-linked processes between companies.

Two keywords, "difference" and "arrival" are important for considering logistics management between companies (Abo, 1998).

(1) Difference: Distribution works to move a product from a manufacturer to consumers. In other words, the basic function of distribution mediates between and connects production and consumption. The differences are (a) a difference of place (the place for consumers is different from the place of manufacturing), (b) a difference of time (the time to use is different from the time to produce), (c) a difference of recognition (the producer can evaluate the quality of products, but the consumers cannot evaluate them adequately), (d) a difference of ownership (there is a person who wants to sell a product, and there is a person who wants to buy a product). The process to overcome these differences leads to creation of value.

(2) Arrival: Value does not increase only by overcoming the differences mentioned above; an arrival theory has been proposed. The amplification of value is not a function of distance. Value is created by the object arriving at a state (that is available) that a customer can use. The purpose of logistics is arrival at consumption.

Logistics management is necessary so that an object arrives at a state that is available and the differences are overcome. Here, we must pay attention to customer satisfaction, which is different from the level of the available state. Various factors, such as whether the correct information is grasped in real time, transportation quality is superior, lead time is short, and correspondence to the inquiry is quick, affect the level of the available state. These factors are mutually related, and the significance varies according to customer needs. For example, it is apparent that the relationship between lead time and customer satisfaction is not linear. Customers need to get the objects just when they are necessary.

The customer service element considered for management in Japanese companies are listed below by the Japan Institute of Logistics Systems. As a matter of course, it must be decided under each corporate strategy which of these customer service elements is focused on.

1. Lead time
2. Correspondence to delivery date and time designation
3. Distribution quality (load damage, erratic delivery and so on)
4. Correspondence to an order
5. Correspondence to lot size
6. Stock availability
7. Provision of information (delivery information, load trace information and so on)
8. Delivery frequency
9. Customer correspondence
10. Capacity to process returned goods

For example, when the logistics between companies at the strategy level is examined, the restructuring of the basic points is very important. A simulation system for basic point restructuring, including a warehouse management system (WMS), is used. By such a system, distribution centers of basic points on a map are displayed and costs are calculated by pathway analysis by considering the customer service elements. Then, the benefit of integration and abolition can be investigated (Amemiya, 2003).

Some tools for assessing the ability to execute the logistics between companies are proposed. One is an ECR scorecard. Efficient consumer response (ECR) refers to actions aiming at efficiency of distribution to cope with consumer needs by collaboration of makers, wholesalers and retailers. The food industry in the United States first promoted ECR. The ECR scorecard is a progressively graded list of marks. It is a checklist that can objectively evaluate trading situations between companies. The Global Commerce Initiative established the international standard of the ECR scorecard. A standard scorecard for Japanese companies has been developed and popularized based on this global ECR scorecard by the Distribution System Development Center of Japan. The items of the scorecard are classified into four categories: demand trend management, supply control, realizable technique and integration instrument method. Furthermore, middle classification and sub-classification have been conducted, and each item was evaluated on a scale from 0 to 4 (http://www.ecrnet.org/).

In addition, the Japan Institute of Logistics Systems suggests an SCM logistics scorecard in cooperation with the Tokyo Institute of Technology (Hamasaki, Arashida and Enkawa, 2003). The SCM logistics scorecard is a self-diagnosis sheet to evaluate from the viewpoint of logistics based on the idea of SCM of customer origin. Four main items are evaluated: cooperation between companies and/or organizations, the executive ability of a plan, logistics performance and utilization power of information technology. It was statistically shown that in high-quality logistics companies (1) the growth rate of the stock turnover period is low, (2) the average of increased income rate is high over the past five years, (3) the cash flow to stock price ratio is high and (4) ROA is high.

5 Green Logistics

The Logistics Environment Meeting of the Japan Institute of Logistics Systems has proposed a green logistics checklist. In the logistics field, necessary corporate activity items for environmental load reduction are summarized. For distribution activities such as transportation, packing, cargo work and safekeeping, 86 items for environment load reduction are shown specifically. The enforcement level (four stages) for each item is indicated to measure the degree of the company's action (JILS, Logistics Environment Meeting, 2008). The main items of the environmental load reduction program, presented by the Logistics Environment Meeting are shown in Table 1.

In addition, to expand voluntary action for the reduction of CO_2 discharge in the logistics field, based on the idea that collaborating across several types of industries and business conditions would be profitable, a Green Distribution Partnership Meeting including several societies was organized by the Ministry of Economy, Trade and Industry and the Ministry of Land, Infrastructure and Transport. The voluntary activity of the companies regarding global warming should be accelerated by utilizing the market mechanism. The government should not force the collaboration only for environmental reasons. Through the partnership meeting, a social movement has been formed with wide participation of the manufacturing industries and logistics companies. The modal shift to rail and

Table 1.   Main items of environmental load reduction program.

	Objectives	Main programs
Attainment of recycling society	Energy saving, CO_2 reduction	
	Improvement of fuel efficiency, CO_2 discharge, necessary amount for product unit	Promotion of eco-drive Hardware correspondence Promotion of modal shift
	Mileage reduction	Review of basic point placement Review of transportation plan Reduction of transportation frequency
	Loading rate improvement	Adjustment of distribution unit and ordering unit Invention to increase amount of loading
	Resource circulation, waste reduction	
	Reducing	Reduction of packaging materials Reduction of firmness, dead stock
	Reuse, recycling	Reuse of returned materials

Source: JILS, Logistics Environment Meeting, 2008.

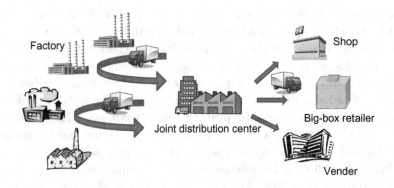

Fig. 2.   Joint delivery system.

ship, cooperative distribution by several companies, distribution efficiency by collection at primary points, efficiency by upsizing distribution facilities, and cooperation between shipping companies and distribution companies are recommended.

Several projects have been performed as follows: the joint delivery (see Fig. 2) and the milk run (collection at primary points and transportation by main lines) shift from transportation by tanker to transportation by soft tank (dissolution of side transportation), modal shift to container-rail transportation and carriage by sea, upsizing of the container-specialized ship, collection at primary stock points through partnership, unification of packing style (returnable packing), energy saving of the work in warehouses by assorted work using radio frequency identification (RFID).

6   Examples of Environmental Load Reduction of Japanese Logistics Companies

In each company, many actions for environmental problems, including improvement of packing processes, loading rate improvement, reform of delivery systems and so on, are promoted actively. Some examples are summarized as follows (Yoshiyuki Nagasaka, 2008).

Nippon Steel Logistics Co., Ltd. has developed a "rack service" for small heavy cargo (http://www.ns-log.co.jp/service/rack/overview.html). Small heavy cargo under four tons on a special steel rack (two varieties) is transported by a 15-ton truck with wings (business started Oct. 2004). A four-ton truck was rented for small cargo (weighing around two tons, such as metal wrought goods or mechanical parts) and long-distance transportation conventionally. It was not efficient. The transportation efficiency, price reduction and the correspondence on delivery time have been improved. If an order is accepted in the morning, delivery is possible the next day.

Nippon Express Co., Ltd. developed ground breaking shipment containers for the distribution of repair products of precision instruments (such as cell phones and note PCs) and applied for a patent in March 2003 as follows: (1) the container can be used repeatedly and thrown away; (2) packing is completed close to the cover (special urethane is adopted and cushioning material such as an air cap is unnecessary); (3) it is adaptable for various kinds of small precision instruments. The containers were used in more than 100,000 cases in 2004. An evaluation of the introduction of this container showed several improvements: (1) reduction of material cost (the quantity of corrugated cardboard disposed was reduced by 35 tons; cost savings were 13 million yen/year); (2) reduction of physical distribution cost (expense reduction for handling the minimum size of general home delivery); (3) efficiency of shipment and packing work (packing time was reduced 916 hours/person compared with corrugated cardboard); (4) customers did not need time for packing. This evaluation was conducted for customer satisfaction improvement.

Noritz Corporation transports bath units. Conventionally, packaging became waste material immediately after a shipment to the construction spot. Since then, simple and returnable packing has been enforced. The rate of occurrence of quality problems (the goal of reject ratio was less than 100 ppm in 2005. 69 ppm was achieved in 2006.) Every transportation was controlled very well and the cost was reduced.

The Kameyama Logistics Center of Sharp Corporation is responsible for delivering and maintaining liquid crystal display panels and televisions. Aiming at balancing cost reduction, efficiency and environmental stewardship, development focused on an eco-band (a band for preventing the collapse of cargo). Stretch films (purchase and disposal) were conventionally used in warehousing for maintaining work, but the eco-band could be used repeatedly and contributed to CO_2 reduction with improvement of operations in 2007.

Mitsui Mining and Smelting Co., Ltd. reduced packing waste in 2007. It improved the loading efficiency from 24 packages/container to 28 packages/container. As a result, overhead expenses for exports could be reduced along with a 12.2% reduction in CO_2 discharges.

In 2008, Johnson & Johnson K.K. Co., Ltd. in Japan developed an intensive delivery system for the disposable contact lens market by collaborating with chain stores considering environmental problems. There were several problems, such as load separation at the same delivery location, unbalanced work loads in the warehouse and mass consumption of packing materials. Due to arranged delivery, the intensive delivery of the JIT box charter flight and the introduction of a foldable container, large reductions not only in working hours but also in CO_2 discharges were achieved. Alliance with a distributor and sharing cost reductions proportionally were also important.

Nagahama Canon Corporation shortened its lead time by using warehouse-less offshore procurement of parts in 2008. To shift maintenance activities, assorted work was done in China which reduced the cost of having to import goods and store them in a warehouse.

Three cosmetics companies, Shiseido Co. Ltd. KOSE Co. and Kanebo Cosmetics Inc., started joint delivery of cosmetics in the Kyushu area of Japan in October 2008. Shipped cosmetic products can be gathered in one branch from each company by consigning the delivery to one company and delivering to stores in bulk. The merits of joint delivery are (1) task-load reduction by decreasing the number of times of reception and classification and (2) approximately 30% of CO_2 reduction in all three companies by removing the redundant trucking.

7 Application of BPM to Green Logistics

To advance green logistics, IT is useful for visualizing the states of SCM encyclopedically. The visualization makes it possible to investigate a remedy that can contribute to cost and environment load reduction at the same time. In addition, it is important that breeding of spot power with pride links to management as well as environmental management be connected with corporate value improvement. Therefore, application of business process management (BPM) is effective (Lee, Kosuge, and Nagasaka, 2006).

The process is constructed with a variety of interdependent activities for the creation of customer value. The output can definitely be distinguished from the input of the process. The processes are structured hierarchically by the level of management (Monden and Lee, 2005).

In other words, BPM can overcome obstacles inside and outside the company. Information and resources can be shared. Several tasks can be bound together and connected as a couple. The flow of tasks can be regarded as a process and managed. Several BPM tools are necessary for monitoring, analyzing and evaluating the progress of processes in a company. This is called business activity monitoring (BAM).

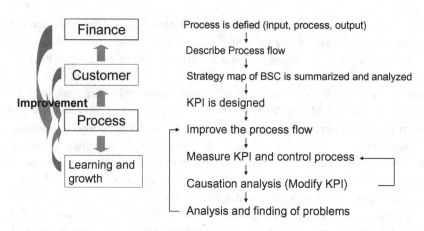

Fig. 3.   BPM applied to BSC.

If BPM is applied to a framework of balanced scorecard (BSC) as shown in Fig. 3, BPM is clearly defined as a BSC approach based on significant process management. Namely, the correction of the key performance indicator (KPI) and the change of business processes are continuously performed by causation analysis in BSC.

The BPM approach is useful for green logistics. It is directly connected with not only cost reduction but also reduction of the environmental load to optimize a delivery process as already mentioned. Data such as position (latitude, longitude), speed, the number of revolutions of the engine, temperature, movement distance, work (load, discharge, break, waiting time), the service situation (high speed, traffic jam) are automatically analyzed in real time by IT. KPI is designed by mixing such data for BPM. A time map (how much time is really needed, what time on what day of the week), an environmental load map (how much CO_2 and NOx discharge on what day of the week), waiting time (for each delivery and each customer) can be visualized and analyzed. CO_2 discharges are different at the same mileage (Nagasaka and Miki, 2002).

8   Summary

It is important to confirm the results of SCM considering environmental problems. SCM has an important role in that the recycling-based manufacturing system is synchronized seamlessly. The basic idea for living together on the Earth is significant. Management with both bird's-eye and worm's-eye views is important across the walls of divisions and companies. Several good practices for the improvement of SCM efficiency in companies are very useful. Visualization of the process of SCM, including arterial and venous logistics coupled with BPM, is helpful for coming up with innovative ideas for sustainability.

References

Abo, E. (1998). Era of Supply chain: Dobunkan (in Japanese).

Amemiya, H. (2003). Most suitable design of base placements and simulation for operation of trucks, *Proceedings* of RAMP 2003.

Arashida, K., Enkawa, T., Hamasaki, A. and Suzuki, S. (2004). Developing the SCM logistics scorecard and analyzing its relation to the managerial performance, *Journal of Japan Industrial Management Association*, 55(2), 95–103.

Hamasaki, A., Ashida, K. and Enkawa, T. (2004). Discussion about roles of division and relations between logistics and management performances using SCM logistics score card, *Journal of Japan Logistics Society*, 12, 89–94 (in Japanese).

JILS refer to email (2008). *Green Logistics Guide*, http://www.logistics.or.jp/green/report/08checklist.html.

JILS Logistics Environment Meeting (2009). http://www.logistics.or.jp/green/words.html.

Lee, G., Kosuga, M. and Nagasaka, Y. (2006). *Strategic Process Management Theory and Practice*, Tokyo: Zeimukeirikyokai (in Japanese).

Monden, Y. and Lee, G. (2005). Conceptual framework and management accounting of process management, *Accounting*, 57(5), 18–25 (in Japanese).

Nagasaka, Y. and Miki, T. (2002). Development of an information analysis system for trucks services, *Journal of Japan Physical Distribution Society*, 10, 49–56.

Nagasaka, Y. (2008). Issues of environmental management from the viewpoint of SCM, *Business Research*, 1015, 41–48 (in Japanese).

Nakano, K. (2007). Report of the 19th strategic integrated manufacturing system society (SiGMA society), Kansai Institute of Industrial Engineering.

Utsumi, M. (2008). Kao Corporation, action of the green SCM activity, *Proceedings of the SCM forum 2008*, JILS.

11

Inter-firm Business Process Management of Companies Specializing in Element Technology: Analysis of a Horizontal Division Network Created by a Cluster of Small Enterprises in Japan

Naoya Yamaguchi

Niigata University

1 Introduction

Business process management (BPM) can be management-based and internal control-based; however, according to various business models and organizations, management-based BPM may involve various approaches.

This chapter deals with the case of horizontal division of work in a network of small buffing companies specializing in an element technology and utilizing industrial accumulation, called the Polishers' Syndicate in Tsubame City, Niigata Prefecture, Japan; the aim is to elucidate the syndicate's characteristics from the perspective of BPM.

Furthermore, this chapter highlights the problems faced by and the requirements for inter-firm BPM that supports the execution of strategies by the companies specializing in an element technology.

2 Polishers' Syndicate

Tsubame City is a domestic center for the production of metal tablewares and housewares, and buffing technology is essential for these products. The Polishers' Syndicate is a joint group by small-sized buffing companies that procures/receives orders, and was formed in January 2003. By taking

171

advantage of the industrial accumulation of metal polishing in Tsubame City and systematizing the horizontal division-of-work network of the small-sized buffing companies as an original brand (product), the syndicate aims to create a new business in polishing technology, independent of wholesalers of metal housewares.

The syndicate uses a system in which several main companies selects a company with orders from amongst them; this company forms a team along with its several affiliated companies and they jointly deal with the order. What began with 5 main, 15 affiliated, and 2 support companies has now increased to 10 main, 16 affiliated, and 14 support companies.

In the syndicate, the Tsubame Chamber of Commerce and Industry (CCI), as the sales office, exclusively manages orders and deals with inquiries from customers. On receiving an order, the CCI faxes inquiries to the main companies, and each company decides whether to accept the order or not, according to various criteria such as quantity, quality, technology level, and delivery time, and conveys its decision to the CCI. If two or more candidates exist, they make a decision by negotiation. If they are unable to do so, they decide by drawing lots. The composition of teams, which includes one main company and several of its affiliated and support companies, changes like an amoeba, according to the condition of order such as quantity, product size, or technology level.

While the main companies handle the evaluation of the order, scheduling, and bill collection, the affiliated and support companies have to steadfastly meet the demand for quality and timely delivery.

Although the syndicate initially received most of its orders from customers within or around the Tsubame area, it now receives polishing orders for parts or metallic molds of cars, semiconductors, nuclear power plants, etc., from outside the Tsubame area. Further, since 2005, it has also engaged in cooperation with metalworking companies. The orders received have been increasing year after year, and now, it is five times the original.

Takaoka points out that, for an industrial accumulation to function as a single system, two subsystems need to function, that is, "the division of work within the accumulation" and "the connections between the accumulation and markets" (Takaoka, 1998). The former is the subsystem for flexible production that best suits the external demand. The latter is the subsystem for reducing the information gap between companies within the accumulation and the external customers as well as for realizing efficient dealings between them.

In addition, Takaoka named linkage companies the companies essential for these two subsystems, that perform the function of transmitting information within the accumulation and markets; she considered the following three functions to be that of the linkage company (Takaoka, 1998).

1. Supply-and-demand coordination function: The linkage companies procure information about technologies from both the supply and demand sides, and thereby reduce the transaction costs in searching for business partners, negotiating with them, and arranging the contracts.
2. Production coordination function: The linkage companies understand the technical level and the capacity use of all the companies within the accumulation that constitute the division-of-work network, and arrange them in order to utilize them effectively.
3. Transaction governance function: The linkage companies that have detailed information about the suppliers and the customers guarantee their sincere dealings, because the suppliers and the customers cannot mutually comprehend their partners' actions directly owing to asymmetries of information and thus the companies control the opportunistic actions of the suppliers and customers.

In the syndicate, while the main companies still manage the production coordination function, the CCI manages the supply-and-demand coordination and transaction governance functions that the metal housewares wholesalers formerly managed. Thus, this can strengthen both the supply-and-demand coordination function that was limited to product handling by metal housewares wholesalers and the transaction governance function of screening customers according to factors such as credit risk.

3   Basic Elements and Approaches of BPM

3.1   *Basic elements of BPM*

Lee *et al.* (2010) define BPM as

> the control and management of transactions between organizations both inside and outside corporations by viewing the transaction flows as processes, which is enabled by breaking up the traditional walls between organizations, sharing information and resources among them, and combining and connecting their transactions

BPM is a business management system that visualizes business flow, within and outside organizations, using the concept of processes, and improves and strengthens both individual processes and relations among the processes continuously, according to the perspective of total optimization.

The four basic elements of BPM are as follows:

1. It treats processes as the objects of management.
2. It visualizes processes within and outside organizations.
3. It improves and strengthens the relations among the processes according to the perspective of total optimization.
4. It repeats the plan-do-check-action (PDCA) cycle.

Among these elements, the repetition of the PDCA cycle requires a set of performance evaluation measures for BPM. Lebas and Euske's (2002) "performance tree" is very useful for this purpose. They portray the causal relationships among performances as a performance tree on the basis of three basic performance components; outcomes, processes, and foundations. Furthermore, they insist that the very process of defining the three components of the model is an essential step in realizing performance.

Among these components, foundations are the prerequisites for processes. The strategic readiness of intangible assets in strategy maps/BSC (balanced scorecard), as theorized by Kaplan and Norton (2004), is contained in the foundation measures.

In BPM, not only the outcome measures but also the process measures are vital. However, if a certain process cannot be executed effectively, some problems might arise in the execution of the process itself or there might be a lack of capability, resources, or time to execute it primarily. Therefore, in order to manage the processes successfully, it is very important that the organization itself manages the process measures as well as the foundation measures as prerequisites of the processes.

Based on this perspective, the template for building the structure of performance measures for BPM is shown in Table 1.

In order to build a relevant structure of performance measures for BPM, it is necessary to make all measures correspond to the three components above, by classifying them into two types of measures, that is, ability measures and key performance indicators, and classifying key performance indicators into process measures (leading indicators) and outcome measures (lagging indicators). Furthermore, it is necessary to set the measures of both the individual processes themselves and the BPCs (business process chains).

Ability measures corresponding to foundations can be roughly classified into capabilities, that refer to the ability elements required for executing a certain process, and capacities, that show the volume of the capabilities.

Table 1.   Template for building the structure of performance measures for BPM.

Three Components of Performance	Foundations		Processes	Outcomes
	Ability Measures		Key Performance Indicators	
Basic Elements of Performance Measures	Capabilities	Capacities	Process measures (leading indicators)	Outcome measures (lagging indicators)
	Readiness	Availability		
			Condition | Activity	
Individual Processes	Ability measures-oriented			
BPCs (business process chains)			Key performance indicators-oriented	

The capacities defined by the traditional cost concept of the capacity theory, for example, according to the National Association of Accountants (NAA, 1963), are measured for individual resources such as machines and equipment. However, the capacities defined here are measured for each capability. If the degree of sufficiency of a certain capability increases, the capacity of the capability and its availability will increase. We can define readiness (the degree of sufficiency) as the measure of capabilities, and availability as the measure of capacities, respectively.

Process measures corresponding to processes are measures of the individual processes themselves and the leading indicators for expected outcomes by executing a series of processes. It is equivalent to the performance driver defined by Kaplan and Norton (1996).

Process measures can be roughly divided into condition indicators, that affect the results of the individual processes such as temperature, humidity, and atmospheric pressure, and activity indicators, that show the volume of operations of the processes, such as the order number, amount of money for ordering, rate of contract, response time, and lead time.

Outcome measures are the measures showing the results of the processes themselves or BPCs such as reprocessing rate, reprocessing time, rate of unsold returned goods, order fulfillment rate, number of complaints from customers, rate of customer satisfaction, sales, sales per person.

In BPM, although both the measures for managing the individual processes and those for managing the relations among processes or BPCs are needed, ability measures will play a more important role in the former, and key performance indicators in the latter.

In addition, even if the process and outcome measures of a certain process itself maintain a high score, and if the process does not constrain the BPC as the bottleneck, the improvement in the process cannot contribute to the outcome of the BPC. Therefore, it should be determined whether or not the operation and the outcome of a certain process itself can contribute to the outcome of the BPC.

3.2 *Approaches of BPM*

Although the approaches of BPM are diverse, they can be classified according to the following three elements:

1. scope of organizations (a single organization, and two or more organizations (organization crossing));
2. function in value chain (designer (coordinator) or pursuer (dependent));
3. purpose of BPM (process improvement, process reform, or process development).

Table 2 classifies the approaches of BPM according to these elements. For the scope of organizations, BPM can be classified into single organizations and two or more organizations. The former can be called intra-firm

Table 2.   Classification of BPM approaches.

Scope of Organizations	Function in Value Chain	Purpose of BPM		
		Process Improvement	Process Reform	Process Development
Intra-firm BPM	Specializing in a single element technology or executing a single process only	Efficiency improvement, capacity enlargement	Flexibility improvement, diversity improvement, capability reinforcement, new process development	
	Executing several processes	BPC optimization	Optimal BPC design	New BPC development
Inter-firm BPM (cooperation between organizations)	Pursuing some processes of the BPC designed by coordinator (dependent)	Process synchronization with BPC, efficiency improvement, capacity enlargement	Existing process review, new process development	
	Designing and managing a BPC (coordinator)	BPC optimization	Optimal BPC design	New BPC development

BPM and the latter can be called inter-firm BPM. Furthermore, intra-firm BPM can be roughly classified into the following cases: specializing in a single element technology or executing a single process only and executing several processes. On the other hand, inter-firm BPM can be roughly classified into the following cases: designing and managing a BPC as a process coordinator and pursuing some processes of the BPC designed by the coordinator as a dependent.

BPM approaches can be diversified according to the purpose, for instance, process improvement, process reform, and process development. However, in the case of specializing in a single element technology or executing a single process, it essentially deals with the strengthening of the single element technology or process, new process development, or process synchronization with BPC. In the case of bundling and managing two or more processes, it essentially deals with BPC optimization, optimal design of BPC, or new BPC development.

4 BPM Features and Problems of Polishers' Syndicate

Table 3 shows the BPM approaches of the Polishers' Syndicate. The syndicate has expanded its business domain until now, because while the Tsubame CCI has exclusively managed the ordering process, small-sized buffing companies have strengthened their polishing process through the horizontal division-of-work network. If it is presumed that the syndicate is a single organization, it can be considered that this approach is an extension from process improvement to process reform and process development of specializing in a single element technology or executing a single process only of intra-firm BPM.

Furthermore, the syndicate is now actively aiming to develop its original brand products, such as stainless steel beer mugs. This approach can be considered to be an extension to new process development, process improvement, and process reform as a coordinator of inter-firm BPM.

Itami lists three basic requirements for the division-of-work accumulations to maintain flexibility, that is, the requirements for flexibility: deep technical accumulation, low division-of-work adjustment cost, and easy foundation (Itami, 1998).

The syndicate has hitherto dealt with the extension of the above mentioned BPM domains by taking advantage of the characteristics of the polishers' horizontal division-of-work network, that is, deep technical accumulation and low division-of-work adjustment cost. As the formal

Table 3. BPM approaches of the Polishers' Syndicate.

Scope of Organizations	Functions in Value Chain	Purpose of BPM		
		Process Improvement	Process Reform	Process Development
Intra-firm BPM	Specializing in a single element technology or executing a single process only	Efficiency improvement, capacity enlargement	Flexibility improvement, diversity improvement, capability reinforcement, new process development	
	Executing several processes	BPC optimization	Optimal BPC design	New BPC development
Inter-firm BPM (cooperation between organizations)	Pursuing some processes of the BPC designed by coordinator (dependent)	Process synchronization with BPC, efficiency improvement, capacity enlargement	Existing process review, new process development	
	Designing and managing a BPC (coordinator)	BPC optimization	Optimal BPC design	New BPC development

information, only order information has been transmitted initially from CCI to the main companies and then from the main companies to their affiliated companies. All other information has been shared through daily private informal communications among the companies.

However, the syndicate is actually not a formal single organization, but only a loose network formed by buff polishers with the same motivation. While this has the advantage of forming good and flexible combinations among the companies according to the kind of order, there are some problems from the BPM perspective as mentioned below.

First, regarding intra-firm BPM, if it is presumed that the syndicate is a single organization, the problem of instability arises. Now, if the syndicate has inquiries about the CCI's treatment of orders, the main companies cannot force their affiliated companies to accept the order, and can only make a suggestion regarding whether to receive the order or not. Therefore, the main companies have to induce the participation and the cooperation of their affiliated companies for every order. That is, the way that the syndicate treats orders will be greatly influenced by the member companies' motivation to actively participate in the syndicate.

Second, the syndicate does not have any formal cost tables for revenue management. Because a significant proportion of the costs of buff polishers consists of personnel expenses, there is almost no room for cost control. However, since polishing services are provided depending on customer specification, that is, polishing objects or materials at customers' request, the syndicate uses its own discretion for pricing. From this perspective, it can be said that the usefulness of cost information for revenue management is high.

Now there is a shift in the polishing of objects from being final consumption goods to production goods. As polishers do not understand the value or the unit price of the production goods themselves, they face a problem in setting low prices according to their previous experiences.

Hence, in the syndicate, the CCI is committed to pricing as a part of the transaction governance function. Although it uses the time-based standard unit price, it prices the orders flexibly according to the objects or materials to be polished, customer request, and customer attribute. As in the present condition, unless there are a certain number of dealings via the syndicate, the syndicate can manage its revenues through the CCI's commitments to pricing in detail. However, as the syndicate's businesses expand further and as the objects for polishing and customer requests diversify further, the need for cost tables for revenue management should increase considerably.

Third, the syndicate does not have a formal information system for capacity and capability management.

As mentioned above, all information, except order information, is shared through daily private informal communications. Naturally, since the main companies should check whether their affiliated companies can afford to deal with the order before making a suggestion to them, they informally check the capacity availability of their affiliated companies for every order inquiry. Nevertheless, even if the capacity information is shared for every partnership that comprises a main company and its affiliated companies, it is not shared within the entire syndicate.

In the conventional vertical division-of-work networks, wherein principal contractors such as housewares wholesalers functioned as the core of the networks, as the objects to be polished were limited, the adjustment costs of the division of work were essentially low and the informal information sharing worked effectively. However, since the adjustment costs will increase as the business domain expands, the formal information system peculiar to the horizontal division-of-work networks is more important.

In regard to this point, as the syndicate is only a voluntary network of small-sized companies, the decision of whether to introduce the information system or not is each individual company's discretion. However, this formal information system cannot adequately exercise its function, unless all or most member companies introduce it. However, for each company, the need for the information system is proportional to the level of its dependence on the network. It is natural for most companies not to appreciate the necessity of the information system as long as the portion of their work via the syndicate is not of immediate importance. Besides, the syndicate uses a system in which the main companies make a decision by negotiation about who accepts the orders passed on by the CCI. Therefore, it is reasonable that most companies cannot identify a need for sharing information within the entire syndicate.

Thus, the syndicate does not have any information system that checks in real time the availability of capacities and the conditions of acquisition or possession of capabilities and shares them mutually among the member companies.

Even if the syndicate cannot detect the availability of capacities in real time, it can satisfactorily deal with specially ordered and small lot-sized products, for which the delivery time is relatively unimportant. However, in the case of quick delivery and large lot-sized mass products, where delivery time is very important, unless the syndicate detects the availability of capacities in real time, the CCI cannot immediately reply whether the syndicate can meet the customers' time-for-delivery demands. As for the customers, because they will be somewhat concerned about the order processing capabilities of the syndicate, they may hesitate to place an order.

Thus, in the case of large lot-sized mass products, as the quantitative capacities create a restraint on their polishing, the importance of capacity management will be high. On the other hand, in the case of complicated-shaped products, materials, and products that require some difficult and advanced techniques, and products that need a high degree of accuracy, as the qualitative capabilities restrain their polishing, the importance of capability management will be high.

Now, the syndicate does not have the demand and supply information on capabilities that constitute the formal information about both the demand trend of each capability, on which the capability demand is concentrated, and the condition of acquisition or possession of each capability. Therefore, member companies cannot share the information about the demand trend of capabilities in the entire network. In addition, if any task is concentrated in particular companies that have the capability required according to the condition of the order, as an entire syndicate, they would not be able to increase the capacity and decrease the lead time by providing the demand and supply of the capability match.

However, all information systems essentially need the formalization and formulation of information. However, capability, by nature, can only be described qualitatively. Nonetheless, the polishers' capabilities are skillful techniques and so difficult to standardize, unlike the capabilities of tangible fixed assets such as machines and equipment. Therefore, it is very difficult to define the polishers' capabilities in definite terms. In addition, regarding the capabilities peculiar to temporary businesses that are not repetitive, the syndicate does not have any merits in defining them. Therefore, there exists some difficulty in the formalization and formulation of the information about capabilities.

Finally, with regard to inter-firm BPM, the syndicate faces a problem — the total optimization in BPC levels. It has designed the products that can optimally utilize the advantages of polishing. However, as no product can be completed only using the polishing technology, in order to produce the original brand products while considering the R&D function, the syndicate must cooperate with other companies with different element technologies in the production stage and systematically combine the polishing technology and other technologies into its original products.

However, the processing ability of the former processes acts as a constraint to BPC. Therefore, unless the syndicate is able to induce strong cooperation in all processes before polishing, the productivity in the BPC level cannot improve regardless of how the syndicate strengthens its polishing process.

Thus, as the process coordinator, the syndicate has to play a role wherein it proposes, coordinates, and secures the strong cooperation of other companies that have different element technologies; this role will become complicated as the product diversifies further.

Therefore, as the original brand (product) grows, the syndicate is required to prepare a plan of production according to the order conditions and deploy it to the plan of each process, in order to manage its constraints and optimize the entire BPC; however, it will be more crucial to construct a system wherein the process information among companies with different technologies is shared.

5 Conclusion

This chapter considers the example of a horizontal division-of-work network specializing in an element technology, called the Polishers' Syndicate, and clarifies the features and problems from the BPM perspective.

Generally, the necessity for the formulation of performance measures and the management accounting system will increase according to the scale of the organization. In the Polishers' Syndicate, the necessity for a formal information system has hitherto been low for most small-sized member companies. However, as the syndicate acts and develops just like a single company and as the member companies' dependence on the syndicate increases, there will be a need for a management accounting system specifically adapted to the network, such as the use of cost tables for revenue management, and a formal information system for capacity and capability management.

However, if both the collapse of industrial accumulation and the acute shortage of successors worsen, the maintenance of this network itself will become more difficult. Thus, it is insufficient to only construct the management information system, given the existent network.

First, the syndicate has to strengthen the network base through the formulation of organization by unifying the member companies and establishing a single company specializing in a new element technology; further, it should prepare a stable business base for securing its successors. Next, it is preferable to deal with the formulation of information. Through the formulation of organization, the syndicate will be able to promote, to some extent, the sharing of the technologies and information, which is difficult to define such as capabilities, through internal training, skill certification systems, etc.

Furthermore, as it is essential to secure a strong cooperation among companies that have different element technologies in order to develop the original brand products, it will be essential to construct some information systems that share the information on processes among the companies to create and implement the plan of production and thus to optimize the entire BPC.

Acknowledgments

I gained a considerable amount of precious knowledge by conversing with Mr. Masaya Takano (Tsubame CCI) and several syndicate members;

I immensely appreciate their kindness. Naturally, I am solely responsible for any errors or misstatements in this chapter.

References

Itami, H. (1998). Meaning and logic of industrial accumulation in Itami, H., Matsushima, S. and Kikkawa, T. (eds.), *Nature of Industrial Accumulation: Condition of Flexible Division of Work and Accumulation*, Tokyo: Yuhikaku, pp. 1 23 (in Japanese).

Kaplan, R.S. and Norton, D.P. (1996). *The Balanced Scorecard: Translating Strategy into Action*, Boston: Harvard Business School Press.

Kaplan, R.S. and Norton, D.P. (2004). *Strategy Maps*, Boston: Harvard Business School Press.

Lebas, M. and Euske, K. (2002). A conceptual and operational delineation of performance in Neely, A. (ed.), *Business Performance Measurement: Theory and Practice*, Cambridge: Cambridge University Press, pp. 65–79.

Lee, G., Kosuga, M., Nagasaka, Y. and Sohn, B. (2010). *Business Process Management of Japanese and Korean Companies*, Singapore: World Scientific.

McNair, C.J. (1994). The hidden costs of capacity, *Journal of Cost Management*, 8, 12–24.

National Association of Accountants (1963). *Accounting for Costs of Capacity*, Research Report No. 39.

Small and Medium Enterprise Agency (1996). *White Paper on Small and Medium Enterprises in Japan: 1996 Edition* (in Japanese).

Small and Medium Enterprise Agency (2007). *White Paper on Small and Medium Enterprises in Japan: 2007 Edition* (in Japanese).

Takaoka, M. (1998). Industrial accumulation and market in Itami, H., Matsushima, S. and Kikkawa, T. (eds.), *Nature of Industrial Accumulation: Condition of Flexible Division of Work and Accumulation*, Tokyo: Yuhikaku, pp. 95–129 (in Japanese).

Yamaguchi, N. (2005). A new capacity concept in management accounting, *Niigata University Annual Report of Economics*, 29, 47–72 (in Japanese).

12
Organizational Capability of Master Data Management for Inter-Firm Integration

Mohammad Aghdassi* and Farzad Movahedi Sobhani†
*Tarbiat Modares University
†Islamic Azad University, Science and Research Branch

1 Introduction

Coordinating operations and harmonizing decisions throughout the value chain are the challenges that today's inter-firm networks are faced with. Inter-firm structures from the time of formation until now have always combined two complementary concepts: integration and fragmentation. With fragmentation the benefit of specialization throughout the value chain is provided. However, integration connects all tasks and activities of the value chain in a logical way so that a coherent set of operations and decisions are obtained.

The basis of integration in inter-firm networks is based on the way master data is managed across the value chain. Master data is the persistent type of data in an organization; without it none of the transactions and operations in the organization can be performed. According to Berson and Dubav (2007), "Master data can be defined as the data that has been cleansed, rationalized, and integrated into an enterprise-wide system of record for core business activities". For example, categories of information subjects such as customer, vendor, material master, chart of accounts, cost center are types of master data.

In an organization, every functional area with regard to its mission is responsible for creating and maintaining the respective master data in order to prepare them for organizational transactions. In fact, this simple concept ensures the integration and harmonization of operations and decisions in the whole value chain. However, in practice, this simple concept does not happen easily. In particular, master data integration is much more complex when the value chain elements are handled by independent specialized business units.

These challenges have not been far from executives' and information technologists' views. In practice several tools and techniques have been crafted in order to manage master data integration. Enterprise resource planning (ERP) is one of the most popular tools that provide the necessary technological infrastructure for integrating master data. But in practice, its implementation has been faced with massive challenges.

Beyond the technological solution, conflict of interest amongst the elements of an inter-firm network is one of the most important barriers that make integration so difficult. In this chapter, based on data gathered from an automotive value chain, the issue of the master data integration is considered from the standpoint of conflicts among network's Inter-firm elements. Moreover, executive solutions and guidelines will be presented for this matter. To achieve this goal, this chapter is organized in six sections. In the next section, a brief definition of master data is introduced and its role in value chain integration is explained. Then in Sections 3 and 4 a real case of an inter-firm network is introduced and the challenges of integration regarding conflict of interest among value chain elements and within an inter-firm network are investigated. Also, in this section it will be mentioned that master data leadership has a critical role. In Sections, based on Adair's Action-Centered Leadership model, the role of leadership and its relation to master data management is investigated, then practical solutions for this issue are presented. Section 6 concludes.

2   Master Data Management and Value Chain Integration

An inter-firm network manages all or a substantial part of the operations in a value chain. A value chain is a chain of related activities and processes in a particular industry that are often carried out by different independent business units. In a value chain, business units do some kind of operational and/or supportive transactions, such as research and development, purchasing, production, sales, after-sales service, and so on.

An organizational transaction that occurs in one element of the value chain affects the operations and decisions of other value chain elements. Furthermore, this transaction may be the result of the decisions and operations of other elements in the value chain. For example, when a customer sends a sales order to a company, all elements of the value chain such as procurement, engineering, production and sales are activated to coordinate their own decisions and operations for manufacturing and delivering goods or services to customers. This coordination is necessarily achieved in an integrated context of operations and decision making processes.

One of the basic principles that guarantees the harmonization of decisions and operations throughout a value chain is master data integration. In the above-mentioned example, the sales order will not be realized properly unless the necessary information, such as material specification, vendor name, delivery time, batch size, production capacity, etc , is already available to the planning and production departments. Vendors also require the latest valid engineering information for the requested material. Furthermore, all changes in this information must be coordinated throughout the value chain. In fact, the inability of a value chain to coordinate master data will cause the sales order to be realized below the expected quality.

Organizational boundaries cause some kind of isolation in value chains. In that way, each particular function in a value chain tends to carry out its own operations and decisions via a series of self-contained, independent islands of systems. Many companies fix this problem by using a kind of integrated information system like ERP. ERP puts information and processes in a systematic integrated infrastructure and provides synchronization among the three flows of material, money and information in a value chain.

One of the advantages of ERP in the value chain is that it provides an appropriate organizational context for managing centralized master data throughout the value chain, independent of organizational boundaries. In fact, each element of the value chain, alone or jointly, is responsible for creating and maintaining a piece of master data. If any of these elements are allowed to manage master data independently or without coordination with other elements, a lack of data integration will occur in the whole value chain and consequently failure in operations will happen. Changing or updating an item of the master data by an organizational unit without awareness of the other units can easily lead to the wrong decisions being made in the value chain.

Although from a technological perspective a lot of innovative solutions have been offered for master data integration, in practice it has not been realized easily. The political structure of each value chain element simply will not allow other elements to interfere with its own master data management procedures. The root of this resistance can be studied from two organizational perspectives, the hard and soft sides of organizations. The hard side of an organization relates to the technical aspects of organizational processes and systems. Many organizational rules and procedures have been combined with the way master data is created and maintained in a company. Therefore, any changes in master data management procedures can lead to changes in the work setting of the company. Obviously, these changes are always accompanied by resistance. However, overcoming organizational resistance stemming from the hard side of an organization is generally achievable.

In terms of the soft side of an organization, resistance against master data integration relates to the attitudes of the people, especially senior managers, towards centralized master data management. The attitude of senior managers has a lot of effect. The rest of this chapter is devoted to defining and analyzing the barriers to master data integration from the standpoint of the soft side of organizations.

3 Methodology

Material presented in this chapter has been obtained following research done in one of the automotive inter-firm networks in the Middle East. Automotive value chains, usually because of the extended operations and high-volume transactions, are much more complex, and therefore integration does not happen easily.

The inter-firm network that we studied in this research manages all elements of the automotive value chain, including new product development, procurement, production, sales and after-sales service via more than 104 business units with independent legal status. In 2005, this company decided to implement SAP R/3 in order to benefit from the integration of business processes. In practice, despite choosing an appropriate technological solution, the advantages of integration were obtained with difficulty.

The investigations done by the authors of this chapter at the same time as ERP implementation project managers in the above-mentioned inter-firm network and academic researchers indicate that the lack of appropriate organizational capability to overcome the conflict of interest between the inter-firm network's elements is one of the most important obstacles to integration in a value chain.

Organizational capability needed for integration in an inter-firm network is related to the managerial attitudes of each value chain element. In the following sections we will present our findings on the relationship between managerial attitudes and resistance to master data integration via centralized management.

4 Case Study

Generally, ERP implementation comes with risk. Using a step-by-step strategy is an approach that is usually adopted to reduce the risk of implementation. In this way, instead of implementing ERP in the whole value chain at once, an appropriate combination of the geographic and process scope of the value chain will be chosen and then ERP will be implemented. Obviously, in this method, implementation will be done through defining a set of related projects.

In our case, the step-by-step strategy was selected and an ERP implementation plan was developed for the whole value chain (Fig. 1). The first step of the implementation plan was common data implementation but it faced from strong opposition SBU and BU's managers. Consequently, it was decided that instead of implementing master data in an independent phase, it would be implemented along with its own process individually. Hence,

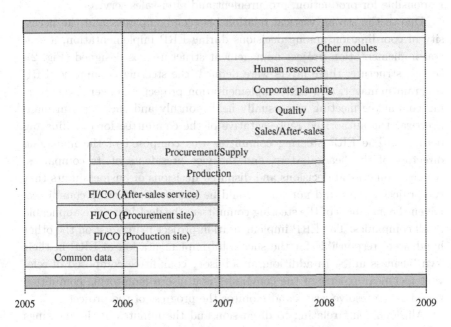

Fig. 1.   ERP implementation plan.

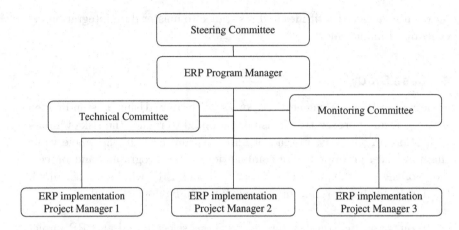

Fig. 2.   ERP Project management organizational structure.

implementation of Accounting (FI/CO) with its master data was the first project, and was started in three independent companies in the value chain responsible for production, procurement and after-sales service.

Due to the strong vertical relation between companies and the necessity of coordination among decisions during ERP implementation, a central implementation project management structure was designed (Fig. 2). In this structure, three layers were defined: the steering committee, ERP program manager, and ERP implementation project manager. The steering committee meeting was usually held monthly and the program manager was the authorized representative of the committee for coordinating decisions. The ERP steering committee was composed of the managing directors of the headquarters, and the vice presidents of its companies. All cross-functional decisions and disputed decisions of business units that the project team could not solve would be sent to the steering committee. Given the members of the steering committee, the decisions were applicable to all companies. The ERP implementation project managers, on the other hand, were responsible for the successful implementation of ERP in their own business units. In addition, an advisory committee composed of relevant technical experts of the companies and also a monitoring committee were held to resolve issues and monitor the progress of the project.

All documents relating to discussion and the minutes of the meetings of the steering, technical and monitoring committees were among the most important sources of information in this research.

5 A Leadership Model for Master Data Management

Dan Power (2008) provides a solution for the political aspect of master data management by mapping the typology of power of organizations involved in the master data management process. He suggests considering the organization chart, and writing beside each element the attitudes of each key manager from the two perspectives of personality and politics. Also he stresses that for doing this work, it is not required to have too much dialogue with people. Then, Power proposes an organization change management (OCM) approach based on education and communication initiatives. He also offers effective ways for managers to set up master data management by defining a three-layer organization for data governance. The three layers are the steering committee, middle level council, and executive agents (stewards) in the fields of business and IT operations. He considers the three-layer organization to be a very wise and political solution that helps the leaders to have successful management of master data. But in terms of individuals, being a capable and powerful manager is not sufficient for master data management. In fact, master data management needs a leadership model to achieve the desired results.

In this study based on Adair's Action-Centered Leadership model, the results of the case study are analyzed and a leadership model for master data management is developed.

5.1 *Adair's action-centered leadership model*

The Center for Leadership Studies (Bolden *et al.*, 2003) provided a comprehensive literature review on leadership to find new occupational standards for management and leadership. Through reviewing all the leadership theories developed during the past 70 years, they showed that leadership theories evolved through seven categories: great man theories, trait theories, behaviorist theories, situational leadership, contingency theories, transactional theories, and transformational theories. They conclude that each of these theories offers some insights into the qualities of successful leaders. However, there has been a shift in focus from the generic characteristics and behaviors of the individual to recognition of the importance of responding to different situations and the leaders' role in relation to followers (Table 1).

Among the situational and contingencies theories, Adair's Action-Centered Leadership model is one that has enough capability to fulfill the purpose of our study. Adair's model (2006) is a simple leadership

Table 1. Review of leadership models and theories (Bolden, 2003).

Great Man Theories	Based on the belief that leaders are exceptional people, born with innate qualities, destined to lead. The use of the term "man" was intentional since until the latter part of the twentieth century leadership was thought of as a primarily male, military and Western concept. This led to the next school of Trait Theories.
Trait Theories	The lists of traits or qualities associated with leadership exist in abundance and continue to be produced. They draw on virtually all the adjectives in the dictionary which describe some positive or virtuous human attribute, from ambition to zest for life.
Behaviorist Theories	These concentrate on what leaders actually do rather than on their qualities. Different patterns of behavior are observed and categorized as styles of leadership. This area has probably attracted the most attention from practising managers.
Situational Leadership	This approach sees leadership as specific to the situation in which it is being exercised. For example, whilst some situations may require an autocratic style, others may need a more participative approach. It also proposes that there may be differences in required leadership styles at different levels in the same organization.
Contingency Theories	This is a refinement of the situational viewpoint and focuses on identifying the situational variables which best predict the most appropriate or effective leadership style to fit the particular circumstances.
Transactional Theories	This approach emphasizes the importance of the relationship between the leader and followers, focusing on the mutual benefits derived from a form of contract through which the leader delivers such things as rewards or recognition in return for the commitment or loyalty of the followers.
Transformational Theories	The central concept here is change and the role of leadership in envisioning and implementing the transformation of organizational performance.

Fig. 3.   Adair's Action-Centered Leadership model.

and management model in which leaders should consider three main areas of actions regarding their situation. Being able to keep the right balance among these three areas is the key to success.

The three areas are commonly represented by three overlapping circles, one of the most iconic symbols in management theory (Fig. 3). These areas are achieving the task, ensuring the Group Functions and Developing the individual.

For each category a number of activities are defined as follows:

Achieve Task

- Defining the task
- Making a plan
- Allocating work and resources
- Controlling quality and tempo of work
- Checking performance

Group Functions

- Establishing clear standards
- Maintaining discipline
- Building team spirit
- Encouraging a sense of purpose

Develop Individuals

- Developing and coaching individuals
- Attending to personal problems
- Offering recognition and status

Using the above-mentioned model in the master data management environment, a powerful management framework will be provided in order to incorporate the local relevant factors and create the respective interpretation.

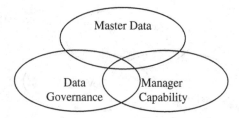

Fig. 4.   Converted Adair's model for management of master data.

5.2   *Adair's Action-Centered Leadership model for master data management*

Adair believes that in accordance with the particular situations and requirements of each of these three factors, we could plan some actions. In the master data management environment, the three elements of Adair's model can be interpreted as depicted in Fig. 4. In this model, "Group Functions" is replaced by a three-layer organization which is responsible for data governance. "Achieve Task" is related to the integrated management of the master data. "Develop Individuals" is related to the capability of people including managers and experts who have a role in the three-layer organization. In the remainder of this chapter, based on the real data gathered from the case study, each element of the model will be described.

5.2.1   *Data Governance as the "Group Functions" in Adair's model*

The contribution of "Group Functions" in Adair's model is a group of people who are responsible for the management of the master data. This group consists of managing directors (key people) of value chain companies who are responsible for data governance. As discussed earlier, data governance is conducted by a three-layer organization. The three-layer organization consists of the following players:

Steering committee: The first layer is the steering committee consisting of the headquarters' managing directors, the headquarters' related vice presidents, and managing directors of the value chain companies.
Project manager: The second layer consists of the headquarters' program manager, and the company implementation project managers. The company project manager is a competent person from each company, who

is responsible for conducting executive operations in the self-contained company with the cooperation of the headquarters' program manager.

Experts: In the third layer, there are full-time experts in IT and business. They have been assigned professional roles in the implementation of ERP.

To understand the role of the three-layer organization in master data management, explanation of layers is required. However, considering the importance of the subject and to avoid prolonged discussion, we will briefly describe the steering committee in the first layers of the three-layer organization.

The steering committee had 46 sessions, each averaging two hours during the ERP implementation project. Subjects discussed in each session were recorded by the head of the monitoring committee. These minutes of meetings were a basis for follow-up actions to be done by the relevant individual in each company.

Using content analysis, ten categories of work or decision were recognized. Table 2 shows these ten types of work together with the frequency and the percentage of occurrence.

Considering these ten types of work, it can be concluded that the steering committee solved the political issues of master data management in the value chain by conducting four essential roles.

Support for project manager: The execution organization, including work teams, supervisors, all people formally assigned to the project, or all people in departments who should provide services for the project, is not motivated by itself or only by the energy of the project manager. It should feel the energy of the top management pushing it forward (note items 2, 3, 6, 7 and 9 in Table 2, which show the steering committee devoted more than 50% of the time to this).

Reducing excuses: The steering committee plays a significant role in reducing the excuses of the companies for not doing their assigned work (note item 9, which forms the majority of the committee's work. Also, note items 6 and 7, which make up 30% of total discussions in meetings. All three items refer to some kind of excuse for cutting work). Reasons for not doing the assigned work may include the following:

- They do not know what should be done and how to do it. But because of the job position or expectations of senior managers, they cannot declare that they do not know.

Table 2. Main issues discussed in steering committee.

	Nature of Work (Motivation for Work)	Total	Percent
1	Help to eliminate the ambiguity in duties determine duties and tasks	54	10
2	Pressure for doing work	91	17
3	Help to find capable people who should participate, or to force corresponding organizational unit to participate	44	8
4	Request from project team or technical and processes analyst team for comments on or approval of their work	44	8
5	Solve human resource allocation problems	94	17
6	Committee informed of deficiency motivation, and lack of serious communication efforts among organizational units	12	2
7	Committee informed of deficiency motivation, and lack of serious efforts to create capacity and capability	28	5
8	Report project progress	51	9
9	Committee informed of the weak participation of experts, so that they have no sense of ownership	112	21
10	Report of termination of work	16	3

- They have incomplete information. So, they are convinced that such a project is not high-priority.
- They have to spend a lot of resources and time for the project, which prevents them from doing their departmental jobs. In addition, evaluation of their performance by their boss is not much adapted to the progress of the project.

Follow-up: Another significant role of the steering committee is to monitor and follow upon the work assigned to the managers. This type of work ranks second among the ten types of work (note that item 2 makes up 17% of the issues). Therefore, the steering committee is a very appropriate tool for follow-up.

Reorganizing: The role of the steering committee in reorganizing the project organization structure is critical. Seventeen percent of the subjects of meetings are about modification of the organization structure chart of the project (see item 5). We often observed discussions in which some managers did not actively participate due to a lack of proper position in the project organization chart. So, an official position is very important for managers and employees to take the responsibility of the assigned role. In this regard, often one of the following two problems has occurred. First, in the project organization, responsibility often is given to a senior manager of an organizational unit but he does not involve his personnel who should carry out their related project duties. Second, in the project organization, responsibility has been assigned to an active and motivated expert in an organizational unit, but his top manager has assigned a lot of tasks to him and so he cannot have acceptable cooperation with the project.

5.2.2 *Master data as the "Achieve Task" in Adair's model*

The scope of master data is very wide and includes customer, product, personnel, financial, vendor and other key business data that can be used for sustainable and integrated business management. Master data is a primary vehicle that creates and maintains on-time and accurate records for business management. For example in a university, educational transactions including course registrations, test scores, accommodation; cultural transactions such as the use of dormitories, student clubs and alumni; and financial transactions including registration fees, cost of facilities and other expenses may be done by separate applications. But if all of these transactions use the same master data, like as student, course, program, and chart of accounts, which is managed in an integrated form, records of these transactions always are highly accurate.

In an enterprise, any company based on its mission has unique capabilities for creating and maintaining a specific kind of master data for conducting organizational and inter-organizational operations. Therefore, based on Adair's converted model each company has the responsibility for maintaining and coordinating its own master data for using all elements in an inter-firm network. Four types of master data and management issues that were recognized in our study are explained below:

Chart of accounts (COA): The finance and accounting department of each company is responsible for creating and maintaining COA. Most of an inter-firm network's transactions are related to the COA. In our case a lot of effort has been made to resolve conflicts among accounting departments and obtain an agreement on the format and content of the COA.

Material master (MM): The engineering department of each company is responsible for creating and maintaining the MM. Once a material master is created by the engineering department the other elements of the inter-firm network (such as production, procurement, after-sales service and even vendors) are allowed to use it. Any changes or updates to the material master have to be done centrally by the engineering department and should be coordinated with other elements of the value chain.

Vendors: The central supplying company is responsible for creating and maintaining vendor data. All contracts and financial transactions related to vendors are directly connected to this kind of data. Vendor data is considered political data because it is related to non-disclosure data.

Customer: The sales department is responsible for creating and maintaining customer master data. All contracts and financial transactions related to customers are directly connected to this kind of data. Like vendor data, customer data is also political data.

5.2.3   Develop the Capability of Managers and Experts as the "Develop Individuals" in Adair's model

The information gathered through interviews with the managing directors of the value chain companies and also the data collected from the meeting that the project manager of the headquarters held with the assigned project managers of value chain companies (i.e., middle management council) revealed four different attitudes toward master data integration. These four types of attitude show behavioral aspects and mental models of key people of the project. By considering each of the features, we are able to approach a specific leadership solution. This is the third aspect of Adair's model (i.e., Develop Individuals). In the following we describe the four types of attitude of the companies towards the inter-firm network.

Non-participatory attitude: Such managers do not allow others to interfere in their work. They believe any kind of headquarter interference may decelerate their work. They state that the headquarters must define the inter-firm network's objectives clearly and then request respective results. These groups believe that centralized master data management does not need the collaboration and elaboration of managers of various companies. They think that holding several meetings about master data is inefficient. They have a simple notion of data transfer between companies. Therefore they are unable to consider the decisions about master data definition as a basic platform for transferring data. They often consider these kinds of decision as operational and not strategic decisions that should be followed by operational people. When these people are criticized for being responsible for the lack of master data integration, they may offer a simple solution, that is, every company which needs data from others should be put on some interface system in the path of receiving information. It seems that they consider the issue of master data just as a topic of information technology, not as a topic of strategic management. So their attitude may lead to very weak local operational control with repeated transactions, mistakes and errors, increased costs, and finally unsatisfied customers.

Information hiding: Managers with this attitude believe that giving the company's data to the headquarters or other value chain companies will endanger the company. They believe that the headquarters' managing director and the managers of other companies should not know their internal business data, and that their awareness of some information of the company will cause that those managing directors to take some decisions which will negatively affect the success of their business strategies. For example, consider a company which is responsible for supplying spare parts and warranty services. Suppose the managing director of the company decides to sign a new contract with one of his vendors in order to provide new services to customers in such a way to enhance their satisfaction and decrease their costs. Now, suppose the managing director of a supplier company is aware of the provisions of the new contract. He may put pressure on the warranty services company (through the managing director of the headquarters) to cancel its new contract just because the contract includes some points which are considered to be outside the agreed strategy of the inter-firm network.

Fear of mistakes: Such managers are afraid of their managerial mistakes being exposed and prefer non-transparency. These people always feel that some of their decisions may be wrong from the viewpoint of the top managers. They think if the headquarters' top managers become aware of their wrong decisions, they may lose their position so it is better not to let them know. Generally, these people are afraid of the supervision of top managers as well as their colleagues. They believe that the solution is a lack of transparency in their business issues.

Laziness: Such managers believe that accepting master data integration policies imposed by the inter-firm network will change many of their business rules and procedures which are working well. For example, if a company changes their chart of accounts (one type of master data), their accounting system will be completely transformed and they must make changes in the accounting processes and organization structure. So they prefer not to spend their time and energy on changing a process that they think does not need change. Often, they are not able to assess the effect of change of master data on their process and business rules, so they may overestimate the required changes. And since they have no clear idea of the benefits of master data integration, they consider changing their process and organization to be onerous and time-consuming work. For example, they don't know how much the volume of transactions decreases due to master data integration and/or they may not know that because of master data management, the number of mistakes will dramatically decrease to almost zero, and customer satisfaction will greatly increase.

6 Conclusions

Master data integration is the key to incorporating decisions and operations in an inter-firm network. However, master data integration is not achieved easily. Beyond the innovative technological solutions that provide an appropriate technical infrastructure for master data integration, the political atmosphere dominating master data makes it very complicated. This political atmosphere is caused by conflicts of interest in different elements of the inter-firm network.

Overcoming the complexity of master data management needs the role of master data leadership for balancing the three areas of "Develop Individuals", "Achieve Task" and "Group Functions" within the value chain.

Master data management in an inter-firm network is faced with two contradicting issues of centralized and participatory decisions making at the business and corporate level. The necessity of participation in decisions comes from the fact that master data is directly related to the daily operations of business units. Therefore any change in format or content of master data without the coordination and verification of independent business units will cause disruption in their current operations. On the other hand, this will create a departmental or sectional view about master data management.

A practical solution for these issues is to transfer the decisions regarding master data from business units to a cross-functional committee with sufficient authority in the inter-firm network. This committee considers the benefit to each element of the inter-firm network and the benefit to the value chain as a whole. However, establishing the cross-functional committee will not be useful by itself and it is essential that its members commit to its decisions. This commitment will be achieved by the leadership of master data in the whole value chain.

When a centralized cross-functional committee as an initial approach cannot solve the political problems of master data management, aligning the attitudes of managers of the inter-firm network with the related decisions of master data management could be considered as a supplementary approach. According to their attitudes towards centralized management of master data, managers of business units are categorized into four types. The practical solutions to the political problems of master data management will be different for each of these types.

More complex problems of master data management that cannot be solved with the two above approaches could be managed by considering the type of master data. So, considering the type of master data in solving political conflicts is the third approach. From the perspective of the impact on value chain integration and its effect on the value chain elements, master data can be divided into several groups. Master data such as customer, vendor, material master, chart of accounts have cross-functional effects in the whole inter-firm network, while the impact of master data such as BOM and controlling object is limited to the internal parts of a business unit. Considering the above approaches, i.e., current management attitudes in each business unit and the type of master data, will create the different styles of leadership in master data management.

References

Adair, J. (2006). *Effective Leadership Development*, Mumbai: Jaico Publishing House.

Berson, A. and Dubov, L. (2007). *Master Data Management and Customer Data Integration for a Global Enterprise*, New York: McGraw Hill.

Bolden, R., Gosling, J., Marturano, A. and Dennison, P. (2003). A review of leadership theory and competency frameworks, Centre for Leadership Studies, University of Exeter.

Power, D. (2008). The politics of master data management and data governance, *DM Review*, 18(3), 24.

13

Deployment of Material Flow Cost Accounting in an Inter-Firm Network

Tomonori Inooka

Kokushikan University

1 Introduction

Environmental issues are contemporary societal problems. The importance of company responses to these issues is increasing. In particular, the effective realization of the three Rs (reduce, reuse, recycle) in inter-company networks may be considered a prerequisite to their permanent contribution to society. Accordingly, this chapter examines which input/output models may be applicable to material flow cost accounting in relation to the three Rs in the venous system of an inter-firm network.

Green supply chain management has been developed as an environmental effort among enterprises. However, in the expansion and application of material flow cost accounting between firms, the effectiveness of that application differs according to the conditions under which such accounting information is shared. Therefore, in this chapter I attempt to apply the simultaneous equation system through the reciprocal allocation method of the service cost to material flow cost accounting cost measurement, as concerns situations in which recycling occurs in inter-firm networks, where cost information is relatively easy to obtain.

2 Environmental Accounting and Material Flow Cost Accounting

The environmental efforts and consideration of firms are becoming more important than ever before. Compliance with legal regulation is not sufficient; the extent to which a firm, as an environmentally friendly business, actively takes up environmental protection activities and how that might appeal to stakeholders is becoming an important issue in business strategy. Firms' efforts towards the environment may be published in environmental reports but it is the part expressed in monetary terms that is particularly important. It is there that the measurement system of a firm's environmental efforts becomes environmental accounting. Environmental accounting includes the capacity to evaluate non-monetary values. However, it also measures in monetary terms the economic activities of firms. As shown in Fig. 1 it can be thought of as a mechanism in which environmental protection activities accompanying a firm's purchasing, manufacturing, logistics, and sales activities are measured mainly in monetary terms.

Business environmental consciousness or efforts cannot sufficiently be put into practice in a single enterprise; integrated joint efforts in the inter-firm arena are necessary. That is to say, the partial optimization of each enterprise does not necessarily lead to total optimization. Because of this, coordination between firms and a management system aiming at total optimization becomes important. With that, environmental efforts in the supply chain have seen various developments in green supply chain management.

In order to manage environmental protection activities the measurement and evaluation of such measures is necessary; however, for company-wide or inter-firm management such monetary measurement is also indispensable. And even if the aim is to be an environmentally friendly enterprise, such

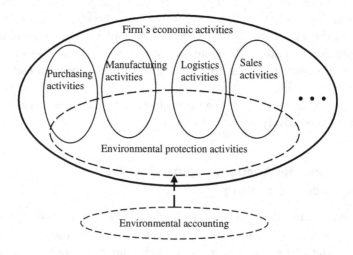

Fig. 1. Firm activity and environmental accounting.

economic support is necessary and it is absolutely necessary to grasp in monetary terms what sacrifices are being made for such activities. So, cost measurement of environmental protection activities is important.

Environmental management accounting is useful for the management of environmental efforts. However, as shown in the *Environmental Management Accounting Method Workbook* (Ministry of Economy, Trade and Industry, 2002, pp. 13–14), there are a wide variety of techniques to be found that may be used as tools of environmental management accounting: environmental quality cost accounting system, environmentally conscious cost management, material flow cost accounting, life cycle costing, and so forth. In this chapter I will emphasize material flow cost accounting (MFCA), and shall consider in which ways MFCA may be used in the analysis of the problem of improving resource productivity in inter-firm networks.

MFCA is concerned with the transfer of material within the enterprise or in the fabrication process through the quantity of input material, and focuses particularly on the loss element which does not make up non-defective goods. This element is called material loss, and through the reduction of such material loss such accounting aims simultaneously to lessen environmental impacts and reduce costs. The cost element in MFCA is divided into material costs, system costs, and delivery and disposal costs, and measured as such.

Material costs consist of all the primary-material expired costs, and also includes the energy expired costs. System costs, made up mainly of such conversion costs as labor costs, depreciation expenses, and so forth, are those costs necessitated by system maintenance. Delivery and disposal costs consist of those costs incurred through the discharge outside the enterprise of finished products and waste products.

MFCA views as material costs those environmentally related costs of business activity, that is to say, input primary materials and various energy costs. The productive activities of enterprises are those activities that create new products and goods through the use of raw materials generated from the Earth's natural resources or energy sourced from such natural resources. However, such new goods may be divided into non-defective products, or "positive products", and waste products, or "negative products". MFCA makes clear the relation between material inflows and stock in a firm's activities and the firm's outflows. MFCA makes clear the relation between cost flows and material flows. In particular with regard to outflows it distinguishes between products and material losses, and determines the outflows. In this way, information is brought to light regarding waste products which do not use the Earth's resources effectively. Through improvements based on this information, improvement of resource productivity, progress in environmental protection activities, and cost reduction may be aimed at.

The productive activities of enterprises consume the world's natural resources, and generate both non-defective goods and losses. MFCA captures the value fluctuations in this through material flows. In order to do this, it is necessary, first of all, to measure quantitatively the material inputs and outputs in those productive activities. This measuring point or area is termed the quantity center. In measuring the output of a given quantity center, the output delivered to the next quantity center and the first center's material loss are measured. Under MFCA, attention is paid to the cost of natural resources, and in order to measure that material cost from the input to the output stage, quantity measurement is necessary, and material unit tracking is very important.

3   MFCA between Firms

Because the environmental measures of individual corporations are not sufficient to solve environmental problems, it follows that aiming for the most appropriate approach through integrated adjustment between firms is necessary. Thus, there is a widening of environmental measures by individual firms to measures through the supply chain, the so-called green supply chain. Green supply chain management is expanding as an area for the solution of environmental problems.

In green supply chain management, the utility is increasing of the employment of MFCA data in analysis for raising resource productivity. This has been observed in research by the US Environmental Protection Agency (EPA) (US EPA, 2000) and in research projects sponsored by the Ministry of Economy, Trade and Industry (METI) in fiscal year 2006.

There has been a series of studies (Kokubu and Shimogaki, 2007; Higashida, 2008; Nakajima, 2009) concerning the expansion of MFCA to the supply chain and which may be considered important in examining environmental issues in the inter-firm realm. I will explain some of those studies below.

According to Kokubu and Shimogaki (2007), the effectiveness of promising productivity enhancement varies in relation to differences in the degree of MFCA data sharing in supply chains into which MFCA is being introduced. The MFCA data which may be shared depends on the relation with the data-sharing counterparty. They distinguish the following three

Table 1. MFCA data-sharing spectrum.

		MFCA Data Which May Be Shared			
		Material quantity data	Material cost data	System cost data	Energy cost data
Data-sharing Counterparty	(1) Same plant	○	□	□	□
	(2) Same company or capital-controlled group	○	□	△	△
	(3) No capital-controlled or controlling relation	○	△	–	–

Source: Kokubu and Shimogaki (2007), p. 39.

types of relation with the data-sharing counterparty: (1) those in another department or division in the same plant; (2) those in the same company or in different plants of other firms in a capital-controlled group of firms; and (3) firms not in capital-controlled or controlling relations. The different implications of these three types of relation on MFCA data sharing are indicated in Table 1.

As may be understood from Table 1, the degree of difficulty in MFCA data sharing, more specifically sharing of material quantity data, material cost data, system cost data, and energy cost data, differs according to whether the counterparty relation is type 1, 2, or 3. The differential is expressed in the table by symbols in the following relation: ○ > □ > △; the symbol "—" indicates that data exchange is very difficult. Kokubu and Shimogaki (2007) go on to analyze case studies of improvement in each scenario. In this chapter, however, demarcation of the three types is what is important and so I shall refrain from further discussion here.

4 Application of the Reciprocal Allocation Method (Simultaneous Equation System) to Service Department Costs under MFCA

I will now discuss the introduction of MFCA in inter-firm networks. Here I assume (a) the three types of relation previously mentioned and (b) that cost information is comparatively easy to obtain in type 1 and type 2 relations.

Wassily Leontief's input-output analysis is applied in a number of fields. Accounting, particularly when using the reciprocal allocation method (simultaneous equation system) in allocating service department costs in cost accounting, is one such field. As is found in various cost accounting texts (Atkinson, Kaplan, and Young, 2004; Horngren, Datar and Foster, 2002, etc.), such cost accounting is an example of the expansion of an input-output model. That is to say, each service department output is taken as an unknown quantity and the service provision proportion is made a coefficient, and a simultaneous input-output equation for each service department is devised. Solution of this simultaneous equation provides the amount allocated to the fabrication department from service costs.

Next, I wish to focus on the cost measurement system of material flow cost. I shall discuss the application of the simultaneous equation system of the reciprocal allocation method of service department costs to measurement of those costs, particularly in situations concerning recycling involving additional treatment.

In order to explain the application of the reciprocal allocation method (simultaneous equation system) to MFCA in an inter-firm network, I shall first provide a simplified example.

In MFCA the measurement of material loss is important. From this, for each quantity center which is emitting a material loss an input-output relation develops. Based on this relation, the gross output value for each quantity center is assigned an unknown value and a simultaneous equation is devised.

By thinking algebraically about the measurement of material flow cost, it may be represented by matrices and vectors, and analyzed. For example, as each element of the coefficient matrix for input-output changes, that is to say the parameters of material loss rate, etc., changes analysis of the effect on cost becomes possible. In this way, it may be useful for a variety of planning and control measures based on material flow cost data.

As an example, I put forward a situation in which a supplier provides components to a maker, from which the maker produces his products. Where some of the components have been recalled from the maker to the supplier they may be processed and input again. However, it is

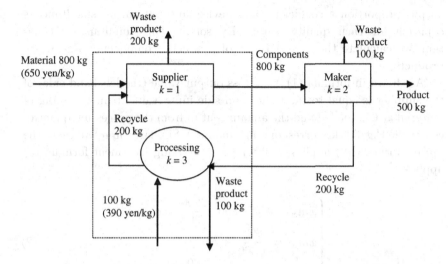

Fig. 2.   Material cost flow.

not necessary for there to be recycling at all quantity centers. I assume that there is recycling at some quantity centers. With regard to recycling, I presuppose the additional input of material or processing treatment. Consequently, in such recycling, material for which the cost has already been paid is input again, and amounts to the input of newly acquired material.

The input-output relation must be understood for each individual quantity center, because the release of waste must be understood for each unit from which such release occurs. In this example, processing is done at the supplier but it is taken as being done at an independent quantity center.

Figure 2 illustrates the following: a supplier puts in 800 kg of material costing 650 yen/kg. Then 200 kg of waste (material loss) are produced, and 800 kg of components are shipped to the maker. The maker puts in the 800 kg of components, and produces 500 kg of product and 100 kg of material loss. Further, 200 kg are recycled at the supplier, with 100 kg put out as material loss. Added to the remaining 100 kg is 100 kg of material priced at 390 yen/kg, with 200 kg being re-used as input at the supplier.

Here I discuss the quantity center. I make the output value for each quantity center an unknown value ($k = 1...3$) and the provided output proportion a coefficient, and devise an input-output simultaneous equation for each quality center. By solving this simultaneous equation, we calculate the material cost of products, components, and waste products.

As shown in formula (1), the gross output value (the left-hand side) of the supplier is equal to the right-hand side input value, namely, 800 kg of material at 650 yen/kg and the amount put in from the processing quantity center (200 kg/300 kg corresponding amounts). Similarly, in reference to the maker, formula (2) applies, and for the processing treatment formula (3) applies.

$$
\begin{cases}
xm_S = 650 \times 800 + \dfrac{200}{300} \times xm_T & (1) \\[2mm]
xm_M = \dfrac{800}{1,000} \times xm_S & (2) \\[2mm]
xm_T = 390 \times 100 + \dfrac{200}{800} \times xm_M & (3)
\end{cases}
$$

If we express this using matrices and vectors, formula (4) applies. The second term 2 of the coefficient matrix on the right-hand side of formula (4) is a transposition of the matrix which takes as its element the provided output proportion of each quantity center. For each element, where there is a provision of goods or recycling the value is not 0, and where there is no such provision the element is 0.

$$
\begin{bmatrix} xm_S \\ xm_M \\ xm_T \end{bmatrix} =
\begin{bmatrix} 650 \times 900 \\ 0 \\ 390 \times 200 \end{bmatrix} +
\begin{bmatrix} 0 & 0 & \dfrac{200}{300} \\[2mm] \dfrac{800}{1,000} & 0 & 0 \\[2mm] 0 & \dfrac{200}{800} & 0 \end{bmatrix}
\begin{bmatrix} xm_S \\ xm_M \\ xm_T \end{bmatrix} \tag{4}
$$

Next, we transpose the second term on the right-hand side of formula (4) to the left-hand side, giving us formula (5).

$$
\left(
\begin{bmatrix} 1 & 0 & 0 \\ 0 & 1 & 0 \\ 0 & 0 & 1 \end{bmatrix} -
\begin{bmatrix} 0 & 0 & \dfrac{200}{300} \\[2mm] \dfrac{800}{1,000} & 0 & 0 \\[2mm] 0 & 0 & \dfrac{200}{800} \end{bmatrix}
\right)
\begin{bmatrix} xm_S \\ xm_M \\ xm_T \end{bmatrix} =
\begin{bmatrix} 650 \times 800 \\ 0 \\ 390 \times 100 \end{bmatrix} \tag{5}
$$

Then, if we solve formula (5), we derive formula (6).

$$
\begin{bmatrix} xm_S \\ xm_M \\ xm_T \end{bmatrix} = \left(\begin{bmatrix} 1 & 0 & 0 \\ 0 & 1 & 0 \\ 0 & 0 & 1 \end{bmatrix} - \begin{bmatrix} 0 & 0 & \dfrac{200}{300} \\ \dfrac{800}{1,000} & 0 & 0 \\ 0 & \dfrac{200}{800} & 0 \end{bmatrix} \right)^{-1} \begin{bmatrix} 650 \times 800 \\ 0 \\ 390 \times 100 \end{bmatrix} \tag{6}
$$

Using the values in formula (6), the gross output values for each quantity center are those in (7).

$$
\begin{bmatrix} xm_S \\ xm_M \\ xm_T \end{bmatrix} = \begin{bmatrix} 630,000 \\ 504,000 \\ 165,000 \end{bmatrix} \tag{7}
$$

If we express the relations of formula (6) by means of matrices and vectors, we arrive at formula (8).

$$
\mathbf{x} = (\mathbf{I} - \mathbf{A})^{-1}\mathbf{b} \tag{8}
$$

However, $\mathbf{I}$ is an identity matrix and $\mathbf{A}$ is a transpose matrix of the provided output proportion between quantity centers. $\mathbf{b}$ is the input cost vector for each quantity center. $(\mathbf{I} - \mathbf{A})^{-1}$ is the inverse matrix of $(\mathbf{I} - \mathbf{A})$. $(\mathbf{I} - \mathbf{A})$ assumes that an inverse matrix exists.

Based on the gross output value of each quantity center being $xm_S = 630,000$ yen, $xm_M = 504,000$ yen, or $xm_T = 165,000$ yen, the supplier's component material cost Cm_{PS}, supplier's waste material cost Cm_{ES}, maker's product material cost Cm_{PM}, maker's waste material cost Cm_{EM}, and waste processing material cost Cm_{ET} may be calculated as follows:

$$
\begin{cases}
Cm_{PS} = 630,000 \times \dfrac{800}{1,000} = 504,000 \text{ yen} \\[2ex]
Cm_{ES} = 630,000 \times \dfrac{200}{1,000} = 126,000 \text{ yen} \\[2ex]
Cm_{PM} = 504,000 \times \dfrac{500}{800} = 315,000 \text{ yen} \\[2ex]
Cm_{EM} = 504,000 \times \dfrac{100}{800} = 63,000 \text{ yen} \\[2ex]
Cm_{ET} = 165,000 \times \dfrac{100}{300} = 55,000 \text{ yen}
\end{cases}
$$

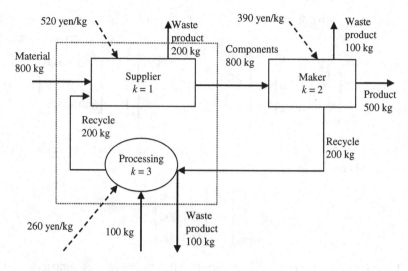

Fig. 3.   System cost flow.

Next, we consider the cost allocation of the system cost for each output. However, the cost allocation is based on the material cost ratio, and the material flow weight is as previously discussed.

As shown in Fig. 3, we assume the following system costs: for the supplier, 520 yen/kg; for the maker, 390 yen/kg; for processing treatment, 260 yen/kg.

With these material costs the following relations may be noted in regard to the gross output value of the system costs in each quantity center.

$$
\begin{cases}
xs_S = 520 \times 1{,}000 + \dfrac{200}{300} \times xs_T \\[2mm]
xs_M = 390 \times 800 + \dfrac{800}{1{,}000} \times xs_S \\[2mm]
xs_T = 260 \times 300 + \dfrac{200}{800} \times xs_M
\end{cases}
$$

This leaves us with the following gross output values: for the supplier $xs_S = 720{,}000$ yen, for the maker $xs_M = 888{,}000$ yen, and for processing treatment $xs_T = 300{,}000$ yen. Based on these results, the supplier's component system cost Cs_{PS}, supplier's waste system cost Cs_{ES}, maker's product system cost Cs_{PM}, maker's waste system cost Cs_{EM}, and waste treatment system cost Cs_{ET}, may be calculated as follows:

$$
\begin{cases}
Cs_{PS} = 720,000 \times \dfrac{800}{1,000} = 576,000 \text{ yen} \\[2mm]
Cs_{ES} = 720,000 \times \dfrac{200}{1,000} = 144,000 \text{ yen} \\[2mm]
Cs_{PM} = 888,000 \times \dfrac{500}{800} = 555,000 \text{ yen} \\[2mm]
Cs_{EM} = 888,000 \times \dfrac{100}{800} = 111,000 \text{ yen} \\[2mm]
Cs_{ET} = 300,000 \times \dfrac{100}{300} = 100,000 \text{ yen}
\end{cases}
$$

Shipping and waste treatment costs include shipping charges and waste treatment costs incurred in relation to the removal outside the enterprise of products and waste. We assume the following. For each 800 kg of the supplier's components, shipping charges amount to 40,000 yen; waste treatment costs of 100 yen/kg of waste material (where 100 yen/kg × 200 kg = 20,000 yen) are incurred; 500 kg of the maker's product incur shipping costs of 45,000 yen; maker's waste treatment costs of 150 yen/kg (where 150 yen/kg × 100 kg = 15,000 yen) are incurred; waste or defective goods returned to the supplier from the maker for recycling incur treatment costs of 120 yen/kg (where 120 yen/kg × 100 kg = 12,000 yen).

If we express the material cost, system cost, and shipping and waste treatment costs for the supplier using the above numerical examples in a material flow cost matrix, we get Table 2.

Waste product 1 is the supplier's waste product, while waste product 2 is recycling waste product.

Table 2. Supplier's material flow cost matrix.

		Production Cost	Material Cost	System Cost	Shipping & Waste Treatment Cost	Total (yen)
Supplier	Components		504,000	576,000	40,000	1,120,000
	Waste product 1		126,000	144,000	20,000	290,000
	Waste product 2		63,000	100,000	12,000	175,000
	Total (yen)		693,000	820,000	72,000	1,585,000

Table 3.   Maker's material flow cost matrix.

		Production Cost	Material Cost	System Cost	Shipping & Waste Treatment Cost	Total (yen)
Maker	Product	315,000	555,000	45,000	915,000
	Waste product	55,000	111,000	15,000	181,000
	Total (yen)	370,000	666,000	60,000	1,096,000

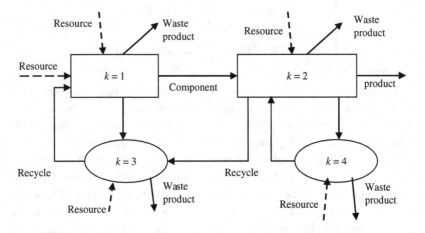

Fig. 4.   Generic material flow.

Next, we express the material cost, system cost, and shipping and waste treatment costs for the maker using the previous numerical examples in a material flow cost matrix (Table 3).

If we add percentages to the material flow cost matrix we are able to summarize the composition of the material flow cost of the components and waste products, etc., creating a material flow cost matrix that is able to provide information useful for environmental protection activities.

As illustrated by Fig. 4, we have a generic situation, namely one in which resources are input according to the materials and processing, etc., at each quantity center ($k = 1\ldots n$). The simultaneous equation system may be applied not only at the quantity center $k = 1$ but also at the quantity center $k = 2$, and when recycling is undertaken. In the coefficient matrix $\mathbf{A}$ of the previously mentioned formula (8), elements that do not have a value of 0 increase.

In a material flow cost cost-measurement system, the application of the simultaneous equation system of the reciprocal allocation method of service costs to the measurement of those material flow costs, through the change of each element of the coefficient matrix which expresses the input-output relation, namely the material loss ratio and other such parameters, allows the analysis of the effect of such changes on the costs. Deployment also becomes possible of a variety of planning and control measures based on material flow cost information.

5 Conclusion

The effectiveness of the application of MFCA from the case of the single firm to the inter-firm area differs in relation to the conditions under which MFCA data sharing occurs. We examined the application of the simultaneous equation method of the service cost reciprocal allocation method to MFCA cost measurement where recycling was occurring in an inter-firm network and where we had assumed that cost information was comparatively easy to obtain. From this we demonstrated that changes in each element of the coefficient matrix which expresses the input-output relation, namely the material loss ratio and other such parameters, allows the analysis of the effect of such changes on the costs. Deployment becomes possible of a variety of planning and control measures based on material flow cost information. Also, consideration of how activity-based costing should be applied to the measurement of system cost becomes necessary.

References

Atkinson, A.A., Kaplan, R.S. and Young, S.M. (2004). *Management Accounting*, 4th ed., New Jersey: Prentice-Hall.

Baker, B.K. and Taylor, R.E. (1979). A linear programming framework for cost allocation and external acquisition when reciprocal services exist, *The Accounting Review* (October), 784–790.

Churchill, N. (1964). Linear algebra and cost allocations: some examples, *The Accounting Review* (October), 894–904.

Higashida, A. (2008). Application of material flow cost accounting for green supply chain management, *Kigyo-Kaikei*, 60(1), 122–129 (in Japanese).

Horngren, C.T., Datar, S.M. and Foster, G. (2002). *Cost Accounting: A Managerial Emphasis*, 11th ed., Upper Saddle River, New Jersey: Prentice-Hall.

IFAC (2005). *International Guidance Document: Environmental Management Accounting*, International Federation of Accountants.

Kaplan, R.S. (1973). Variable and self-service cost in reciprocal allocation models, *The Accounting Review* (October), 738–748.

Kokubu, K. (2010). The essence of MFCA: From the viewpoint of material flow and money flow, *Communication of Japan Industrial Management Association*, 20(1), 3–7 (in Japanese).

Kokubu, K. and Nakajima, M. (2009). *Material Flow Cost Accounting*, Tokyo: Nikkei Publishing Inc. (in Japanese).

Kokubu, K. and Shimogaki, A. (2007). Development of MFCA in supply chain: Significance of MFCA information sharing, *Environmental Management*, 43(11), 37–43 (in Japanese).

Livingstone, J.L. (1968). Matrix algebra and cost allocation, *The Accounting Review* (July) 503–508.

Livingstone, J.L. (1969). Input-output analysis for cost accounting, planning and control, *The Accounting Review* (January), 48–64.

Manes, R.P., Park, S.H. and Jensen, R. (1982). Relevant cost of intermediate goods and services, *The Accounting Review* (July), 594–606.

Minch, R. and Petri, E. (1972). Matrix models of reciprocal service cost allocation, *The Accounting Review* (July), 576–580.

Ministry of Economy, Trade and Industry (2002). *Environmental Management Accounting (EMA) Workbook*, Japan: Ministry of Economy, Trade and Industry.

Nakajima, M. (2009). Significance of supply chain management by material flow cost accounting: Possibilities of an environment-conscious 'KEIRETSU', *Environmental Management*, 45(4) 60–65 (in Japanese).

Nakajima, M. (2010). The development of MFCA: MFCA management in supply chain, *Communication of Japan Industrial Management Association*, 20(1) 8–12 (in Japanese).

US EPA (2000). *The Lean and Green Supply Chain: A Practical Guide for Material Managers and Supply Chain Managers to Reduce Costs and Improve Environmental Performance*, EPA742-R-00-001.

Williams, T.H. and Griffin, C.H. (1946). Matrix theory and cost allocation, *The Accounting Review* (July), 671–678.

14

Coordinating Supply Chains by Controlling Capacity Usage Rate in the Japanese Car Industry

Fumiko Kurokawa

Dokkyo University

1 Introduction

There has been a great deal of research into the success factors of build-to-order supply chain management (Blackhurst *et al.*, 2005; Christensen *et al.*, 2005; Holweg *et al.*, 2005; Mukhopadhyay and Setoputro, 2005).

A quasi build-to-order production system tends to cause large fluctuation in the capacity usage rate, which adversely affects productivity and profitability. This chapter will examine how the car industry copes with fluctuations in the capacity usage rate and how stocks in the supply chain influence the productivity and financial performance of both car makers and suppliers. In 1999, Renault acquired a 36.8% share in Nissan and the long-standing keiretsu system, which this chapter looks at, disappeared. Most of the data, therefore, refers to the pre-1999 period.

2 The Demand-Supply Gap in Toyota and Nissan

Figure 1 shows the fluctuations in the number of cars sold by Toyota, Nissan, Honda and Mazda during the 26 months from June 2003 to July 2005. This chapter will focus on Toyota and Nissan. By comparing the data from Fig. 1 with Figs. 2, 3 and 4, it can be seen that the number of produced cars comes close to the number of sold cars if the ratio of build-to-order production increases. However, if the ratio of scheduled production increases, the demand-supply gap also increases, which leads to pileups, or shortages, of stocks.

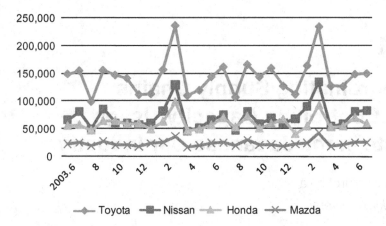

Fig. 1.   The number of cars sold by Toyota, Nissan, Honda and Mazda (June 2003–July 2005).
Source: Raw data from *Automobile Monthly Statistics*, Japan Automobile Manufacturers Association.

Figure 1 shows that car sales are not consistent throughout the year in Japan. Sales in March are extremely high for every company. If a build-to-order production system were exclusively implemented, the maximum operating capacity of factories would have to be set for March, when sales peak. However, as sales decrease in other months, the capacity usage rate also decreases and the production capacity is not fully utilized. Therefore, the question arises of whether or not automakers are gearing production to sales.

Figure 2 shows the number of domestically produced cars, the number of domestically sold cars and the number of domestically produced cars minus the number of exported cars for Toyota. It can be seen that altering production volume directly according to the sales demands is not fully implemented. It also shows that the number of domestically produced cars is always greater than the number of domestically sold cars. The number of domestically produced cars each month averages about 300,000, fluctuating from about 250,000 to 350,000. Therefore, 250,000 would appear to be the lower limit for profitable business and 350,000 maximum capacity at full operation. The number of domestically produced cars minus the number of exported cars is equal to the domestic stock. The lines showing domestic stock and the number of domestically sold cars follow each other closely. That is, demand and supply are nearly in balance for Toyota. The average

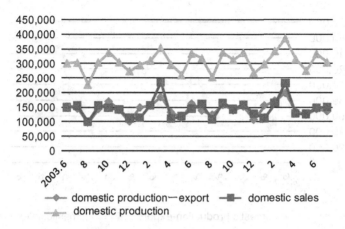

Fig. 2. Number of domestically produced cars, number of domestically sold cars and number of domestically produced cars minus the number of exported cars for Toyota.
Source: Raw data from *Automobile Monthly Statistics*, Japan Automobile Manufacturers Association.

monthly domestic sales figure for Toyota during this period is 145,016. The difference between the number of sold cars and domestic stock is 14,758 over the 26-month period, that is, only 568 a month. Toyota, therefore, seems to maintain a production system which adjusts well to fluctuation in sales.

Figure 3 shows the number of domestically produced cars, the number of domestically sold cars, and the number of domestically produced cars minus the number of exported cars for Nissan, the second biggest car maker in Japan. Fluctuation in domestic sales is larger than fluctuation in domestic production and is therefore more problematic than that seen in Fig. 2. Nissan also appears to try to keep the production volume within a limited range (100,000–140,000). The two lines for the number of domestically produced cars minus the number of exported cars and the number of domestically sold cars are close, except in March, but not as close as those for Toyota. The average monthly domestic sales for Nissan during this period is 71,498. The difference between the number of sold cars and domestic stock is 194,810 for the 26-month period, or 7,493 a month. The demand-supply gap for Nissan, therefore, is very large compared to that for Toyota.

Figure 4 shows the number of domestically sold cars minus the number of domestically produced cars less the number of exported cars for Toyota and Nissan over a 26-month period. It is, respectively, 14,758 for Toyota and 194,810 for Nissan. The demand-supply gap for Toyota is considerably

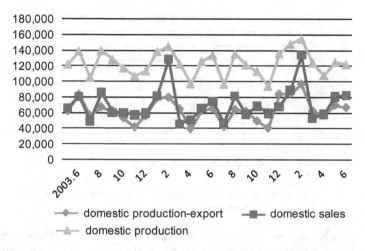

Fig. 3. Number of domestically produced cars, number of domestically sold cars and number of domestically produced cars minus the number of exported cars for Nissan.
Source: Raw data from *Automobile Monthly Statistics*, Japan Automobile Manufacturers Association.

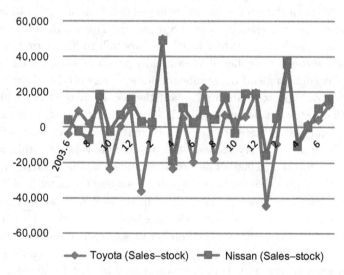

Fig. 4. Number of sold cars − (number of domestic produced cars less the number of exported cars) for Toyota and Nissan.
Source: Raw data from *Automobile Monthly Statistics*, Japan Automobile Manufacturers Association.

smaller than that for Nissan. This is because at Toyota, the demand-supply gap has been counterbalanced. At Nissan, demand is mostly greater than supply.

The figures for the demand and supply gap divided by the average number of cars sold in a month for Toyota and Nissan are as follows:

$$\text{Toyota: } 568/145{,}016 = 0.4\%$$

$$\text{Nissan: } 7{,}493/71{,}498 = 10.5\%$$

Considering that monthly sales for Toyota are twice those of Nissan, the balance between supply and demand at Toyota seems miraculous. Toyota has high production flexibility which smoothly adjusts to changing demand and achieves this fine balance between demand and supply by having a four-tier production strategy, that is, a yearly strategy; a three-, two- and one-month strategy; a strategy for the first, second, third ten days of the month; and then, between one week and three days before actual production day, a quasi-build-to-order production plan. However, the changing range of options and specifications by build-to-order is between 10% and 20%. Figures greater than 20% would create problems for suppliers and would adversely affect the production efficiency at Toyota. The build-to-order rate in Toyota is 70% of total production and scheduled production makes up 30%. In this way, the final production plan achieves an optimal balance between demand, supply and production efficiency. The build-to-order entry system is heavily supported by sophisticated information technology. Orders from customers are input by car dealers and transferred directly to the Toyota production system. Suppliers also connect directly with Toyota's production information system for parts orders in real time.

3 Parts Stocks and Operating Profit to Sales Ratio in the Toyota and Nissan Groups

It would seem that Toyota could minimize the risk of holding excessive stock by simply balancing demand and supply over the year. However, the situation is a little more complex in relation to parts stocks for the main suppliers of the Toyota Group and for Toyota itself. Figure 5 shows total parts stocks held by the 21 parts suppliers of the Toyota Group and by Toyota itself, divided by Toyota's revenue from 1985 to 1998. The ratio of parts stocks held by the 21 parts suppliers to raw material and work-in-process goods in Toyota to parts stocks in Toyota is 5:2:3. Therefore, parts

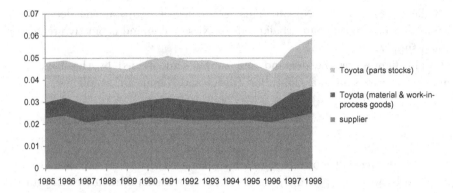

Fig. 5.   Total parts stocks. Toyota's divided by revenue.
Note: Lower layer: Toyota's 21 suppliers' parts stocks; middle layer: Toyota's
stocks (raw material & work-in-process goods); upper layer: Toyota's parts stocks.
Source: Shimono, Y. (2005). Profit and risk distribution in supply chain:
Comparison of the Toyota and Nissan Groups, *Organizational Science*, 39(2), 71.

are stocked in the ratio of 1:1 in Toyota and its parts suppliers through
the supply chain. Though parts are delivered to Toyota by the just-in-time
(JIT) system, Toyota has a buffer zone of both outsourced and made-in-
house stocks.

Figure 6 shows parts stocks for the Nissan Group. The ratio of parts
stocks held by the 20 parts suppliers to raw material and work-in-process
goods at Nissan to parts stocks at Nissan is 3:3:4. Therefore, parts are
stocked in the ratio of 7:3 at Nissan and its parts suppliers. Toyota clearly
has the advantage of holding less in-company stocks than Nissan.

Denso, the biggest parts supplier of the Toyota Group, is a good example of how the JIT delivery system works. As stated earlier, in Toyota the
second tier of planning is decided three months before production. However,
the actual final production order is decided three to four days before production day, according to the actual orders from car dealers. Denso delivers
parts according to a paper order form, or kanban. Kanban deliveries of
eight or more times a day account for 80% of all deliveries. The other 20%
of kanban deliveries of lower frequency are mostly of standardized parts.
Car components which vary according to customer orders, such as ABS
options and various options of interiors, arrive in the order in which they
will be required for assembly.

Production volume for Toyota changes day by day at Denso though,
as stated earlier, the variation from the original scheduled production plan

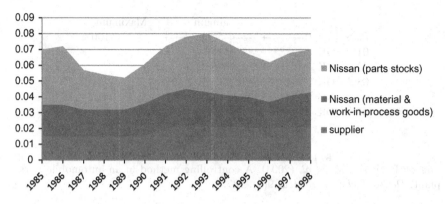

Fig. 6.   Total parts stocks. Nissan's divided by revenue.
Note: Lower layer: Nissan's 20 suppliers' parts stocks; middle layer: Nissan's stocks (raw material & work-in-process goods); upper layer: Nissan's parts stocks.
Source: Shimono, Y. (2005). Profit and risk distribution in supply chain: Comparison of the Toyota and Nissan Groups, *Organizational Science*, 39(2), 71.

is only 10–20%. This avoids major supply problems for the parts maker; however, despite this reasonably accurate forecast of demand from Toyota, the fine tuning represents a problem for Denso, as capacity usage rate is not fully realized.

The final order for car parts comes by kanban from Toyota just before the delivery. Denso needs to maintain a certain amount of parts in stock as, in most cases, it is difficult to produce parts on demand. When the quantity of stock falls to a fixed minimum point, the assembly line automatically receives instruction to begin to produce the parts, as shown in Fig. 7. The maximum level of stock volume avoids having too much upfront investment and high storage costs. The quasi build-to-order system makes it more difficult to keep capacity usage rate high for both suppliers and car makers. Suppliers try to realize high capacity usage rate by production smoothing and JIT delivery; however, they cannot avoid having a certain volume of parts in stock. Denso applies this production smoothing technique in its meter factory. As a result, it has been able to reduce fluctuation of production volume from 14.7% to 2.4% as shown in Fig. 8.

Throughout its supply chain, these efforts help keep the stock volume of the Toyota Group within an acceptable range, as shown in Fig. 5.

It is difficult, even with an automated production system, to achieve compatibility between high productivity and adaptability to market demand fluctuation. However, Denso comes very close to achieving this

```
                       Minimum          Maximum
Parts     0---------+---------50 ---------+-------------100
01   OK   ***************
02   OK   *******************
03   OK   ***********************
04   NG   ***********
05   OK   **********************************
```

Fig. 7.   Control of stock volume at Denso.

Source: Ishibashi, M. *et al.* (2004). A controlling method in an automobile part plant, *Denso Technical Review*, 9(1), 137.

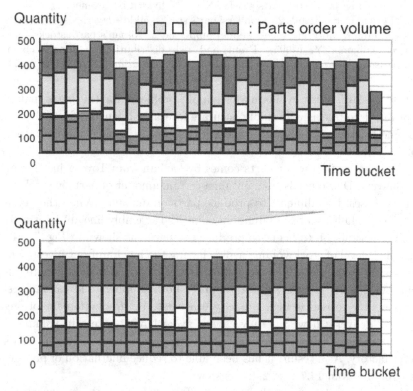

Fig. 8.   Order volume on a meter assembly line.

Source: Ishibashi, M. *et al.* (2004). A controlling method in an automobile part plant, *Denso Technical Review*, 9(1), 137.

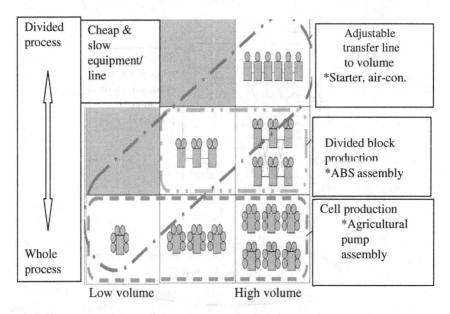

Fig. 9.   Classification of the manufacturing system corresponding to quantity change in Denso.
Source: Kojima, F. (2004). Current status and future perspective of manufacturing system technologies in Denso, *Denso Technical Review*, 9(1), 9.

balance. In order to maximize capacity usage rate, Denso uses three patterns of production system as shown in Fig. 9.

The production system shown in the lowest (i.e., cell production) level is used for producing agricultural pumps, supplied to another Denso customer. Different pump models are wholly manufactured in independent work cells. If there is no more demand for a particular pump, that work cell is cut, thus reducing the total number of cells.

The production system shown in the middle (i.e., divided block production system) level is used for producing anti-lock braking systems (ABS). The production volume of ABS fluctuates dramatically from 50,000 to 110,000 a month. New series of ABS are regularly launched but many common parts are used in the various versions. In Denso's Oyasu factory, its divided block production system, or the middle level, can deal with fluctuations in volume and achieve the same productivity as that of the transfer line, or upper level. At this upper level, there is a quality control check for each process, unlike the lower level individual cell system, and faults in the process are easier to locate. The middle level is similar to the upper level in

Fumiko Kurokawa

Process flow

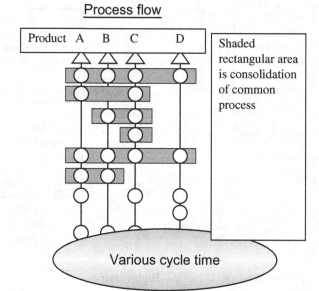

Fig. 10.   Divided block production.

Source: Yamazaki, Y. *et al.* (2004). Production system design adapted to production volume and product variety change in market demand, *Denso Technical Review*, 9(1), 31.

terms of quality control. The middle level production system, the divided block system, has multiple production lines, where each line connects similar processes and different processes, as shown in Fig. 10. A machine can be plugged in or out of each line to easily adapt to a variety of products. This divided block production system, therefore, can keep working even when the life cycle of one specific model of ABS ends and the life cycle of a new ABS model begins.

The production system shown in the upper level (i.e., adaptive transfer line to production volume) is used when production volume is relatively large and stable. At Denso, this system is available for producing starters and air conditioners for cars. If market demand for these products fluctuates, production volume can be adjusted by increasing, or decreasing, the number of mobile robots in the line and by changing the number of tasks each robot carries out. When market demand is weak, the number of mobile robots is reduced but the number of tasks they carry out is increased. A mobile robot can sense if its neighboring robot is busy or

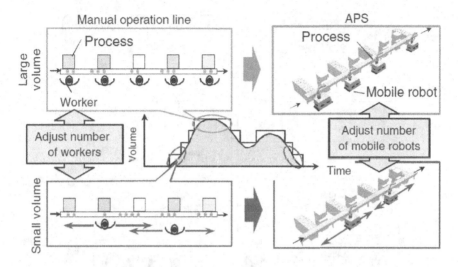

Fig. 11.   Characteristics of the adaptive production system (APS).
Source: Mitsuyuki, K. (2004). Efficient and agile production system development using information technology: Risk assessment using production system simulation and simulation environment for distributed engineering, *Denso Technical Review*, 9(1), 123.

not and, as it is also programmed to do its neighbor's task, can prevent hold-ups in production. When demand is strong, the number of mobile robots is increased but the number of tasks they carry out is reduced, as shown in Fig. 11, and the product moves through the production process at a greater speed. In Denso's Nishio factory, where air conditioners for car are produced, the adaptive transfer line was developed. When the production volume is small, one robot can work on six processes. When the production volume is large, more robots are added to the assembly line and they work on fewer processes.

Investment costs for mobile robots rise considerably if many functions are combined into one robot. However, such a multiple-function robot can adapt to fluctuations in production volume and product variety. If the economic risk of low capacity usage rate caused by fluctuations in market demand is greater than the investment cost for mobile robots or equipment, then multiple functions should be introduced under following two conditions:

1. The system layout is easily adaptable to having equipment added or removed.

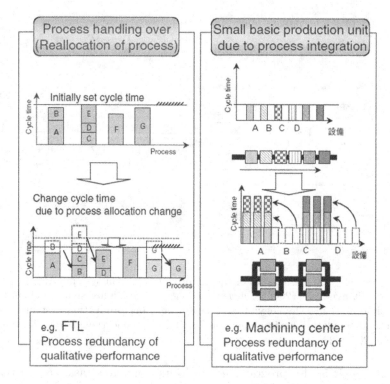

Fig. 12. Equalized and maximized efficiency without quantity prerequisite.
Source: Yamazaki, Y. *et al.* (2004). Production system design adapted to production volume and product variety change in market demand, *Denso Technical Review*, 9(1), 28.

2. Software for each piece of equipment is independent but includes the
   capability of carrying out its neighbor's tasks.

Figure 12 shows a system layout which achieves equalized and maximized efficiency without a quantity prerequisite. When production volume demand is high, reallocation of processes is implemented by handing over certain processes to the neighboring piece of equipment. Line balance in the shorter cycle time is maintained by leveling of the process load. Conversely, process integration is implemented with low production volume. Small production units carrying out multiple processes require longer cycle times.

As well as maintaining high capacity usage rate, Denso keeps the stock volume of Toyota parts within an acceptable range by implementing the JIT delivery system which is fine-tuned by the quasi build-to-order system.

A certain volume of Toyota parts are stocked at Denso, rather than at Toyota, in order to optimize the quasi build-to-order supply chain. Toyota takes advantage of their suppliers' stocks and JIT delivery capability to lower its own stock costs. This would seem to be unfair to the suppliers; however, as can be seen in Fig. 13, there is an advantage for the suppliers in this system.

Figure 13 shows the operating profit to sales ratio in the Toyota and Nissan Groups from 1985 to 1998. The profits of Toyota's suppliers are kept steady compared to the profits for Toyota itself, that is, Toyota takes the risk when there is a downtrend in the operating profit to sales ratio of the Toyota Group. However, when the trend is rising profits in the Toyota Group, Toyota takes a lot of profit as the risk premium. This can be explained by the research of Asanuma and Kikutani (1992) which shows

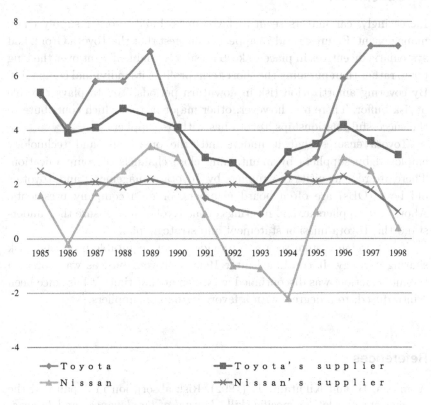

Fig. 13.   Operating profit to sales ratio.
Source: Shimono, Y. Profit and risk distribution in supply chain: Comparison of the Toyota and Nissan Groups, *Organizational Science*, 39(2), 73.

that the increase in the material cost of parts is shifted to the trading price of parts to the car maker and the expense to suppliers of under-depreciated press dies is covered by the car maker when parts trade stops before the originally estimated volume is achieved. This cuts into the car maker's profits. However, when press dies amortization is fully achieved, the trading price of parts is lowered, which increases the car maker's profits.

In the Nissan Group, however, Nissan alone takes the risk in low profit periods. In high profit periods, Nissan does not benefit from the risk premium. Parts suppliers' profits have always been kept high. It seems, therefore, that from 1985 to 1998 Nissan was not able to control its suppliers, in the way that Toyota was.

4 Conclusion

Increasingly, car makers seem to favor quasi build-to-order supply chain management. Figures 5 and 13 appear to suggest that the Toyota Group had systematic incentives in place to keep its supply chain efficient over the long term, rather than pursuing the short-term profit of its individual companies. By covering amortization risk in downturn periods, Toyota plays the role of risk buffer. There are, however, other major factors which contribute to the successful relationships Toyota has with its suppliers.

Toyota ensures that it understands the operations and technology employed by suppliers by maintaining close channels of communication. There are regular visits to suppliers by Toyota management, and Toyota's old boys (OBs) are often board members, or even company presidents. About 210 suppliers attend meetings of the Kyohokai to ensure they understand the Toyota mission statement and strategic plans.

The keiretsu system seems to provide a more equitable profit and risk sharing strategy. It continued after 1999 at Toyota but, as was noted in the introduction, was discontinued at Nissan at that time. It has since been reintroduced, to a degree, with a favored group of suppliers.

References

Asanuma, B. and Kikutani, T. (1992). Risk absorption in Japan and the concept of relation-specific skill, *Journal of the Japanese and International Economies*, 6, 1–29.

Blackhurst, J., Wu, T. and O'Grady, P. (2005). PCDM: A decision support modeling methodology for supply chain, product and process design decisions, *Journal of Operations Management*, 23, 325–343.

Christensen, W.J., Germain, R. and Biron, L. (2005). Build-to-order and just-in-time as predictors of applied supply chain knowledge and market performance, *Journal of Operations Management*, 23(5), 470–481.

Holweg, M., Disney, S.M., Hines, P. and Naim, M.M. (2005). Towards responsive vehicle supply: A simulation-based investigation into automotive scheduling systems, *Journal of Operations Management*, 23(5), 507–530.

Kurokawa, F. (2008). *Strategy of Automobile Industry in the 21st Century*, Tokyo: Zeimukeirikyoukai.

Mukhopadhyay, S.K. and Setoputro, R. (2005). Optimal return policy and modular design for build-to-order products, *Journal of Operations Management*, 23(5), 496–506.

15

Human Capital Strategy of an Inter-Firm Network: Contribution to the Evolution of the Management Accounting System, and Examples Thereof

Noriyuki Imai

Toyota Financial Services Corporation

1   Introduction

Management theories in the 20th century, after their early developments before World War II, evolved around management strategy theories, such as the corporate strategy theory advocated by Ansoff (1965) and the competition strategy theory advocated by Porter (1980), in an environment marked by the creation and development of inter-firm networks with the advance of postwar economic growth. In general, management strategy is thought to have three principal functions: (1) domain identity, (2) establishment of core competence and (3) allocation of management resources. The allocation of management resources is interpreted to mean the strategic allocation of three main factors of management — personnel, goods and money — and has been put into practice in real management scenarios by companies or company groups. Personnel, as a management resource, primarily refers to workers as a quantitative resource, and companies or company groups have taken a top-down approach to the deployment or redeployment of personnel as a quantitative resource to strategically important domains or functional areas based on formulated management strategies.

The management of personnel, a management resource, from the quantitative viewpoint functioned relatively effectively in the period of high economic growth. However, in the 1980s, the US manufacturing industry was faced with a drop in its international competitiveness. As a result, the necessity of revamping management techniques was pointed out, and, regarding personnel as a management resource, the importance of fostering human capacity from the qualitative as well as the quantitative viewpoint came to be recognized more than ever. The concept of human capital (Becker, 1975) was born in the above-mentioned circumstances, and with the advance of social and economic maturity, the efforts of companies or company groups to foster human capacity with the aim of retaining or strengthening their competitiveness have become increasingly intense.

In Japan, companies or company groups have made efforts relatively widely to foster human capacity from the human qualitative viewpoint, mainly in the manufacturing industry. Such efforts are summarized by the Toyota Group's statement, "The matter most essential to manufacturing is fostering personnel", and are exemplified by the practical approach of *kaizen*. The Toyota Group has adhered to both of these ideas at its production sites for more than half a century, ever since the establishment of the Toyota Production System (TPS) in the 1950s.

This chapter positions the continuous organizational fostering of human capacity as a factor of corporate competitiveness suitable for the management environment of the 21st century, in which society and economy are becoming increasingly complex and mature, and conceptualizes it as "relationship management" by way of human capital strategy. It also discusses cases experienced by the Toyota Group from the perspective of the contribution to the evolution of the management accounting system.

2   Relationship Management by Way of Human Capital Strategy

2.1   *Background: Views on management and human behavior*

The beginning of the 20th century, when management theories were born in the US, corresponded to the period of the business scale expansion of companies or company groups based on a wide variety of basic technologies established by the Industrial Revolution, etc. For the management theories in this period, it was necessary to create a methodology for controlling the work of workers in order to maintain or improve the efficiency of the operations of companies or company groups. It can be said that American management theories, such as scientific management advocated by Taylor

(1911), the mass production system advocated by Ford (1923) and theories on bureaucracy and divisional organization based on the division-of-labor theory advocated by Adam Smith (1776), were born in such circumstances.

If these management theories are viewed from the perspective of personnel, a management resource, it is hardly deniable that while personnel has mainly been recognized as a quantitative source of labor force and the maximization of its input efficiency has been aimed at, the qualitative aspects of personnel, such as autonomy, creativity, innovativeness and cooperativeness, have been treated rather lightly. It is likely that the top down control of on-site employees by the management of companies or company groups, based on a dichotomic view of human relationships between controlling people and controlled people, prevented them from building interrelationships on-site based on the autonomous behaviors of the personnel and from developing qualitative aspects of the personnel, such as creativity and innovativeness, based thereon. Also, it is possible to speculate that this management view of personnel was locked in as a schema (psychological framework) in the management of companies or company groups in the US and that subsequent management strategy theories succeeded to this management view.

Meanwhile, in Japan, Deming's (1982) quality control theory, which was introduced into Japan as a total quality control (TQC) theory at the beginning of the 1950s and became widespread in the Japanese industry, particularly in the manufacturing industry, had an enormous effect on the management view of personnel. Deming advocated that, in order to improve product quality, the top executive of each company or company group must establish a system of quality improvement through close cooperation with the personnel of each company or company group, including the production sites. Such advocacy derived from his belief that the enhancement of the problem-solving capacity of the personnel, by emphasizing the qualitative aspect of the personnel, facilitating the autonomous behaviors of the personnel, facilitating the establishment of a wide variety of interrelationships, and facilitating the practice of quality improvement based thereon, would lead to the strengthening of competitiveness in manufacturing.

The subsequent prosperity of the companies which won the Deming Prize in Japan, and the differences in the competitiveness of the industries, mainly the manufacturing industry, in the US and Japan clearly show the importance of perspectives such as putting emphasis on the qualitative aspects, including creativity and innovativeness, of the personnel, establishing interrelationships based on autonomous behaviors and fostering the problem-solving capacity of the personnel through cooperation. It can be said that one essential factor for maintaining and strengthening the competitiveness of the industries, mainly the manufacturing industry, is management geared toward the strengthening of cooperative relationships within each company or company group based on the autonomous activities of the employees.

2.2 *Background: Epistemology and human thinking*

In general, it is said that the scientific way of thinking derives from the physics of medieval Europe. Its reductive way of thinking, which saw its most spectacular manifestation in the classical dynamics of Newton, consists of the following procedure: first, an "entirety" is divided into or reduced to small parts; then, the logic of each part is examined; finally, all the parts are combined again to comprehend the "entirety". It is true that the reductive way of thinking, which is based on a mechanistic worldview where the world is supposed to be an enormous machine to be disassembled, examined in great detail, and reassembled, has produced a number of great scientific results. Behind this way of thinking, there is an epistemology in which each component is deemed to be functionally independent from all others, despite the fact that it is a part of the mechanistic whole.

In recent years, however, an interactive way of thinking, on which the new science, including quantum mechanics, and the complex adaptive system theory (Waldrop, 1992; Gell-Mann, 1994) advocated by Waldrop, Gell-Mann *et al.*, are based, has gathered momentum, fueled by the relativity theory of Einstein. In essence, the universe, the Earth, nature, society, etc., acquire new properties upon exceeding a certain threshold of complexity: this means that the newly acquired properties cannot be explained by dividing the whole and reducing it to its components based on the reductionist paradigm. This interactive approach is grounded on the epistemological concept of the formation of the "entirety" as a result of the existence of complex interrelationships and interactions between components; it aspires to go beyond the limits of reductionism typical of modern science.

It is difficult to deny the view that the reductive way of thinking, as a traditional scientific approach, has produced enormously valuable results over many years, has made a major contribution to the shaping of human thought in social activities in general, including business and management, through education, etc., and has been locked in as a schema. Meanwhile, it can be said that the rapid advance of complexity in society and economy, unprecedented in human history since the end of the 20th century, demands a radical change in the way of thinking even in the management of companies or company groups, in the same way as the change in paradigm from the reductive way of thinking to the interactive way of thinking in science. That is, the capacity to accurately determine the true cause of management problems from among all the complex interrelationships and interactions between many factors related to those problems is becoming essential.

The basis therefor was introduced in the form of TQC, as per the said quality control theory advocated by Deming, and has contributed to the fostering of employees' problem-solving skills through the practice of quality improvement. It is worthy of attention that, in recent years, the approach of determining the real cause of problems from among all the complex interrelationships and interactions between factors has become widespread among employees as a problem-solving method, and is now applied generally to any business area, functional area and business process in companies or company groups, including production and development sites.

2.3 *Concept of relationship management*

Based on the above background information, the concept of relationship management for the continuous organizational fostering of human capacity suitable for the management environment of the 21st century, in which complexity and maturity grow steadily, is presented below. Please keep in mind that this concept is applicable to company groups which exist within the framework of an inter-firm network.

Relationship management consists of two factors: (1) management by quantitative indices and (2) management above quantitative indices. The gist of relationship management is (2), and (1) is a supporting function of (2).

The foundation of management by quantitative indices is the problem-solving technique, which is the technique or approach that determines the real cause of problems from among the interrelationships and interactions between multiple factors. The requisites for utilizing this technique for fostering human capacity in a company group are the following:

(1) Although the main body of the problem-solving technique is factor analysis, the analysis task (function) is not outsourced to anyone outside the company group. Also, the relevant task (function) is not concentrated on any specific company, specific department, or specific specialist in the company group.

(2) An internal educational system is created so that every employee in the company group can equally learn the problem-solving technique to foster his or her capacity. A mechanism for the synergistic cultivation of the capacity of every employee of the company group is introduced by producing lecturers for inner education within the company group.

(3) The state of permanently improving the capacity of every employee through practice in everyday work is created by the introduction of the level of understanding and learning of the problem-solving technique into the employee evaluation system.

Next, the main factor of relationship management is management above quantitative indices. Such management facilitates the creation of interrelationships in a company group based on the autonomous behaviors of employees, unrealizable by management as per quantitative indices.

The significance of management above quantitative indices lies in the hierarchy of management information (Table 1). It can be said that information in terms of monetary amounts in management accounting, etc., or quantitative information in production management, etc., that is, management information expressed in quantitative indices, is a mapping cut for a certain purpose out of the real image, which is the scene information at a process site in a company group. Meanwhile, the autonomous behaviors of employees who establish interrelationships within a company group derive from "noticing" which is an inducement to improvement or problem solving, and most of the "noticing" is obtained from the real image rather than the mapping expressed in quantitative indices. Although management information expressed in quantitative indices is one of the necessary tools for company group management, it is difficult to maintain that this tool is also sufficient from the perspective of cultivating employees' problem-solving capacity or the continuous organizational fostering of human capacity in a company group.

Table 1.   Hierarchy of management information.

Hierarchy	Contents of Info	Image Property	Type of Info	Expression Form
Uppermost layer	Accounting	Mapping	Data	Numerical value
Upper layer	Material amount	Mapping	Data	Numerical value
Bottom layer	*Genchi genbutsu*	Real image	Scene info	Phrase

The requirements for utilizing management above quantitative indices for the cultivation of human capacity in a company group are the following:

(1) Emphasis is placed on qualitative aspects such as autonomy, creativity, innovativeness and cooperativeness in the employees of the company group, and the sense of value or code of conduct that should be held in common by all employees of the company group is clarified with the aim of creating interrelationships and interactions within the company group based on the autonomous behaviors of the employees and facilitating the cultivation of the problem-solving capacity through cooperation within the company group.

(2) The clarified sense of value or code of conduct is repeatedly and in various forms passed from the top executive of each company of the company group to the on-site employees, so that such clarified sense of value or code of conduct may infiltrate into the minds of all the employees in each company.

(3) An internal educational system is created so that all the employees of the company group can equally learn and understand such a sense of value or code of conduct. A mechanism for facilitating the understanding thereof by the employees of the company group in a synergistic manner is created by fostering, through the company group's own efforts, lecturers for internal education.

(4) The state of permanently improving the understanding of such a sense of value or code of conduct by every employee through practise in everyday work is created by the introduction of the level of understanding of the sense of value or code of conduct in the employee evaluation system.

As mentioned above, the nucleus of the concept of relationship management is to release the employees who belong to inter-firm networks of company groups, etc., from the traditional schema of top-down control and the simple and linear reductive way of thinking, and to let them shift to the way of thinking and behavior based on the epistemology of a network of elaborate interrelationships and interactions.

3 Relationship Management in the Toyota Group

3.1 *Characteristics*

The Toyota Group has consistently expanded its scale of operation and strengthened its management for about 70 years since its foundation, based on the following management principles: "We will devote our energies to meeting social needs and enriching people's lives through the manufacturing of automobiles", and "We will devote our energies to creating jobs and contributing to the prosperity of the local economy as a company firmly rooted in the region".

Although the Toyota Group has frequently been faced with grave operational difficulties, such as the management crisis in 1950, the pollution problem and oil shock in the 1970s, and the trade issue and voluntary export restriction in the 1980s, the Toyota Group has overcome such difficulties by focusing on technological innovation suitable for the changing times and on productivity improvement together with its dealers and parts suppliers throughout the world, under the slogans of "Customer first" and "*Genchi genbutsu*" (the actual place and the actual thing).

The Toyota Group has survived such frequent crises thanks to its product capability, technological capability, supply capability and sales capability, all of which have been driving forces of the long-term stable growth of the Toyota Group, its quality and cost competitiveness which has supported such capabilities, and the qualitative improvement of its human resources based on the fostering of human capacity. Without the qualitative improvement of its human resources, such competitiveness would never have been possible.

The Toyota Group's mid- and long-term tasks are to step up management centered on products and management centered on markets based on its managerial creed, i.e., contribution to local communities through car manufacturing, and to step up technological development to meet the needs of the times, such as environmental technology, including low fuel consumption, for the realization of a low-carbon society, technology for joyful and delightful driving, and other technology in anticipation of customer needs. These tasks cannot be fulfilled without the qualitative improvement of human resources based on the fostering of human capacity.

The cultivation of human capacity in the Toyota Group is based on the Toyota Production System (TPS). TPS aims at the total optimization of the Toyota Group by way of the just-in-time (JIT) system, based on the interrelationships between all the production lines across the Toyota Group, considering the production lines as a continuum of individual processes. Since the ultimate purpose of TPS is to enhance the quality of each process based on the concept of Jidoka (autonomation), the capacity to determine the real cause of any quality problem from among complex interrelationships between factors in the group and the creation of various cooperative relationships between processes and functions based on autonomous improvement efforts are required of each on-site employee of the group. This is a TPS concept, summed up by the phrase "Manufacturing means the development of human resources".

In terms of relationship management, the nucleus of management by quantitative indices in the Toyota Group is the problem-solving technique, that is, the technique or way of thinking in which the real cause of any problem is determined from the complicated interrelationships between factors in the group in order to fulfill each task successfully. For the determination of the real cause of any problem, the establishment of close cooperative relationships within the group based on the thorough checking of interactions between the functions related to the real cause is required of the group's employees.

Management by quantitative indices in the Toyota Group, from the perspective of the cultivation of human capacity, has the following two characteristics:

(1) In the group, there are units in charge of putting together and systemizing the know-how related to problem-solving techniques (in the form of cooperation among the units of companies in the group). However, in principle, the tasks (functions) of factor analysis, etc., in problem solving are not concentrated in a specific unit or specialist in the group. Also, as a rule, any total outsourcing to outsiders is excluded.

(2) In principle, each employee of the group enjoys an equal opportunity to become a trainee of the internal training program (created by the above unit) to learn problem-solving techniques. The internal training program is carried out in an overlapping manner for each workplace, for each level of problem-solving capacity, etc. Also, some employees are trained as lecturers for the training program, and they account for a part of all the lecturers.

From the first, the Toyota Group has attached great importance to management above quantitative indices, which is the main factor of relationship management. Its core is "The Toyota Way", the mindset of TPS, which had been imparted to the employees at the production sites of the Toyota Group as implied knowledge for more than half a century, until it became formal knowledge in 2001. The Toyota Way is a sense of value or code of conduct that should be held in common by all the employees of the Toyota Group with the aim of facilitating autonomy, creativity, innovativeness and on-site cooperation. The Toyota Way consists of the following components:

(1) Continuous improvement

- Challenge: The challenge of realizing dreams with vision, courage and a creative mind.
- *Kaizen*: Making incessant efforts toward improvement, for constant evolution and innovation.
- *Genchi genbutsu* (the actual place and the actual thing): Ascertaining the essence of things, coming to agreement and deciding without delay, and implementing with utmost effort, based on the way of thinking summed up by "*Genchi genbutsu*".

(2) Respect for people

- Respect: Respect for others, making earnest efforts at mutual understanding, and fulfilling each responsibility.
- Teamwork: Cultivating human resources and mobilizing individual capacities.

The Toyota Way drastically strengthens the relationships between processes/functions within the group and facilitates the development of human resources through improvement activities pursued stubbornly and relentlessly, involving the entire group. The group's functions, such as development, procurement, production technology, production, physical distribution and sales, are organically integrated, centering on goods and processes. The strength of the cooperation across the group and the high problem-solving capacity of the group's employees are a significant part of the underpinning of the mid- and long-term competitiveness of the Toyota Group.

Relationship management above quantitative indices in the Toyota Group, as viewed from the perspective of the development of human capacity, has the following three characteristics:

(1) The Toyota Way, which is a sense of value or code of conduct to be held in common by all the employees of the Toyota Group, attaches great importance to qualitative aspects such as autonomy, creativity, innovativeness and cooperativeness. The Toyota Way, held in common by all the employees of the Toyota Group, facilitates the forging of interrelationships within the group based on the autonomous behaviors

of the group's employees, as well as the development of the employees' problem-solving capacity by way of cooperation within the group.

(2) The Toyota Way is frequently conveyed in various forms, including in writing, through electronic media and through oral explanations, by the top executive of each company of the group to the on-site employees.

(3) In principle, the opportunity to learn and understand the Toyota Way through internal training is given equally to every employee of the group. Furthermore, the Toyota Way is an integral part of the mindset of the employees of all global Toyota Group entities, and cultivates those employees who think and act on their own throughout the world, via the trainer educational program, etc., of the Toyota Group.

As mentioned above, it can be said that the cultivation, by the Toyota Group as a whole, of human capacity, summed up by the phrase "Manufacturing means the development of human resources", basically corresponds to the concept of relationship management presented in this chapter. It can be said that management which facilitates relationships, including the improvement of the problem-solving capacity (above all the capacity to determine the real cause of any problem) of every employee within the group, the sense of value that encourages on-site relationships within the group, and the cultivation of the problem-solving capacity of the group's employees through consistent improvement activities, is a significant part of the underpinning of the mid- and long-term competitiveness of the Toyota Group.

3.2   *Cases of contribution to the evolution of the management accounting system*

The characteristics of relationship management as a human capital strategy in the Toyota Group were mentioned above. Now, cases experienced by the Toyota Group will be discussed mainly from the perspective of their contribution to the evolution of the management accounting system. Cases belonging to the following three areas are examined: (1) cost planning, (2) cost improvement and (3) improvement of order delivery.

(1) Cost planning: Regarding the development process for new products in the Toyota Group, simultaneous engineering (SE) activities, in which design engineers who belong to the technological development field and production engineers who belong to the production field of the

companies across the group undertake the development of new products while cooperating and coordinating concurrently with one another, have taken root in the group.

In the process of developing new products, the so-called large-room activities, an expanded version of the SE activities, have been conducted in recent years. In large-room activities, many representatives in charge of the various functions of a product meet in a large room from the very beginning of the development process of the product. Together, they attempt to find the optimal solution through stubborn and consistent efforts of adjustment, even between conflicting functions, toward maximization of production efficiency, by incorporating beforehand the factors for realizing the development concept of the relevant product, introduction of epoch-making technologies and manufacturability in the mass production stage into the design information, and toward the realization of ultimate improvements, that is, improvements of tens of percent or even several hundred percent as compared to improvements of a few percent in ordinary companies.

This ultimate concept was brought to perfection by the continuous organizational cultivation of human capacity by the Toyota Group, based on the human capital strategy of relationship management. From the perspective of management accounting, improvements of tens of percent or even several hundred percent are unrealizable, if the objective is to effect an improvement of merely a few percent, as observed in the profit plans of ordinary companies. The capacity of adjustment between different departments and the realization of ultimate improvements by the sublation of contradictory factors, which have been cultivated for a long time within the group through relationship management, have remarkably improved the effectiveness of the cost planning system of the Toyota Group.

(2) Cost improvement: In general, most results of cost improvement activities are realized through productivity improvement at each company's own plants by its own effort, but one of the characteristics of cost improvement activities in the Toyota Group is that, in addition thereto, improvement results unrealizable by one company are realized through cooperation between companies within the group.

Therefore, in the Toyota Group, negotiations on discounts for sales transactions between companies within the group are usually not conducted. Instead, with the help of an improvement support function created within the group, multidimensional activities geared toward

radically improving the quality, cost and delivery (QCD) and strengthening management vitality among the group's companies that have
business connections are promoted. All the companies involved enjoy
the fruits of such activities on an equitable basis. Also, in the group,
there is a system of promoting further cost improvements by granting awards to those units that are found to have obtained excellent
improvement results, upon examining them by using the evaluation
system set up by the improvement support function in the group. This
is also an example of the evolution of the Toyota Group's management
accounting system derived from relationship management.

(3) Improvement of the flow from order to delivery: In the supply chain
process of the Toyota Group, customers, sales companies, physical distribution companies, assembly plants, parts plants, suppliers, etc., are
integrated organically by means of a certain information infrastructure, with the production lines, which play a key role in TPS, as a
nucleus. Based on the integrated information infrastructure, TPS aims
at realizing the just-in-time smooth flow of goods throughout the process, starting from the customers' orders. However, the best method
of ensuring a smooth just-in-time process flow among customers, sales
companies and production lines has been a longstanding issue for the
Toyota Group.

Regarding this issue, thanks to the project team activities for the
entire group in recent years, various improvements have been made,
including the radical reduction of the lead time from the customer's
order to delivery, the emptying of stock and accumulation of goods
throughout the supply chain, the improvement of customer satisfaction by immediately dispatching a notice on the delivery date, and the
new mechanism of business management featuring an improvement of
cash flow and a reduction in capital cost. This also is an example of
the evolution of the management accounting system made possible by
relationship management.

4   Conclusion

Since the birth of management theories at the beginning of the 20th century
in the United States, the search for efficiency has consistently been the core
issue in the management of companies or company groups. The rapid social
and economic development and progress have put pressure on companies

and company groups to supply products and services in larger quantities, more quickly and at lower prices, and they have met these requirements by adapting their management systems thereto. To meet such requirements, it was necessary at one time to strengthen the top-down linear control for the purpose of maximizing efficiency. As a result, it was difficult to broaden relationships or allow employees to express their individuality. However, US companies and company groups, mainly in the manufacturing industry, gradually lost their competitiveness due to their rigid management system, the decrease in the autonomy of the employees, the promotion of the partial optimization way of thinking, etc.

On the other hand, it is said that the essence of Japanese management lies in the cultivation of human capacity based on a long-term perspective. If management is conducted so that each on-site employee is fostered as a human being who retains and improves his or her will, thought and energy instead of a mere worker, those functions which constitute a company or company group will be organically integrated and on-site tacit knowledge will be improved, thereby leading to the basic strengthening of the competitiveness of the company or company group, as demonstrated by the trajectory of management theories in the last century.

The society and economy since the end of the 20th century have become increasingly complex and mature on an unprecedented scale and at an unprecedented speed, as seen, for example, in the development and sophistication of inter-firm networks, and are now in a period of transition. If the management of a company or company group is to adapt itself to the prevailing social and economic changes, the key to such adaptation should lie in the way relationships are promoted based on respect for humanity. Management that promotes relationships as a human capital strategy for the continuous organizational cultivation of human capacity should be one of the cardinal factors of competitiveness suited to the management environment of the 21st century.

References

Ansoff, H.I. (1965). *Corporate Strategy*, New York: McGraw-Hill Education.
Becker, G. (1975). *Human Capital*, Chicago: University of Chicago Press.
Deming, W.E. (1982). *Out of the Crisis*, Cambridge, MA: MIT Press.
Ford, H. (1923). *My Life and Work*, London: Heinemann.
Gell-Mann, M. (1994). *The Quark and the Jaguar: Adventures in the Simple and the Complex*, New York: W.H. Freeman & Co.

Porter, M. (1980). *Competitive Strategy: Techniques for Analyzing Industries and Competitors*, New York: Free Press.

Smith, A. (1776). *An Inquiry into the Nature and Causes of the Wealth of Nations*, London: W. Strahan and T. Cadell.

Taylor, F. (1911). *The Principles of Scientific Management*, New York: Harper Brothers.

Waldrop, M. (1992). *Complexity: The Emerging Science at the Edge of Order and Chaos*, New York: Simon & Schuster.

Index

About the Editor

Yasuhiro Monden is Professor Emeritus of the University of Tsukuba and currently serving as Visiting Professor at the Global MBA Program of the Nagoya University of Commerce and Business, both in Japan. He has been majoring in production management and managerial accounting. He received his PhD from the University of Tsukuba, where he also served as Chairperson of the Institute and Dean of the Graduate Program of Management Sciences and Public Policy Studies.

Monden has gained valuable practical knowledge and experience from his research and related activities in the Japanese automobile industry. He was instrumental in introducing the Just-In-Time (JIT) production system to the United States. His book, *Toyota Production System* (Engineering and Management Press: IIE, 1983, 1993, 1998 and 2011 forthcoming) published in English, is recognized as a JIT classic; it was awarded the 1984 Nikkei Prize by the *Nikkei Economic Journal*.

Monden was a Visiting Professor at the State University of New York at Buffalo in 1980–1981, at California State University, Los Angeles in 1991–1992 and at Stockholm School of Economics, Sweden in 1996. He is also a board member and advisor for the Production and Operations Management Society (POMS) and an international director of the Management Accounting Section of the American Accounting Association.

Other English-language books written by Monden include: *Cost Reduction System: Target Costing and Kaizen Costing* (Productivity Press, 1995), *Japanese Management Accounting* (Productivity Press, 1989); *Value-Based Management of the Rising Sun* (World Scientific Publishing Company, 2006), *Japanese Management Accounting Today* (World Scientific Publishing Company, 2007).

Monden's professional activities in the business world include practical guidance on JIT system and strategic cost management in Singapore and Thailand as an expert of JICA (Japan International Cooperation Agency), an agency of the Japanese Ministry of Foreign Affairs, and his service as a committee member of the second examination of Certified Public Accountant in Japan.